CARIBBEAN WOMEN WRITERS

CARIBBEAN WOMEN WRITERS

Edited and with an Introduction by

Harold Bloom

CHELSEA HOUSE PUBLISHERS

Philadelphia

ON THE COVER: *Simbi Haiti*, 1994, watercolor, 24" x 18" by Lois Mailou Jones.

CHELSEA HOUSE PUBLISHERS

EDITORIAL DIRECTOR   Richard Rennert
PRODUCTION MANAGER   Pamela Loos
PICTURE EDITOR   Judy Hasday
ART DIRECTOR   Sara Davis
SENIOR PRODUCTION EDITOR   Lisa Chippendale

WOMEN WRITERS OF ENGLISH AND THEIR WORKS:
  Caribbean Women Writers

SERIES EDITOR   Jane Shumate
CONTRIBUTING EDITOR   Piper Kendrix
INTERIOR AND COVER DESIGNER   Alison Burnside
EDITORIAL ASSISTANT   Anne Merlino

Introduction © 1997 by Harold Bloom

First Printing
1 3 5 7 9 8 6 4 2

Library of Congress Cataloging-in-Publication Data

Caribbean women writers / edited with an introduction by
  Harold Bloom.
      p.   cm. — (Women writers of English and their works)
    Includes bibliographical references and index.
    ISBN 0-7910-4476-9 (hardcover). — ISBN 0-7910-4492-0 (pbk.)
      1. Caribbean literature (English)—Women authors—Bio
  -bibliography—Dictionaries. 2. Women and literature—Caribbean Area—
  Dictionaries. 3. Women authors, Caribbean—Biography—Dictionaries. 4. Caribbean
  Area—In literature—Dictionaries.   I. Bloom, Harold. II. Series.
  PR9205.05.C37 1997
  810.9' 9287' 09729—dc21
  [B]   97-4276
                                                                                 CIP

CONTENTS

JEAN RHYS   134

OLIVE SENIOR 150

THE ANALYSIS OF WOMEN WRITERS

HAROLD BLOOM

I APPROACH THIS SERIES with a certain wariness, since so much of classical feminist literary criticism has founded itself upon arguments with that phase of my own work that began with *The Anxiety of Influence* (first published in January 1973). Someone who has been raised to that bad eminence—*The Patriarchal Critic*—is well advised that he trespasses upon sacred ground when he ventures to inquire whether indeed there are indisputable differences, imaginative and cognitive, between the literary works of women and those of men. If these differences are so substantial as pragmatically to make an authentic difference, does that in turn make necessary different aesthetic standards for judging the achievements of men and of women writers? Is Emily Dickinson to be read as though she has more in common with Elizabeth Barrett Browning than with Ralph Waldo Emerson?

Is Elizabeth Bishop a great poet because she triumphantly meets the same aesthetic criteria satisfied by Wallace Stevens, or should we evaluate her by criteria she shares with Marianne Moore, but not with Stevens? Are there crucial gender-based differences in the representations of Esther Summerson by Charles Dickens in *Bleak House*, and of Dorothea Brooke by George Eliot in *Middlemarch*? Does Samuel Richardson's Clarissa Harlowe convince us that her author was a male when we contrast her with Jane Austen's Elizabeth Bennet? Do women poets have a less agonistic relationship to female precursors than male poets have to their forerunners? Two eminent pioneers of feminist criticism, Sandra Gilbert and Susan Gubar, have suggested that women writers suffer more from an anxiety of authorship than they do from influence anxieties, while another important feminist critic, Elaine Showalter, has suggested that women writers, early and late, work together in a kind of quiltmaking, each doing her share while avoiding any contamination of creative envy in regard to other writers, provided that they be women. Can it be true that, in the aesthetic sphere, women do not beware women and do not suffer from the competitiveness and jealousy that alas do exist in the professional and sexual domains? Is there something in the area of literature, when practiced by women, that changes and purifies mere human nature?

I cannot answer any of these questions, yet I do think it is vital and clarifying to raise them. There is a current fashion, in many of our institutions of higher education, to insist that English Romantic poetry cannot be studied in the old way, with an exclusive emphasis upon the works of William Blake, William Wordsworth, Samuel Taylor Coleridge, Lord Byron, Percy Bysshe Shelley, John Keats, and John Clare. Instead, the Romantic poets are taken to include Felicia Hemans, Laetitia Landon, Charlotte Smith, and Mary Tighe, among others. It would be heartening if we could believe that these are unjustly neglected poets, but their current revival will be brief. Similarly, anthologies of 17th-century English literature now tend to include the Duchess of Newcastle as well as Aphra Behn, Lady Mary Chudleigh, Anne Killigrew, Anne Finch, Countess of Winchilsea, and others. Some of these—Anne Finch in particular—wrote well, but a situation in which they are more read and studied than John Milton is not one that is likely to endure forever. The consequences of making gender a criterion for aesthetic choice must finally destroy all serious study of imaginative literature as such.

In their *Norton Anthology of Literature by Women*, Sandra Gilbert and Susan Gubar conclude their introduction to Elizabeth Barrett Browning by saying that "she constantly tested herself against the highest standards of male-defined poetic genres," a true if ambiguous observation. They then print her famous "The Cry of the Children," an admirably passionate ode that protests the cruel employment of little children in British Victorian mines and factories. Unfortunately, this well-meant prophetic affirmation ends with this, doubtless its finest stanza:

XIII
They look up with their pale and sunken faces,
    And their look is dread to see,
For they mind you of their angels in high places,
    With eyes turned on Deity.
"How long," they say, "how long, O cruel nation,
    Will you stand, to move the world, on a child's heart,—
Stifle down with a mailèd heel its palpitation,
    And tread onward to your throne amid the mart?
Our blood splashes upward, O goldheaper,
    And your purple shows your path!
But the child's sob in the silence curses deeper
    Than the strong man in his wrath."

If you read this aloud, then you may find yourself uncomfortable, on a strictly aesthetic basis, which would not vary if you were told that this had been composed by a male Victorian poet. In their selections from Elizabeth Bishop, Gilbert and Gubar courageously reprint Bishop's superb statement explaining her refusal to permit her poems to be included in anthologies of women's writing:

> Undoubtedly gender does play an important part in the making of any art, but art is art and to separate writings, paintings, musical compositions, etc., into sexes is to emphasize values in them that are *not* art.

That credo of Elizabeth Bishop's is to me the Alpha and Omega of critical wisdom in regard to all feminist literary criticism. Gender studies are precisely that: they study gender, and not aesthetic value. If your priorities are historical, social, political, and ideological, then gender studies clearly are more than justified. Perhaps they are a way to justice, or at least to more justice than women have received throughout thousands of years of male domination and aggression. Yet that is a very different matter from the now vexed issue of aesthetic value. Biographical criticism, like the different modes of historicist and psychological criticism, always has relied upon a kind of implicit gender studies and doubtless will benefit, as other modes will, by a making explicit of such considerations, particularly in regard to women writers.

Each volume in this series contains copious refutations of, and replies to, the traditionally aesthetic stance that I have advocated here. These introductory remarks aspire only to a questioning, and not a challenging, of feminist literary criticism. There are no longer any Patriarchal Critics; they are all dinosaurs, fabulous beasts fit for revival only in horror films. Sometimes I sadly think of myself as Bloom Brontosaurus, amiably left behind by the fire and the flood. But more often I go on reading the great women writers, searching for the aesthetic difference that yet may prove to be there, but which has not yet been found.

INTRODUCTION

BY GENERAL CRITICAL CONSENT, the principal women writers in English to emerge, so far, from the Caribbean are the properly varied trio of Jamaica Kincaid (Elaine Potter Richardson) of Antigua, Paule Marshall of Brooklyn and Barbados, and Jean Rhys of Dominica. I say "properly varied" because the immensely mixed political and social history of the Caribbean is reflected by and in its writers. It would be useless to search for common elements in the art of Kincaid, Marshall, and Rhys, and no such attempt will be ventured here.

Kincaid, the most experimental of the three, is seen by her admirers as a deliberate subverter of Dead White European Male modes of narrative. Yet any reader deeply immersed in Western literature will recognize that prose poetry, Kincaid's medium, always has been one of the staples of literary fantasy or mythological romance, including much of what we call "children's literature." Centering almost always upon the mother-daughter relationship, Kincaid returns us inevitably to perspectives familiar from our experience of the fantasy narratives of childhood.

This childlike element most powerfully informs Kincaid's short stories—to call them that, since really they are prose poems. One of the briefest, "Girl" (1984), is an uncanny chant or litany that stays with one for its hypnotic rhythms, evocative of the girl's voice speaking to itself, yet rehearsing always the admonitions of the dominant mother:

> [T]his is how you grow okra—far from the house, because okra tree harbors red ants; when you are growing dasheen, make sure it gets plenty of water or else it makes your throat itch when you are eating it; this is how you sweep a corner; this is how you sweep a whole house; this is how you sweep a yard; this is how you smile to someone you don't like too much; this is how you smile to someone you don't like at all; this is how you smile to someone you like completely; this is how you set a table for tea; this is how you set a table for dinner; this is how you set a table for dinner with an important guest; this is how you set a table for lunch; this is how you set a table for breakfast; this is how to behave in the presence of men who don't know you very well, and this way they won't recognize immediately the slut I have warned you against becoming; be sure to wash every day, even if it is with your own spit; don't squat down to play marbles—you are not a boy, you know; don't pick people's flowers—you might catch something; don't throw stones at blackbirds, because it might not be a blackbird at all . . . .

This is distinctive and deliberate, but wholly traditional if we are fully aware of how complex and multiform the literary tradition always has been.

Jamaica Kincaid, particularly in *Annie John*, extends the tradition without subverting it, in regard to questions of form and style. Her ideology is explicitly subversive of all Caribbean neocolonialism, but as a literary artist her stance is rather less revolutionary than her highly ideological critical supporters stress it as being.

Paule Marshall, very much a black feminist, attempts few formal innovations and centers her energies upon trying to create black women rebels. As a forerunner of Toni Morrison and of Alice Walker, Marshall probably will retain the interest of literary historians, but the conventional style and sentimental characterizations of her work are likely to diminish the intrinsic importance of her achievement.

Jean Rhys, of creole Dominican descent, is a formidable contrast to Marshall and seems to me the major figure to emerge thus far among Caribbean women writers. Though she lived mostly in Paris and England, the imagination of Rhys came fully alive in her novel of 1966, *Wide Sargasso Sea*, a remarkable retelling of Charlotte Brontë's *Jane Eyre* from the perspective of Bertha Mason, Rochester's mad first wife. The terrifying predicament of the 19th-century creole women of the West Indies, regarded as "white niggers" by colonialists and as European oppressors by blacks, is presented by Rhys with unforgettable poignance and force. Shrewdly exploiting the modernist formal originalities of her mentor, Ford Madox Ford, Rhys achieved a near masterpiece in *Wide Sargasso Sea*. Allusive, parodistic, and intensely wrought, the novel remains the most successful prose fiction in English to emerge from the Caribbean matrix.

PHYLLIS SHAND ALLFREY

1915–1986

PHYLLIS SHAND ALLFREY was born Phyllis Byam Shand in
Dominica on October 24, 1915, the second of four daughters of
Francis Shand, Crown attorney on the island, and his wife, Elfreda.
With no formal education, Allfrey was privately tutored on the island
before leaving to study in Belgium, France, Germany, and England.
She married Robert Allfrey, an Englishman, with whom she had a son
and a daughter, later adopting two Carib sons and an Afro-Caribbean
daughter. Although the Allfreys spent the early years of their marriage
in the United States, they returned to London during the Depression.
In London, Allfrey became a member of the Labour Party, the Fabian
Society, and the Parliamentary Committee for West Indian Affairs.

In 1953, Allfrey won second prize in a world poetry contest, and
her first novel, *The Orchid House*, was published in London and the
U.S.; *La maison des orchidees*, a French translation, was published in 1954.
The novel represents the shift in power from colonizer to colonized
in Dominica through its story of a white creole family on the island.
The story is told by the family's black nurse, Lally, and focuses on the
family's women, tracing the father's decline and the simultaneous rise
of the colored middle class and the black laborers in Dominica.
Allfrey's novel successfully weaves aspects of her own personal family
history with the larger cultural history of the West Indies. Allfrey also
published four collections of poems and wrote a number of short
stories published in newspapers, magazines, and anthologies.

Returning to Dominica in 1954, Allfrey became involved in the
island's political activity. She cofounded the Dominica Labour Party,
was made a minister of the federal government, and was elected as one
of the federal members of parliament for Dominica. In 1958 Allfrey
moved to Port of Spain, Trinidad, to serve as minister of labor and
social affairs in the West Indian federal government (1958–62),
returning to Dominica when the federation was dissolved in 1962.
Allfrey edited the *Dominica Herald*, a weekly paper, until 1965, when
she and her husband began publication of *The Star*, an oppositional
paper that encouraged local writers.

After retiring from active politics, Allfrey returned to her literary
pursuits and began working on a second novel, *In the Cabinet*, an auto-

biographical political novel modeled after her own career. However, when her only natural daughter, Josephine, was killed in Botswana in 1977, she abandoned the project.

In 1979 Heinemann publishers considered reprinting *The Orchid House* as part of its Caribbean Writers Series; however, their Caribbean office issued a marketing report advising against the plan. Elaine Campbell, the editor of the most recent edition of the novel, interprets the rejection of Allfrey's book as part of a larger prejudice facing Caribbean writers of European descent. In her introduction to the novel Campbell offers a quote from Edward Brathwaite, a well-regarded Caribbean critic, to support this claim: "When most of us speak of 'the West Indian,' we think of someone of African descent. . . . There are of course, 'white people' in the West Indies, but they are regarded either as too far apart to count or too inextricably mixed into the whole problem to be considered as separate." *The Orchid House* was eventually reprinted in 1985 by Three Continents Press. Allfrey died in 1986.

C R I T I C A L   E X T R A C T S

KENNETH RAMCHAND

The publication in 1966 of Jean Rhys's *Wide Sargasso Sea* directs attention to at least three other novels by people of European origin who were born or who grew up in the islands (P. Shand Allfrey, *The Orchid House*, 1953; Geoffrey Drayton, *Christopher*, 1959; J. B. Emtage, *Brown Sugar*, 1966). The four writers belong to a group called white West Indians. ⟨. . .⟩

⟨. . .⟩ With differing degrees of intensity, the three novels reflect a significant, but in these days forgotten, aspect of West Indian experience:

> . . . [D]ecolonization is always a violent phenomenon . . . Its unusual importance is that it constitutes, from the very first day, the minimum demands of the colonized. To tell the truth, the proof of success lies in a whole social structure being changed from the bottom up. The extraordinary importance of this change is that it is willed, called for, demanded. The need for this change exists in its crude state, impetuous and compelling, in the consciousness and in the lives of the men and women who are colonized. *But the possibility of this change is equally experienced in the form of a terrifying future in the consciousness of another 'species' of men and women: the colonizers* (Franz Fanon, *The Wretched of the Earth*, 1965, p. 29; my italics).

Adapting from Fanon we might use the phrase 'terrified consciousness' to suggest the white minority's sensations of shock and disorientation as a massive and smouldering black population is released into an awareness of its power. To consider the three novels in this light is to insist upon their social relevance. To consider them at all is to bring forward some imaginative works that tend to be neglected in the demanding contexts of black nationalism.

The Orchid House is narrated in the first person by a peripheral character, Lally—the long-serving Negro nurse of a white family in a fictional island modelled upon Dominica. Lally's memory spans three generations. It is part of the author's purpose to convey a particular sense of the decline of the class to which the planter family belong and to comment on the emergence of the new economic and ruling forces: the novel satirizes the power complex of Church and business in the island and it expresses, and places, the hot-house life of the white characters.

Mrs Allfrey uses the experience of the First World War as the immediate cause of the present Master's state of shock and dope-addiction, but that this is only an intensification of something pervasive is readily apparent: Lally describes the Old Master's habit of insulating himself for 'hours and hours' in the strange shapes, scents and colours of his orchid house at L'Aromatique; and Andrew, the cousin of the Master's three daughters, is given as dying slowly of consumption, without the will to live, in a retreat called Petit Cul-de-Sac. The malaise in the novel thus spreads from the time of the Old Master to his grandchildren's day.

—Kenneth Ramchand, "Terrified Consciousness," *The Journal of Commonwealth Literature* 7 (July 1969): 8–10

BARRIE DAVIS

Phyllis Allfrey's novel is a memorable one in several ways. Not the least of these are the absence of self-conscious West Indian detail and her refusal to purvey the clichés of race, colour, and class. Instead she offers something more subtle and enduring, a sustained and sensitive analysis of Dominican society. She pursues her theme with a single-mindedness which does not exclude the feeling for a whole society, economically caught in the rich metaphor of her prose.

The society, emblematized by the Orchid House itself, is already decaying, though it still remains aloof from the new forces which are stirring and must ultimately sweep it away or leave it stranded. The central impulse in the novel is to preserve, incorporate, and render meaningful to the present what it felt to be valuable in the past. But the tone is one of regret, arising out of the helplessness before irreconcilables.

Likewise the central characters are felt to be part of what is almost oblivion, are activated by their desire to ward off the present, or, attempting to give the present meaning through recollection, experience a frustration which finalises their exile. Past and present are woven together in the figure of the old nurse, Lally. She is the centre from which the major contrasts of the book operate. But she herself is caught in the change, and dying of a tumour, "nurses her complaint" (p. 8). Her winding, retrospective rhythms dimly restore what has gone, but fail to give meaning to the present.

The Master, shattered by his experiences in the First World War, flees the present. Having hurled his medals and the puppy "Flanders" from the window, he has retired into drug-sustained reminiscence, maintained by the sinister Lillipoulala, the embodiment of escape. The Master takes with him the two women who love him. His wife and Mamselle ally themselves for his protection. Mamselle, who after her visit to Europe prided herself on her elegant French and fashionable clothes, now speaks patois and her clothes are faded and démodés.

It is against this that the three daughters returning from exile are matched. Each one demands change. ⟨. . .⟩

⟨One⟩ of the central motifs of the novel ⟨is⟩ the orchid. This beautiful flower needs a living organism to grow upon, but does not suck life from that organism; instead it beautifies. It derives its moisture from the air because the roots never penetrate the earth. The emerging society might have its roots in the land and produce a flower as beautiful and more permanent. Hence the tragedy of the people of Orchid House. Their relationship with the islands is epiphytic. They are people who embellish with their beauty, are made tragic by their transience, are not of the land, are part of a moment, in flux.

The world of *Orchid House* has a metaphorical intensity and is convincing because it is all-pervasive. It enlarges our understanding of human frailty. There is nothing hackneyed, no comment, no moralising, no bitter flourish. Instead there is quiet pathos for people matched against an inscrutable and inexorable historical process.

—Barrie Davis, "Neglected West Indian Writers," *World Literature Written in English* 11, no. 2 (November 1972): 81–83

IRVING W. ANDRE

Allfrey's novel contains an element of social realism which cannot be ignored in an analysis of it. This assumption might not be illogical since Allfrey, a former Fabian Socialist, implicitly acknowledged that creative activity, whether political or literary, had to be grounded in reality in order to be meaningful. While the white family in *The Orchid House* might be a fictitious one, it reflects the circumstances of a whole generation of white settlers in Dominica, the

West-Indian island in which Allfrey bases her story. The symptoms of financial adversity, physical/psychological disease occasioned by adverse circumstances, and migration encompass the realities of a number of white settlers after World War I, the period in which *The Orchid House* unravels.

However, while the author maintains fidelity to the general aspects of this decline, the manner in which she combines character and circumstance to create a story is based entirely on her imagination. Indeed Allfrey's *The Orchid House* exists as an imaginative account of one white family's encounter with self and society in a former 'adjunct of empire'.

Plot and Theme

The 'plot' is simplicity itself. A servant, Lally, narrates the fortunes of the unnamed family after the 'Old Master's' return from World War I. Benumbed by his experiences during the war, he initially settles into a town house, Maison Rose, and later moves to L'Aromatique, the family's old estate house. Lally's account proceeds with the return of the three daughters from overseas, each singularly bent on recapping 'lost time' occasioned by their exile. All reveal that their lives abroad comprised a listless journey without arrival and their return to the island implies a psychic resuscitation for each. All three perform acts which collectively provide plot and 'intrigue' within the novel. Stella, the eldest, attempts to arrest her father's descent into becoming a drug addict by destroying the dope-peddler Mr Lillipoulala. Joan returns from an uneasy marriage to take up the cause of the labourers while the frivolous Natalie rescues her cousin Andrew from the illicit relationship and tuberculosis in which he languishes.

The novel highlights two important themes ⟨. . . .⟩ Allfrey's emphasis on the disease and beauty of the landscape elaborates the view that Dominica possesses 'the fatal gift of beauty'. The relative inaccessibility of the interior, the source of the island's beauty, has militated against economic development and decay has been the inevitable result of neglect. The Moyne Commission Report for example, noted that 'of all the British West-Indian islands Dominica presents the most striking contrast between the great poverty of a large proportion of the population and the beauty . . . of the island'.

The theme of return also receives expression in the novel. In 'Temps Perdi', one of Rhys's short stories depicting her return to Dominica in 1938, the author implicitly expresses nostalgia for a life she 'lost' by leaving the island. All three sisters in *The Orchid House* express a similar sentiment. However, Allfrey makes a precise reference to Marcel Proust's *A La Recherche du Temps Perdu*, the meaning of which is lost in Lally. Yet as Mamselle Bosquet, former tutor to the girls, observes, it implies being,

> In search of the past . . . of lost days . . . but the effort is nearly
> always useless. (p. 45) ⟨. . .⟩

The emphasis on the past however, does not constitute the thematic centre of *The Orchid House*. While the three sisters return to recover 'lost' time, the
slow march of historical changes within the society continues unabated. The
social world of the white creole slowly deteriorates under the siege of
'coloured' aspirations. As the coloured elites encroach on the economic privileges of the whites, the latter take refuge in a literal/psychological 'Petit Cul
de Sac' as Andrew does. ⟨. . .⟩

Allfrey/Lally did not restrict herself to simple narrative to portray the fate
of the family in the context of the slow evolution of the society. The novel is
replete with symbolism which highlights themes of death and decay, sickness
and redemption in the novel.

Images of disease and beauty commingle to create an atmosphere of ominous foreboding. Strange events occur without explanation. The mysterious
fall of the puppy Flanders (p. 33) prefigures the death of Mr Lilipoulala who
'falls' from a swingbridge. Miss Joan notes: 'a hummingbird flew in through my
bedroom window and beat itself to death against the ceiling' (p. 178). Its
patois name *fou-fou* underscores the madness and desperation slowly overtak-
ing Andrew and the Old Master. On the other hand, *La Belle*, a firefly, suggests
light and redemption. The narrator therefore says that 'one of these La Belles
flew in and settled on my Bible' (p. 175).

Then there are those symbols suggestive of death providing life for
others. In the forest, a beautiful bromeliad sapped a tree 'like a disease but
growing to be even stronger and more beautiful than the tree itself' (p. 178).
Again too, a great whale washes up the Roseau seashore, its bloated carcass
providing sustenance for the labourers.

The latter symbol seems a fitting image for the white family washed
ashore by the ebbing tide of fortunes on one hand and bad marriages on the
other. The coloured middle classes slowly gnaw away at the fortunes of the
whites, purchasing old estates too encumbered by debts to be productive. The
author seems to be implying that the persistence of the world of the white signifies an abortion of the lives of the rest of the society. However, even while
the coloureds are consolidating their control, a labour organization emerges.
Allfrey, the Fabian Socialist, seems to suggest that each social reality contains
within it the means whereby it will finally be superseded.

—Irving W. Andre, "The Social World of Phyllis Shand Allfrey's *The Orchid House*," *Caribbean
Quarterly* 29, no. 2 (June 1983): 11–13, 20–21

ELIZABETH NUNEZ-HARRELL

Shand Allfrey presents a sun-drenched landscape teeming with breathtaking flora and fauna, but that, nevertheless, can be casually destroyed by the very environment that engenders it. The people take their lessons from nature and accept disease as a natural phenomenon, doing little to fight against it in a place where beauty thrives indiscriminately. Lally, for example, refuses to remove a tumor that is ravishing her body. Both Stella and Joan reject the people's position, their refusal to struggle against the status quo. Stella does so for personal reasons, because she wishes to save Andrew and her father; and Joan, because she perceives that the people's attitude toward nature extends toward their passive acceptance of the status accorded them by the monied class and of the corruption that surrounds them. ⟨. . .⟩

Joan, the second sister to return to Dominica, represents the solution that Shand Allfrey offers to the white creole woman, and one she personally sought. Joan, of all the sisters, will remain in Dominica to contribute her talents to the removal of social evils on the island. Married to a Fabian Marxist who is a veteran of the Spanish Civil War, Joan is poor but as intensely committed to social reform as her husband. She returns from England to Dominica to assist Baptiste, the educated black son of her mother's cook, in leading a labor reform movement in Dominica. To her, class division, not racism, is the root of evil in Dominica. Responding to Cornélie's comment that in Dominica "the condition of the coloured people is improving every year," Joan says bluntly:

> Of the coloured merchants, the educated people, yes, their condition is improving every year. They are taking the responsibility over from us—we are now the poor whites, we have no longer any power. But I don't notice any greater tenderness in their attitude towards those landless, shoeless devils. . . . (184)

She identifies the plight of the poor white creoles after the political independence of the Caribbean from colonialism with that of the oppressed black peasant class. From this point of view she perceives it as her responsibility to fight against the island's corruptions: the destruction of the island culture, the suppression of patois, the decline of calypso, the removal of the forest trees, the control of the press by the merchant class, the pettiness and greed of the Church, and the materialistic influence of Europe and America. ⟨. . .⟩

As her father represents the end of the white Caribbean class that made its living from the sweat and blood of blacks, so Joan represents the new white creole. ⟨. . .⟩

Joan, disassociating herself from the dying white colonial class of the past, remarks, "Ah . . . I don't suppose I shall ever see a bromeliad. I haven't the time to climb so high." And Baptiste, reinforcing Shand Allfrey's position that greed transcends ethnic distinctions, that blacks as well as whites are guilty, adds mysteriously, "They live also in the lower slopes" (178–179).

If, then, Shand Allfrey tells the white creole woman that her place is in the Caribbean and that her quest for belonging can end only when she assumes responsibility with the rest of the Caribbean people for ending corruption in her native land, she has a message as well for the black Caribbean person. The enemy in the Caribbean is not white people, but greed, an evil common to all humans. And if in this novel Shand Allfrey paints a Caribbean landscape that breeds disease and corruption in the midst of intoxicating beauty, she willingly informs us also that much of the disease and ugliness was brought to the island from England.

—Elizabeth Nunez-Harrell, "The Paradoxes of Belonging: The White West Indian Woman in Fiction," *Modern Fiction Studies* 31, no. 2 (Summer 1985): 284–86

ELAINE CAMPBELL

In ⟨*The Orchid House*⟩, Allfrey assumed responsibility for a certain degree of autobiography, but her notion of autobiography in art was as an expression of a hidden self. She saw the black nursemaid-narrator, Lally, as her persona—a persona who expressed Allfrey's desire to be counted among the accepted majority population of Afro-Caribbeans rather than among the rejected minority white Creoles of the West Indies. However, Lally functions more effectively as the traditional narrator who binds together the various threads of the novel than she does as the author's persona. The character of Joan, one of the three sisters who returns to L'Aromatique—the Orchid House—after expatriation overseas, provides, in fact, a closer approximation of the autobiographical elements in Allfrey's first novel. Joan, the political activist who organizes agricultural labourers into a trade union, mirrors Allfrey's own career as political activist, labour union founder, and finally, cabinet member of the West Indian Federation government that lasted from 1958 to 1962.

Now, thirty years later, Allfrey has come to a literary admission that it is indeed Joan, rather than Lally, who expresses her autobiographical presence in *The Orchid House*. Her admission takes the form of returning Joan to the literary scene of the Dominican landscape. Joan is both narrator and protagonist of *In the Cabinet*. She represents so close an expression of Allfrey's ideas that the reader is uneasy in identifying *In the Cabinet* as a novel in the usual sense of the genre. It seems, perhaps too much, to be an outlet for Allfrey's disillusionment over West Indian politics and over the sad turn her personal life has taken. A woman who has devoted her life to improving the lot of her fellow-Dominicans, she comes through in Joan's musings as a disillusioned idealist: not a cynic, not a sceptic, but a broken and defeated idealist.

There is much personal anguish behind the genesis of *In the Cabinet* as well as behind Allfrey's difficulty in completing it. One strong impulse is her desire to commemorate her daughter, Josephine Allfrey. While telling her own story of political activity in the West Indian Federation government, Allfrey has also produced a memorial to her steadfast husband, Robert, and to her beautiful daughter, Pheena, who died a violent death in Botswana. Pheena serves as a sort of alter-ego in the new novel, asking the questions that Allfrey wishes to answer publicly. Because of Allfrey's mourning for the real Pheena, named Andrina in *In the Cabinet*, the world of the new novel becomes claustrophobically personal, quite unlike the outward-moving world of *The Orchid House*. Further, the fictionalization of Dominica into Anonica is as thinly veiled as the pseudonym suggests. There is no attempt to make Anonica the sort of composite West Indian island that John Hearne created in Cayuna or George Lamming created in San Cristobal. Anonica *is* Dominica, acquiring historic specificity at the very opening of the novel which is set in the immediate post-Hurricane David devastation of the island.

The devastation of Dominica is so much a correlative of the devastation of Joan's political ideals that it takes a very small stretch of the imagination to read Joan as a human embodiment of the island. This reading may be rejected by Caribbeanists who might prefer to see a woman of African ancestry as an embodiment of West Indian life, but here too history and biography invade the novel by way of Allfrey's belief that her West Indian heritage of over three hundred years makes her as authentically West Indian as the later arrivals from Africa. Whether or not this is a self-defensive position, as Kenneth Ramchand suggests in *The West Indian Novel and Its Background*, the fact remains that autobiography is a form of history—personal history—and there are connections between personal history and national history. It is this recognition that invigorates the Latin American novels of magical realism; consequently, to a limited degree, *In the Cabinet* displays more hints of magical realism than do most of the West Indian novels of childhood, setting (yard), and class (peasant).

—Elaine Campbell, "*In the Cabinet*: A Novelistic Rendition of Federation Politics," *Ariel* 17, no. 4 (October 1986): 117–19

EVELYN O'CALLAGHAN

⟨While⟩ it is true that the white creole writer (and protagonist)—especially the female of the species—represents the 'outsider's voice', yet this voice is an integral part of a Caribbean literary tradition. The perspective on West Indian reality articulated by these 'outsiders', "the other side", cannot be provided by the expatriate European or the native Afro-Caribbean writer. And though this perspective, and the reality it presents, may be outmoded or even archaic, it is after all this reality, experience of and contact with this world-view, which gave impetus to the writing of much of early West Indian "mainstream" literature. ⟨. . .⟩

⟨. . .⟩ It is precisely because of this paradoxical place in West Indian socio-history—distanced from, yet bound up in the cultural emergence of the "broadly ex-African base"—that the white creole woman writer can make a valuable literary contribution to the developing tradition.

The 'outsider's voice', then, constitutes an important thread in the fabric of any Caribbean literary tradition, and one can focus on this particular perspective as expressed in three novels: Jean Rhys's *Wide Sargasso Sea* (1966), Eliot Bliss' *Luminous Isle* (1934) and Phyllis Shand Allfrey's *The Orchid House* (1953).

Phyllis Shand Allfrey (born Dominica, 1915) sets *The Orchid House* (*OH*) on an island based on post-colonial Dominica, now ruled by coloured merchants, civil servants and the Catholic church. The novel harks back to childhood in the 1920s, but the concern with transitional politics suggests that the bulk of the action takes place in the 1940s–1950s period. Allfrey's theme is a society in change, mirrored in the microcosm of one white creole family. The old dispensation of the benevolent colonial patriarchy—Shand Allfrey's West Indian roots go back centuries—has given way to that of 'the master', emotionally crippled by his war experiences; in turn, he passes control to the three daughters, Stella, Joan and Natalie, on whom the narrative focuses. Their maturation, departures from and returns to the island are related by their old black nurse, Lally, and the constant juxtaposition of past and present social orders adds depth to the superficially simple family chronicle.

OH continues the span of political history covered in the other fictions—from Emancipation through Crown Colony to early representative government. Again, the interculturation of, and changing relations between, white creole elite, coloured middle class and black peasantry are dealt with.

⟨. . .⟩ ⟨I⟩mplicit questions are raised regarding the place and contribution of the white creole minority in the organization of West Indian society: again, the ambivalent nature of ties between colony and metropole is examined from the perspective of the white Creole; and, of course, male-female tensions permeate the narrative.

—Evelyn O'Callaghan, " 'The Outsider's Voice': White Creole Women Novelists in the Caribbean Literary Tradition," *Journal of West Indian Literature* 1, no. 1 (October 1986): 77–80

HERB WYLIE

Surprisingly little attention ⟨. . .⟩ has been paid to technique in *The Orchid House*, and a stronger argument can be made for the pertinence of Allfrey's work in West Indian writing by paying greater attention to the technical aspects of the novel and to how technique—in particular, narrative perspective—is used to develop the socio-historical perspective of the novel, and serves to reflect, to a much greater degree, the problematic position of Allfrey as a West Indian writer.

One particularly significant aspect of the novel that has been largely neglected is the figure of Lally, the primary narrator of *The Orchid House*. It is curious that, in a literature in which colour is such a central preoccupation, such little notice should be taken of the use of a black narrator by a white novelist. *The Orchid House* is a story about a white family narrated by their black nurse, Lally, and the simple fact that Lally is the figure who presents the story, one would think, would be enough to merit special consideration. Instead, Lally's role has been largely neglected, much to the detriment of the novel's reputation. Kenneth Ramchand's assessment of Lally is not atypical in its brevity: "*The Orchid House* is narrated in the first person by a peripheral character, Lally."

On the contrary, the nature of Lally's involvement with the story and the extent and intensity of that involvement suggest that Lally is critical to *The Orchid House*. The first-person narrative of *The Orchid House* is not simply the story being reported through a peripheral character—Lally is not a peripheral character, and Allfrey's use of her as a narrator is far from simplistic. Lally is not just the "location" of the telling of the story; she influences the story as well as reports it, she constitutes it through her constant efforts to gain access to it, and she is an active participant in that story. Her function in the novel is multifaceted, and not only is she more involved in the story than most accounts of the novel have suggested, but by exploring the position of Lally it is possible to gain greater insight into the complexity of the novel and of Allfrey's relation to the society she is portraying. ⟨. . .⟩

The relation of the obsolescence of Lally's devotion to the family to the effects of colonialism is an important part of Allfrey's depiction of this juncture in West Indian history. If the family gives Lally a sense of comfort, a sense of purpose, it also dominates her life. Just as Lally, as the primary narrator of the novel, constitutes the story of the family through her persistence in gaining possession of as much of it as possible, she is herself constituted by that story. While working for the family she must neglect everything else: her health, the beauty of the island, and her people. ⟨. . .⟩

Lally has, in a way, been colonized by the family story, and her narrative, in that sense, is an exploration of colonialism. Although Lally's attitudes are modified somewhat between the time of the girls' childhood and the time of their return, reflecting changes in the social order of the island, her concerns are clearly not her own, and the values she espouses are largely those of the passing colonial order: political conservatism, a recognition and respect of colour divisions, and a general desire to preserve the status quo.

This colonization of Lally by the family becomes even more interesting when one takes into consideration Allfrey's professed identification, not with Joan ⟨. . .⟩ but with Lally. ⟨. . .⟩

⟨. . .⟩ Allfrey's exploration of the colonization of Lally's life by the story of the family makes her portrait of the island as a microcosm of West Indian society somewhat more balanced, and prevents the novel from being simply an elegy for the white Creole in West Indian society, fortified by the moral that greed and exploitation have no colour—as the emerging brown merchant class in the novel is intended to demonstrate.

But at the same time, there are problems with Lally's character which point to the paradoxical position of Allfrey as a writer and modify the extent to which her vision of West Indian society is a balanced one. In attempting to qualify her relatively elegiac vision of a white family in colonial society by using a black narrator whose fascination with that family dramatizes the effects of colonialism, Allfrey seems to be trying, with questionable results, to have her cake and eat it too. While the self-consciousness of the narrative draws attention to the fact that Lally has, in a sense, been colonized, the validity of her devotion to the story and of the self-effacement that devotion involves is not apparently questioned in the novel, and is, if anything, supported.

The portrait of Lally ultimately points to a tension which is at the heart of the novel and perhaps at the heart of Allfrey's position as a West Indian writer: that because Allfrey seems to share the kind of devotion which in Lally's case is symptomatic of a kind of colonization, she is ultimately unable to portray that devotion in a negative light. And because of the lack of resolution of this tension, because the implications of Lally's character are not effectively addressed in the novel, the various objections to the portrait of Lally—that she is too sentimentally portrayed and lacking in credibility, and that she has been appropriated to tell a story which is not her own—can, in the final analysis, be sustained.

Allfrey's skill at presenting a comprehensive picture of West Indian society has been recognized, but the complexity and problematic nature of *The Orchid House* have been consistently underestimated, because her subtle deployment of Lally—as a narrator and as a figure in this society—to dramatize the ugliness of colonial society and her paradoxical attraction to it has been overlooked. By recognizing both the extent of Lally's role in the novel and the tensions which are ultimately evident in her portrait, it is possible to appreciate to a greater degree the complexity of Allfrey's vision of West Indian society and history, and to come to a better understanding of the problematic and paradoxical place of the white creole woman in that society.

—Herb Wylie, "Narrator/Narrated: The Position of Lally in *The Orchid House*," *World Literature Written in English* 31, no. 1 (Spring 1991): 21–22, 29–30, 32–33

B I B L I O G R A P H Y

In Circles: Poems. 1940.
Palm and Oak: Poems. 1950.
Governor Pod. 1951.
The Orchid House. 1953.
Contrast: Poems. 1955.
Palm and Oak II. 1973.

ERNA BRODBER

B. 1940

ERNA BRODBER was born in Woodside, St. Mary, Jamaica, in 1940 to Ernest Brodber, a farmer, and his wife, Lucy, a teacher. After attending the Woodside Elementary School, where her mother taught, Brodber moved to Kingston to live with relatives and attend Excelsior High School, from which she graduated in 1958. Brodber worked as a civil servant and teacher in Montego Bay before entering the University College of the West Indies (now the University of the West Indies). When Jamaica gained its independence in 1962, Brodber was in her third year studying history.

After receiving her bachelor's degree in 1963, Brodber was awarded a University of the West Indies postgraduate scholarship but took a year off from her studies to work as the director of history at St. Augustine's School for Girls in Trinidad. Returning to Jamaica the following year, Brodber turned her attention to the social sciences, a discipline she hoped would fill the void she felt that history left when it offered accounts of the past that insufficiently treated Caribbean history. However, Brodber found social science research equally lacking in its consideration of Caribbean peoples. Attempting to find an approach to these disciplines that would meet her commitments both to academics and activism, Brodber studied social psychology at the McGill University in Canada.

In 1967, Brodber won a Ford Foundation predoctoral fellowship to study child psychology at the University of Washington in Seattle; there she was exposed to the black power and feminist movements, whose ideologies enhanced her own thoughts about race and gender politics in Jamaica. She returned to Jamaica in 1968 to finish her master's degree in sociology from the University of the West Indies, while working as a research assistant at the university's sociology department, where she subsequently was a lecturer until 1974, when she left to work at the Institute of Social Change and Economic Research (ISER). It was during the nine years that Brodber was on staff at the ISER that her work as a nonfiction writer established her importance in the discipline, while her more creative pursuits established her as a fiction writer. Since 1976 Brodber has been a member of Twelve Tribes of Israel, a Rastafarian sect.

Brodber's first novel, *Jane and Louisa Will Soon Come Home* (1980), was originally conceived as a fictional "case study" for her social psychology students, redressing the lack of Jamaican participants in studies about personality disorders. Focusing on Nellie's psychological fragmentation, the novel tells of her journey to recovery. The novel highlights the negotiation between traditional conceptualizations of womanhood and the reality of sexually motivated violence against women necessary in Nellie's eventual interpretation of herself as a unified being.

In 1983, Brodber left the ISER to found Black Space, a research company in Woodside, St. Mary, Jamaica. After completing her dissertation and receiving her Ph.D. in history at the University of the West Indies in 1984, she published her second novel, *Myal* (1988). The novel takes its title from "myalism," an Afro-Jamaican religion practiced on slave plantations in the 18th century. Brodber expands on the work done in *Jane and Louisa Will Soon Come Home*, stressing the importance of an individual's link with her past and her community. The novel focuses on Ella, a young light-skinned woman, and the small Jamaican community that attempts to help her recover from the "spirit theft" or "zombification" often produced by colonialism and European influence.

Brodber's most recent novel, *Louisiana* (1994), tells the story of a young Caribbean anthropologist who travels to Louisiana to research folk life.

Brodber lives with her son, Timothy, in Woodside, where she continues to work as a freelance writer and researcher.

CRITICAL EXTRACTS

PAM MORDECAI

Miss Brodber occupies a strategic place in the emerging tradition of women prose writers. Someone—I forget who—has made the useful distinction between "the tale of the telling" and the "telling of the tale". In "the tale of the telling", the how of what is being said becomes itself a significant part of the statement; in "the telling of the tale", form is a part of the statement only inso-

far as it is its channel or vehicle. Up to now novels of Caribbean women writers have been concerned with telling the tale. A novel like Paule Marshall's *A
Chosen Place, A Timeless People* ⟨1969⟩ suffers to some extent because the burden
of the tale weighs so heavily on the telling. On the other hand, Simone
Schwarz-Bart's *The Bridge of Beyond* ⟨1975⟩ achieves, even in translation, a special exuberance because the raconteur is as crafty with the form of the telling
as with the content of the tale. In *Jane and Louisa* the balance between artful tale
and crafted telling is tipped in favour of the telling. Brodber's tale is as much
about the felt shapes of the people, the configurations of their language and
the rich texture of their place, as these are received into her young heroine, as
it is about what happens to Nellie. Rather than subject being embedded in setting, the two are made to coalesce by the author's particular choice of narrative mode. The places and times, moods and events *are* the remembering of
Nellie: the story of her progress through experience is the account of how,
from her revisioning of her ancestors, she discovers, or begins to discover, her
own integrity, or, as her Aunt Alice puts it, how to "do her part". It is from the
rehearsing of their experience (revitalized in her recalling in such a way that
the choice, and shape, of the language of memory, is itself the revivification)
that Nellie becomes able to discover and assert herself. By this process of
exhuming the being, wit and wisdom of her people, Nellie learns to operate as
Anancy counsels Tacuma to do:

> Don't follow no firefly boy. Look inside of yourself and row. Them
> will los' you. Them will put you out of your way . . . when you find
> out where you want to go, you watch for them other one what going
> there and you use their light. (p 124)

Dialogue and interior monologue carry the burden of the telling. The
story traverses diachronic space at will, from the generation of Albert and
Elizabeth Whiting, poor-white great-great grandparents of Nellie, the heroine, through Tia and William Alexander Whiting, to Kitty and Puppa Rich-
mond, and to Nellie's own parents, and Nellie's own growing-up time. ⟨. . .⟩

Jane and Louisa is special ⟨. . .⟩ because it departs from the simple linear narrative, or the kinds of variations of this chronology that other Caribbean novelists have up to now employed (Naipaul in *The Mimic Men* or Lamming in *Water
with Berries*, for instance). The difference lies in the fact that the interest in this
book is not so much in the nature of events, the "external action" of the tale,
as in their psychic repercussions, the "internal action". Consequently events
often have less significance in themselves than they have as symbols, shapes
resonating in Nellie's psyche with a power beyond the cumulative effect of
their sequential development. ⟨. . .⟩

Indisputably an important part of the achievement of the book is the author's use of language. Brodber ranges through the overlapping system of dialects from Creole to "standard" English, deploying them at will, code-sliding and code-switching through registers and formal and informal linguistic devices with a kind of abandon that seems, increasingly, a special talent of the women writers in the region. (Compare, for instance, the short stories of Olive Senior and Velma Pollard, and the poetry of Lorna Goodison.) Among the male novelists only Selvon and Lovelace and perhaps Austin Clarke manage the range of Caribbean language with this kind of freedom and authority.
—Pam Mordecai, " 'Into this Beautiful Garden'— Some Comments on Erna Brodber's *Jane and Louisa*," *Caribbean Quarterly* 29, no. 2 (June 1983): 44–45, 47–48

YAKINI KEMP

For Nellie of *Jane and Louisa Will Soon Come Home*, the search for selfhood is a complex, integral and lifesaving need because without a successful redefinition and unification of selfhood, she will return to her alienated, dysfunctional existence that led to a mental breakdown.

Through the fragmented sketches of her childhood which the novel offers, Nellie's upbringing by solid Jamaican peasant stock in a tightly circled rural community accounts for her distraught adult personality. Nellie must reconcile and resolve misguided attitudes toward individual and community relations, women's roles and sexuality, and family lineage and heritage. She develops these attitudes primarily from the influence of her Aunt Becca, who like Tee's Aunt Beatrice ⟨in Merle Hodge's *Crick Crack Monkey*⟩, is determined to eradicate all vestiges of her peasant class origins. ⟨. . .⟩

⟨. . .⟩ Aunt Becca, who gave up sexual love and motherhood for higher social status, offers Nellie guilt-ridden warnings rather than helpful advice, which prevents a close bond between the aunt and niece. Nevertheless, the views take root with Nellie, she acquiesces to them, breaking the rules only after she goes to college in the U.S. and even then feeling guilt.

Nellie grows up to become a college-educated, sexually repressed and intellectually alienated woman. She exists within a "kumbla," which is the symbolic representation of her alienation which Brodber uses throughout the novel. In order for Nellie to withdraw from the kumbla, from her protective enclosure which her middle-class aunt has so carefully taught her "how to wear," she must form real human bonds. She does form two: the first is with Baba Ruddick, her childhood friend who, in saviour-like white attire, destroys her self-deceiving role of secretary of a group of alienated pseudo-radical intellectuals. The second important bond is formed with her Aunt Alice, and it is the one which effectively saves her life. ⟨. . .⟩ Aunt Alice is oblivious to the conflicts caused by unwed motherhood and female sexuality, just as she is unaware of those created by class perspectives and arbitrary human bias because while she was still a child, "it had become crystal clear that little Alice was not quite right in the head" (*Jane*, p. 140).

The mental journey through the history of her father's family, starting with the white ancestor, the great-grandfather and his common-law wife, Tia Maria, who "did everything to annihilate herself . . . her skin, her dress, her smell" (*Jane*, p. 139), is what makes Nellie whole again. Recapturing the family history through the aid of a woman who is outside the realm of society's pressures and biases allows Nellie a full perspective of her origins in the community. It gives her the material to piece together the social and psychological origins of her Aunt Becca's worldview. It also provides Nellie with the strength and courage to emerge from her "kumbla." Building upon the warmth and friendship that her Aunt Alice offered her as a child, Nellie actually reestablishes communication with her self, the self which has been buried, confused and denied by Aunt Becca's teachings and society's contradictory messages about women's roles.

—Yakini Kemp, "Woman and Womanchild: Bonding and Selfhood in Three West Indian Novels by Women," *Sage* 2, no. 1 (Spring 1985): 26–27

BRUCE WOODCOCK

Jane and Louisa Will Soon Come Home ⟨. . .⟩ exploits contradictions in style which relate to, and perhaps derive from, the debates about the Caribbean aesthetic. It has an illusion of oral intimacy appropriate to the traditions recorded by Jamaica's folk poet Louise Bennett. In that sense, *Jane and Louisa Will Soon Come Home* has the popular 'urgency' which Lamming applauds as the central element in the emergent literary cultures of the Caribbean. ⟨*The Pleasure of Exile*, 1960, p. 38⟩. At the same time, like Lamming's own work, Erna Brodber's book is highly sophisticated in narrative and form. This contradiction between a sophisticated literary awareness and a deference to folk-oral traditions accounts in part for the dynamics of the novel. It crystalises around the use of a cultural symbol, the kumbla, which is made a recurrent motif in the text. The kumbla is the camouflaged egg of the August worm and in the text it comes to signify, among other things, cultural aspirations to hide behind an assumed identity. In one respect, it symbolises what Franz Fanon described in his analysis of the 'white masks' adopted by the upwardly-mobile coloured bourgeoisie in post-colonial situations ⟨*Black Skins, White Masks*, 1967⟩. But the way Erna Brodber uses the kumbla as a symbol effectively counteracts the implications of such cultural submergence. The kumbla image receives some of its meanings in the text through the recitation of a 'nancy' story, one of the residual elements of African tradition which have become so important for a diverse range of groups, from the Rastafarians to artists such as Brathwaite. The reassertion of links with Africa can act to counter the colonial legacy by asserting a view of history which is oppositional to the European view. This is very much to Erna Brodber's purpose. She uses the consciousness of her character Nellie to mediate a nexus of relationships and interrelationships, building an intricate web from the reveries and reflections of past and present. Scenes of oral immediacy or of bizarre surrealism mix to make up a patchwork of episodes, coming to resemble the 'scraps of news' which Nellie gradually hears about her family's history, and which were 'tucked away in our unconscious waiting for the other pieces to fit the jigsaw puzzle' ⟨p. 97⟩. The scattered pieces of the past hold clues as to the nature of the present. What is also revealed ⟨. . .⟩ is the process of becoming gendered, 'Wearing my label called woman. Upon my lapel called normal' ⟨p. 29⟩.

—Bruce Woodcock, "Post-1975 Caribbean Fiction and the Challenge to English Literature," *Critical Quarterly* 28, no. 4 (Winter 1986): 89–90

JOYCE WALKER-JOHNSON

Jane and Louisa Will Soon Come Home makes selective use of the author's experience in mediating a variety of themes. Discussion of this novel so far has concentrated on Nellie's experience as a reflection of that of the Caribbean woman, with considerable attention also being given to stylistic and structural aspects of the novel and to the central image of the Kumbla. Brodber's concern with communal ancestry has also been noted, and it has been generally recognized by her critics that Nellie's search for autonomy represents more than a search for a personal direction. The main purpose of this further examination is to show how she uses Nellie's experiences and those of other women whom she depicts to allude to specific incidents or events in her society's history, going back as far as the immediate post-emancipation period. The portrait of the society is strengthened both by the parallel between Nellie's circumstances and those of the society and the way in which the outlook of the women portrayed relates to particular periods of Jamaican social history. The Caribbean woman's behaviour, as Brodber has described it, has been formed very much in the same way as that of the slaves, to avoid conflict and to promote survival. In responding to experience in the way they do, she demonstrates, women become accomplices in their own oppression. Wittingly and unwittingly they create myths and perpetrate deceptions by which they are themselves controlled. Parallels with the colonial society caught up in the hoax of history are thus suggested. Furthermore, Nellie's attempt to free herself from the safe "womb" of inherited ideas evokes extreme schizophrenia comparable to the confusion and disaffection created within the social organ-ism attempting to re-orient itself. The new level of awareness which she achieves, through her re-examination of the past, is far removed from that of her grandmother, Granny Tucker. Nellie's changed outlook may be compared with that of the ex-colonial society in the 1970s, which has come to view its colonial heritage dispassionately.

The title of the novel directs attention to the heroine as prototype and to the fictional aspect of the story. This title, taken from a song which accompa-nies a ring game, both universalizes the reference of the experiences described and associates the novel with the folk/popular tradition. The continued refer-ence to the song "Jane and Louisa" in the section headings highlights the dom-inant theme of homecoming, the basic motif of journeying, and the important image of the garden, which links the novel with a variety of literary antecedents. Through the title, the author signals her intention to combine formal realism with fantasy and make-believe and to describe one set of rela-tions in terms of another. Thus, what advertises itself as a personal autobiog-raphy, primarily because of the narrative method employed, may be read also as a social history. ⟨. . .⟩

Jane and Louisa Will Soon Come Home, ostensibly the story of single individ-ual, ⟨. . .⟩ reflects phases in Jamaica's social development. Part One, which cov-ers Nellie's youth in the village, her high school and university career, refers to the period between World War II and Jamaica's achievement of political independence. Part Two alludes to events in the 1960s and 1970s, and Part Three takes the reader back to the village of Nellie's youth to recall some of the personal tragedies of which, as a child, she was vaguely aware. From her changed perspective, Nellie can understand the reasons for these tragedies. "The Moving Camera" restates and highlights Brodber's preoccupation with sociological analysis.

The novel ⟨. . .⟩ may be seen as an arrangement of facts of experience, apprehended through a single consciousness to create a metaphorical frame-work for projecting a view of history and society. Brodber uses the novel to demonstrate how history can be found in "the work patterns, the dances, the dreams, the songs and the memories of your forefathers" ⟨"Oral Sources and the Creation of Social History of the Caribbean," *Jamaica Journal* 4 (1983): 3⟩. The novel form, in this instance, provides only the vehicle for her attempt to relieve "the pain of history-lessness".

—Joyce Walker-Johnson, "Autobiography, History, and the Novel: Erna Brodber's *Jane and Louisa Will Soon Come Home*," *Journal of West Indian Literature* 3, no. 1 (January 1989): 47–48, 58

MICHAEL G. COOKE

Jane and Louisa Will Soon Come Home ⟨1980⟩ takes its title from a common children's song, the basis of a ring dance performed some evenings by little boys and girls in the yard or at the beach, anywhere outdoors, usually with adults helping out. Brodber takes the words and makes them into social commentary, then into talismans, then into mythic concentrations of the whole complex of Caribbean experience: childhood, city and country, the extended family, social mores and biases, sexual emergencies, political structures, and travel and study abroad (with all that these entail of culture shock and culture clarification and culture enlargement and culture reaffirmation). ⟨. . .⟩

The text is replete with images of enclosure, refining, revising, compounding, enriching one another and the mind of the central speaker. We find enclosure as imprisonment ("I was being choked. . . . I needed out" [p. 70], and as potential site of germination and growth ("immaculate egg" [p. 70], and the image of menstruation as a thing in its own space).

The kumbla is the ultimate image of enclosure in *Jane and Louisa*, and it is used with structural brilliance to resolve the contradictions and anxieties of the garden—the claustrophobia and paranoia and disgrace (since menstruation raises the danger of sexual capture and pregnancy, with its terminal confinement). The kumbla is the space of the self and space for the self, and is as versatile in form as our needs may be various: beachball, eggshell, light bulb, calabash, shell, parachute, womb, and, of course, the omnipresent ring of the title song. Where the garden gives space, the kumbla goes one better by giving both space and time—its only requirement is that one not stay in it too long, for fear of turning albino from lack of sun. The kumbla is the space-time for an apocalypse that is not yonder and happenstance in character, but the sum and product of experience that is illumined in our embrace. ⟨. . .⟩

⟨Another⟩ Brodber technique for capturing the innermost reaches of an idle children's song involves the remaking of the female role in the very edifice of language. What others try to cover over with language ⟨. . .⟩ Brodber insists on naming plain, and she does it with wicked irony: "the pee-pee chin tree in dem front yard, it don't name so no more. Is spathodia, if you please" (p. 40). Her men and women stand in the kitchen "staring past each other. Waiting. Perhaps for a language." And men sit at a bar "staring in the direction of the road. Wordlessly . . . waiting. Waiting for what? Perhaps for their women" (p. 41). If the women they are waiting for are all around them, perhaps the language is all around too, to recognize and to use. But instead of recognition and use, there is the double tableau of kitchen and bar, and silence besets the characters in the novel because of various looming customs.

But Brodber has one pivotal scene where the customary silence is broken and the female speaker explodes with expletives. This gives her the full diapason of national modern speech, unprecedented for a woman. It is a moment of some discomfort for Nellie: "Am I a fishwife?" (p. 71). It works, though, because it is logical, just, and expert. She has been manipulated and provoked. She could remain proper, but not if she is to become herself. She has used Barry's slang term, "bull shit," and apologized for it (p. 50). Now she uses her own curse words, with no apology. To curse *can* be proper for anyone not the mere property of custom.

Whether in vernacular rage or in sophisticated excavations of a children's song, Brodber enters into fresh territory for growing up, for adventure, and for tradition in the West Indies. What had never been dared or imagined stands suddenly integrated into the cultural scheme. The novel ends with an image of a complexly metamorphosed pregnancy, where the woman's belly is a gold-fish bowl, and the child a parrot fish that "no amount of bearing down could give birth to" (p. 147). That the "bearing down" cannot be completed is true to tradition and its adventure, and so no wonder: "I felt neither sadness nor frustration" (p. 147). Besides, by the recurrent imagery of the spying-glass and of the fowl brooding its eggs in December, Brodber makes it clear that, beyond the customary (the spying-glass) and *through* it a new life of the under-standing may be reached. For the thing seen is not just a momentarily fetch-ing object but also a subject that grows within us (the egg), even in the least favourable season (December). She does so without exaggerating the power of Brathwaite's great traditions (the sun is weak). Under our edifices, under our very bodies, a new state of being emerges.

—Michael G. Cooke, "The Strains of Apocalypse: Lamming's *Castle* and Brodber's *Jane and Louisa*," *Journal of West Indian Literature* 4, no. 1 (January 1990): 36–39

Carolyn Cooper

The landscape of Erna Brodber's *Jane and Louisa Will Soon Come Home* is largely that of rural Jamaica, a setting in which family ties are complicated by the sin-uous bonds of colour and class; a context within which an oral tradition of long-time story, family history and pure gossip flourishes alongside the world of books and distant town. Brodber's narrative method exemplifies an inter-penetration of scribal and oral literary forms: a modernist, stream-of-consciousness narrative voice holds easy dialogue with the traditional teller of tales, the transmitter of anansi story, proverb, folk song and dance.

Brodber's experiment in form is underscored by the writer's deliberately ingenuous assertion that *Jane and Louisa Will Soon Come Home* was not conceived as a novel: she set out to write a case study in Abnormal Psychology. But lit-erary critics have appropriated the work, recognizing in its dense patterns of allusive imagery, its evocative language and its carefully etched characterizations, the sensibility of the creative writer. The "functionalist" intention of the social psychologist appears divergent from the "structuralist" analysis of the literary critic. But, Brodber's "faction" can be categorized with a Neo-African folk aesthetic of functional form: literature as wordhoard, the repository of the accumulated wisdom of the community, the creative medium through which the norms of appropriate social behaviour can be elaborated metaphorically.

The Afro-Jamaican folk ethos of *Jane and Louisa Will Soon Come Home* is evident in the organizing metaphors of the work, derived from the folk culture, and in its primary theme: the healing of the protagonist Nellie, who travels to "foreign" to study, and returns home to a profound sense of homelessness, from which she is redeemed only when she comes to understand the oral accounts of her fragmented family history, and the distorted perceptions of female identity and sexuality that she has internalized in childhood. The therapeutic power of the word is the subject and medium of Brodber's fictive art.

Thus Brodber employs the central framing device of the creolized English quadrille dance, and the children's ring game derived from it, "Jane and Louisa Will Soon Come Home," to suggest, imagistically, the adaptive capacity of Neo-African folk culture in Jamaica, its conscription of English folk traditions for its own enrichment: fiddling with their dance! It is this very egalitarian resilience that the contemporary Caribbean intellectual needs to relearn. ⟨. . .⟩

Brodber herself, as social historian, asserts in her polemical essay, "Oral Sources and the Creation of a Social History of the Caribbean," that the Eurocentrically disposed Caribbean intellectual, like Nellie, must revitalize the severed linkages with the nurturing folk culture, for sanity's sake. The deliberate attempt to remember the past—both personal and racial/cultural—restores the breach of history.

—Carolyn Cooper, "Afro-Jamaican Folk Elements in Brodber's *Jane and Louisa Will Soon Come Home*," *Out of the Kumbla: Caribbean Women and Literature*, ed. Carole Boyce Davies and Elaine Savory Fido (Trenton: Africa World Press, Inc., 1990), 279–81

RHONDA COBHAM

How ⟨. . .⟩ to avoid the familiar heresy that the very pathology of ⟨the strength invested in Caribbean women⟩ is responsible for the emasculation of the Black man and the impoverishment of Afro-Caribbean culture?

Caribbean women writers have approached this issue by redefining the notion of motherhood itself. ⟨. . .⟩

Rather than celebrating the maternal in themselves or acting out their victimization as daughters, the symbolic arena of conflict between mother and daughter is removed from the realm of individual psychoanalysis and worked out in terms of community. In this way the inevitable link between biological

and social mothering is ruptured. Maternal caring, involving nurture, discipline and unconditional affection which one normally associates with the
mother figure is provided ⟨. . .⟩ by an assortment of Aunts, grandparents, god-
mothers, elderly neighbors and youthful, often unemployed male family connections. ⟨. . .⟩

⟨Such a⟩ relationship exists between Nellie and Mass Mehiah in *Jane and
Louisa*. The description of their interaction is redolent with sights, sounds and
smells commonly associated with maternal dialogue:

> I loved Mass Stanley and nobody seemed to mind. There were
> pimento trees in his yard growing out of rocks. And the rocks were
> peculiar too. They were full of holes. You had to walk carefully for if
> you stubbed your toe, it was liable to get stuck and break off alto-
> gether. And the rocks had a smell. Sometimes of coffee and tobacco
> and sometimes of sweet soap as if Miss Sada washed them . . . They
> liked to have me creeping into their house too. I would walk in and
> sit at the doorway and Mass Stanley, smoking his pipe in his rocking
> chair by the door, would crinkle his eyes and start talking to me.
> (Brodber 103)

Such fictive scenarios coincide closely with the reality of the extended
family as it exists in New World Black communities, where migration, crowded
living conditions, long working hours for women and relatively high rates of
death in childbirth severely limit the probability that any child grows up in a
one-to-one relationship with both its biological parents. In addition, children
must often live away from home to attend school and the notion of kin is less
a matter of blood ties than of shared exigency. However, none of this is viewed
in the novels as deviancy from the norm. On the contrary, once again an actual
cultural precedent, which in this case necessitates the separation of social and
biological aspects of mothering, is used as the basis of an alternative vision.
The wide network of social support and interaction such a system of social
mothering provides is contrasted favorably with the efforts of some of the
girls' kin to lock them into monolithic, emotionally overcharged relationships
with specific mother figures. ⟨. . .⟩

In keeping with the comparatively denser symbolic structure of *Jane and
Louisa*, social mothering in Nellie's community is presented in a variety of situations, involving many other children besides the protagonists. Baba's
upbringing by his grandparents, Mass Stanley and Miss Elsada is a typical
example. Having acted out the standard oedipal conflict between himself and
his son, Mass Mehiah finds himself saddled with the upbringing of this son's
offspring, Baba, who has been abandoned by both his natural parents. Rather
than being drawn as a child under a curse, Baba is presented as a special gift

whose presence heals the cycles of oedipal frustration within his grandfather's household (Brodber 110).

The complex interaction between parenting and community is presented in synchronic and diachronic terms. Thus, the beautiful garden into which Nellie's Great Aunt Alice leads her is planted with family members, past and present, all of whom have contributed to the strengths and weaknesses which are part of Nellie's psyche. The intricate weave of relationships finds its profoundest symbol in the dance that Nellie watches all the adults in her community perform at the village fair (Brodber 101–2). Its continuous exchange of partners is reminiscent of the children's game for which the novel is named.

—Rhonda Cobham, "Revisioning Our Kumblas: Transforming Feminist and Nationalist Agendas in Three Caribbean Women's Texts," *Callaloo* 16, no. 1 (Winter 1993): 57–58

SHALINI PURI

In her attempt to understand Jamaican society, Brodber grapples with the bitter (post)colonial phenomenon of "prejudice against blacks in a country of blacks. The enemy was a ghost that talked through black faces" ("Fiction" 165). Her novel, *Myal*, is in many ways a literalization of that metaphor. The novel is erected around the mulatto child Ella O'Grady. It spans the years 1913–20, Ella's fourteenth to twenty-first year. As a story of education and coming to consciousness, the novel functions at least partly in the tradition of the Bildungsroman. However, it does not proceed in the linear fashion of the traditional Bildungsroman, but through a complex series of halvings and doublings. At the beginning of her story—though not at the beginning of the novel—we see Ella reciting Kipling's "The White Man's Burden." It is quite literally the colonizer's voice that speaks through her. At the time, she is unaware of the implications of a colonial text that describes her people, a colonized people, as "half-devil, half child" (6). She does, however, know the pain of being a half-caste; like her mother, she knows what it is like to be a "long face, thin lip, pointed nose soul in a round face, thick lip, big eye country" (8). With her racial doubleness born of a forcible colonial coupling, Ella is not-quite-black-enough for most blacks to be comfortable with her; she is just-black-enough to be exotic and exciting to her white American husband; she is not-quite-white-enough to be worthy of carrying his children. We can reconstruct the novel as tracking Ella's development, from unconscious quiescence to the colonialist text, through complicity with the text, and recognition that "the half has not been told," to resistance to the text. ⟨. . .⟩

⟨. . .⟩ *Myal* locates the violence of colonial domination in its "halving" of mind and body, its narrative reduction of the Others to half-wits, and its suppression of "half" the story. That is why the novel is haunted by the insistent refrain: "the half has never been told" (34–35). At the heart of *Myal*, then, is a critique of binaristic narratives. If indeed it is by "halving," by suppressing heterogeneity or doubleness, that domination functions, then resistance to domination must involve the recovery of doubleness. That is why not linearity but doubleness becomes the cornerstone of *Myal*'s poetics. It manifests itself in the controlling concept-metaphor of spirit possession or zombification. For while spirit possession functions in the text as a figure for domination, it also "doubles" as a figure for the survival of disallowed African-derived cultural practices. Helen Tiffin notes that "[m]yalism also returns the Jamaicans to their African ancestry, and thus to the source of the original animal fables, which, taken via the Arab slaving routes through North Africa to the Mediterranean, were spread across Europe as Greek, as 'Aesop's fables'—a very early example of spirit thievery" (33). Spirit possession in the novel thus represents not only domination and theft but also the possibility of connection with the half that has not been told: ancestral beliefs, oral traditions, religions, and healing practices. ⟨. . .⟩

Both by authoring new texts and by opening up alternative reading positions in existing texts, *Myal* tries to tell the half that has not been told. The novel is thus deeply attentive to the multiple and complex ways in which our experience is textualized. To make sense of the multi-storied and temporally interrupted novel, the reader of *Myal* has to occupy a position similar to Ella's. Both readers have to weigh competing narratives, dislodge previous knowledges, and slowly piece meaning together. To use a metaphor from the novel, interpreting the text involves "fishing the bits out like a doctor carefully treating a wound" (90). Making sense of the texts thus involves bringing to the surface hidden stories and obfuscated truths. In "Mr. Joe's Farm," "all the animals . . . are ignorant all the time" (106). The novel's task is to bring to light that which the colonialist narratives render opaque: the possibilities of the Other half. Against the colonialist's linear and "transparent" narrative, which suppresses half the story, *Myal* sets its narrative of doubling, a narrative that is dense with possibilities.

—Shalini Puri, "An 'Other' Realism: Erna Brodber's *Myal*," *Ariel* 24, no. 3 (July 1993): 99–101, 111–12

CATHERINE NELSON-McDERMOTT

Erna Brodber's *Myal: a novel* (1988) ⟨identifies⟩ "contemporary" local and global levels and processes of imperialist cultural and social "spirit thievery." This text ultimately, however, constructs an active, supportive community which both deals with the problems of the colonial dialectical space and moves beyond them to begin building a non-colonized, and non-colonizable, social space. In doing so, *Myal* intervenes in critical debates about the place and nature of education in the Caribbean, the actual and ideal sites of cultural production and identity (including gendered identity), and the possible constitutions of community.

Myal may be said to consist of two intertwined plots, both of which focus on a young woman. In one, Anita is the object of the aging Mass Levi's spirit thievery as he atttempts to prop up his failing sexual powers by stealing her energy, psychically raping her. In the other, Ella becomes the object of spirit thievery when her foreign husband, Selwyn Langley, takes her memories of Grove Town and crafts them into an extremely racist, and very profitable, coon show. *Myal* focusses on the cultural and social processes leading up to the thieveries, while at the same time exploring the myal-ing which purges the characters and the Morant Bay community of exploitative activities. The two nonlinear plots are linked through a series of characters who live "doubled" lives and who heal on both an individual and a social level.

Myal interrogates the results and causes of an iniquitous vertical power system, colonialism. The text is a tale of the positionality of individuals functioning within and without Jamaica told through the psychic and physical landscape of Jamaica. In *Myal*, the process of spirit thievery is paradigmatic of the issues postcolonial cultures face on a day-to-day basis. On a very basic level, spirit thievery is the illegitimate use of another person's body or energy (usually for nefarious purposes). According to the text's Reverend Simpson, however, spirit thievery is also a process whereby persons, both individually and as a people, are convinced by "Conjure men, voodoo men, wizards and priests" (66) of their inadequacy to hold power; they therefore give up a way of looking at life, a way of knowing, that empowers: "The two first principles of spirit thievery [are to] let [people] feel that there is nowhere for them to grow to. Stunt them. . . . [and] Let them see their brightest ones as the dumbest ever. Alienate them" (98). Thus, the unscrupulous have ruled those split from themselves, "working zombie[s]" (67), from the time of Joseph and the Pharaohs. And given Erna Brodber's membership in the Twelve Tribes of Israel ⟨Evelyn O'Callaghan, "Erna Brodber," *Fifty Caribbean Writers*, ed. Daryl Cumber Dance, 1986, 73⟩ and G. E. Simpson's (perhaps suspect) proposal that Rastafarians believe "black men are the reincarnations of the ancient Israelites and were exiled to the West Indies [hell] because of their transgressions" ⟨Aggrey Brown, *Color, Class, and Politics in Jamaica*, 1979, 128⟩, Brodber's choice to locate the origins of spirit thievery (sin) with those involved in the sale of Joseph in Egypt (66) leads to interesting conjectures about the nature of the West Indies as home. Willie's contention that "some have to root" (67) where they are, creating a type of "practice pitch" (68) for those who might one day "make [their] way home," returning to Africa on Marcus Garvey's "Black Star line" (67), also gives rise to such conjectures. While G. E. Simpson contends that Rastafarians believe "the emperor of Ethiopia will arrange for African expatriates to be returned to the homeland [heaven]" (Brown 128), *Myal* clearly proposes a process of "redemption" much more active, communal in nature, and Jamaica-based than this.

—Catherine Nelson-McDermott, "Myal-ing Criticism: Beyond Colonizing Dialectics," *Ariel* 24, no. 4 (October 1993): 53–55

HELEN TIFFIN

Recent West Indian literature by women offers a locus of debate over the retrieval of the body from and within western discursive erasure. This erasure of the female body and its possible reclamation is of course central to contemporary feminist debate, and has its own genealogy within feminist discourse. My interest in this question, however, is in the ways in which colonialism's discursive and institutional apparatuses obliterated and continue to obliterate the colonised (specifically female) body, and the counter-colonial strategies by which this "lost" body might be reclaimed. In ⟨her⟩ fiction Erna Brodber ⟨. . .⟩ ⟨anatomizes⟩ the body's erasure under a colonialist scriptive drive and explores potentials for the re/cognition of corporeality and sexuality.

In Brodber's *Jane and Louisa Will Soon Come Home* the Victorian legacy of middle class sexual repression, collusive with a history of racist oppression, results in the denial of female sexuality, and is imaged here as a persistent attempt by blacks themselves to eradicate the "black womb," to "breed out" blackness. The result is profound self-denigration and a paranoid repression of sexuality. The children's ring game of "Jane and Louisa" introduces the possibility of overcoming that suppression, and thus of the "homecoming" of sexuality and the retrieval of women's bodies from a brutal history of racism and slavery. Once again a deeply interpellative education system ⟨. . .⟩ is figured as the institutional agent of a scribal Euro-colonialism that perpetuates the denigration and/or erasure of women's bodies. Alienated from their own bodies, women become speaking puppets of a deeply classed and gendered Anglo-imperialism. And once again it is a return to folkways and to oral Jamaican tradition which counteracts four centuries of damage.

—Helen Tiffin, "Cold Hearts and (Foreign) Tongues: Recitations and the Reclamation of the Female Body in the Works of Erna Brodber and Jamaica Kincaid," *Callaloo* 16, no. 4 (Fall 1993): 909, 912–13

B I B L I O G R A P H Y

Abandonment of Children in Jamaica. 1974.

A Study of the Yards in the City of Kingston. 1975.

Jane and Louisa Will Soon Come Home. 1980.

Perceptions of Caribbean Women: Towards a Documentation of Stereotypes. 1982.

Rural-urban Migration and the Jamaican Child. 1986.

Reggae and Cultural Identity in Jamaica (with J. Edward Greene). 1986.

Myal. 1988.

Louisiana. 1994.

MICHELLE CLIFF

B. 1946

MICHELLE CLIFF was born on November 2, 1946, in Kingston, Jamaica. When she was a young child, she and her family moved to New York, where she attended public schools. In 1969 she graduated from Wagner College with a bachelor's degree in European history. After working for a year in New York at the publishing house W. W. Norton, Cliff moved to London to attend the Warburg Institute. In 1974 she received her master's degree in philosophy, focusing on languages and comparative historical studies of the Italian Renaissance.

Returning to Norton in 1974, Cliff edited and copublished with Adrienne Rich *Sinister Wisdom*, a feminist journal, from 1981 to 1983, while she was a member of the editorial board of *Signs* from 1980 until 1989. Cliff has taught at a number of institutions, including the New School for Social Research (1974–76); Women Writers Center, Cazenovia College (1982); University of California, Santa Cruz (1987); and Stanford University (1987–1991).

All of Cliff's writing—poetry, fiction, and nonfiction—reflects her interest in histories of struggle, revolution, and political action, both personal and public, silenced and voiced. Her work also explores how identity is shaped by racism and sexism: a book she edited in 1978, *The Winner Names the Age: A Collection of Writing by Lillian Smith*, explores these issues in the context of the American South. In her first book, the semiautobiographical prose poem *Claiming an Identity They Taught Me to Despise* (1980), Cliff traces the intraracial prejudice in the creole community in Jamaica. The poem tells the story of a Jamaican mulatto who embraces her African heritage despite her family's desire for her to do the opposite.

Cliff's first two novels (*Abeng*, 1984; *No Telephone to Heaven*, 1988) continue this theme. They tell the story of Clare Savage as she negotiates the two worlds represented in her family. On her father's side, Clare is descended from slave owners, and on her mother's, from maroon society and the peasantry. While her family celebrates the plantocracy represented by her father's people, Clare only learns of her mother's history from stories told to her by her maternal grandmother. *Abeng* focuses on Clare's adolescent struggles, which are mirrored in the larger context of the search for identity in Jamaica. In *No Telephone to Heaven*, Clare's exile in the United States leads her back to Jamaica to participate in the revolutionary struggle as she searches for "spiritual integrity." Cliff weaves a number of interlocking themes in the novel, including politics, myth, colonialism, and race.

Cliff has also published a collection of poetry and prose (*The Land of Look Behind*, 1985), a collection of short stories (*Bodies of Water*, 1990), and a number of nonfiction essays (in *Sojourner, American Voice*, and *The Voice Literary Supplement*). She has been awarded a Fulbright scholarship (1988) and fellowships by the National Endowment for the Arts (1984 and 1989).

Free Enterprise (1993), Cliff's most recent novel, is considered by many of her critics as her strongest yet. It tells of women revolutionaries and their involvement in John Brown's raid on Harper's Ferry, following the friendship between the sole fictional character, Annie Christmas, and Mary Ellen Pleasant, an entrepreneur in San Francisco in the 19th century. The novel offers various histories—oral, symbolic, and written; American, Caribbean, and African—to tell its story.

Since 1993 Cliff has been a contributing editor of *American Voice*. She is currently the Allan K. Smith Professor of English Language and Literature at Trinity College in Hartford, Connecticut.

C R I T I C A L   E X T R A C T S

CAREN KAPLAN

A world which brings people, information, objects, and images across enormous distances at rapid speeds destabilizes the conventions of identity traditionally found in the culture of the first world during the first half of this century. "Deterritorialization" is one term for the displacement of identities, persons, and meanings that is endemic to the postmodern world system. ⟨. . .⟩

In *Claiming an Identity They Taught Me to Despise* Michelle Cliff describes the process of finding a social space to inhabit that will not deny any of the complicated parts of her identity and history. Radically deterritorialized from a Caribbean culture and a race by a family conspiracy of silence and denial, she explores the parameters of identity and the limits of privilege. Separated from her home and family by geography, education, and experience, Cliff articulates the boundaries between homelessness and origin, between exile and belonging. She must, as she puts it, "untangle the filaments of my history" ⟨7⟩.

The first move Cliff makes in her autobiographical memoir is a return to the territory of her childhood. This trip into memory uncovers a primal injunction. "Isolate yourself," she was told:

> If they find out about you it's all over. Forget about your great-grandfather with the darkest skin . . . . Go to college. Go to England to study. Learn about the Italian Renaissance and forget that they kept slaves. Ignore the tears of the Indians. Black Americans don't understand us either . . . . Blend in . . .

In order to understand her refusal to blend in, Cliff begins to explore what is at stake in her mother's efforts to obscure her racial identity. She has to learn the history of white, black, and mulatto people in Jamaica, the island where she was born. It is a history of divisions, violence, and suppression. A creole culture with no single origin, Jamaica exists in many levels and time periods. Cliff moves through several of these identities. She rewrites her history to "claim" an identity through her powers of story-telling and imagination.

Turning her memories of childhood over and over, Cliff begins with the terrain of the island. Looking for a firm foundation for her identity she finds instead that the geography of that time is "obsolete." There is no possibility of return to that innocent land. Instead, she moves through each place she has lived, asking, "What is here for me: where do these things lead?" ⟨20⟩. At first Cliff discovers the pain that her family had struggled to spare her. Behind each nostalgic memory lies a history of oppression ⟨. . . .⟩ Her new view of her past and her life has to contain all of these images and kinds of knowledge. They become materials for Cliff to discover and use, stories to listen to again, photographs to review, a landscape to rewrite. Mining her memories of both Jamaica and New York she is no longer able to remain separated from the full range of experiences and identities available to her in the past and present.

—Caren Kaplan, "Deterritorializations: The Rewriting of Home and Exile in Western Feminist Discourse," *Cultural Critique* 6 (Spring 1987): 188, 195–96

LIZABETH PARAVISINI AND BARBARA WEBB

The "pairing of two girls" is also the focus of Michelle Cliff's treatment of the Caribbean adolescent's quest for adulthood in *Abeng*. ⟨The⟩ adolescent heroine ⟨of *Abeng*⟩ grows up in a colonial society divided by issues of race, color and class. The relationship between the legacy of colonialism and sexism ⟨is⟩ explicit in this novel, which in many ways is a feminist parable that illustrates how race and class influence our notions of female empowerment and sisterhood. The title of Cliff's novel is the African word for the conch shell used by the Maroons to sound out calls of rebellion. Since the conch shell also suggests the shape of the womb, her title is symbolic of the synthesis of history, rebellion and the feminist perspective that she attempts in the narrative.

The adolescent heroine, twelve-year old Clare, is the oldest daughter of a Jamaican family that has lost its former wealth but that nevertheless clings to the delusion of status based on color. Her father, James Arthur Savage (Boy), is the descendant of an English official who came to Jamaica in the early nineteenth century. If nothing else, Boy Savage inherits his ancestor's arrogance. Since his main purpose in life is the "preservation of whiteness and obliteration of darkness" (129), he lays claim to his beautiful, fair-skinned daughter as the true heir of the Savage family's privileged past. He treats Clare as he would a son, which gives her the false impression that her sex has no boundaries.

Clare's mother, Kitty, is from a family of small farmers, poor by Savage standards and somewhat lower in the caste system based on color. Unlike her husband, she feels a strong connection to the land and people of Jamaica, but her marriage to Boy puts an end to her youthful dreams of building a school in the country where she would teach her people an appreciation of their own island. In what Cliff describes as a misguided act of defiance, Kitty retreats into silence. Her repressed love for the poor Black people of Jamaica and her refusal to share these feelings, or any form of intimacy for that matter, deprives Clare of an important alternative to her father's pretensions.

Through self-deception and denial, her parents obscure the true nature of their pasts. Young Clare is therefore faced with the task of sorting out the family "mythology". Since an understanding of her parents' "separate histories" is crucial to her development, the narrative is composed of contrasting segments of family and social history; her father is associated with the falsified glory of the colonizer and her mother with the "untold" history of Jamaica, the legacy of the maroon rebellions, especially as they relate to the role of women such as the legendary Nanny. In order to become a responsible adult with a clear sense of who she is, Clare needs to know her connection to that history.

—Lizabeth Paravisini and Barbara Webb, "On the Threshold of Becoming: Caribbean Women Writers," *Cimarron* 1, no. 3 (Spring 1988): 113–14

LEMUEL A. JOHNSON

Michelle Cliff 〈. . .〉 insists on a vision of history as blood/lines: as "an intricate weave, at the heart of which was enforced labor of one kind or another." The pattern holds from Cape-to-Cairo; from the tea plantations of Ceylon and China to the coffee ones of Sumatra and Colombia. There are, too, "the mills of Lowell. Manchester. Leeds. Marseilles. The mines of Wales. Alsace-Lorraine. The railroads of Union Pacific." Under such circumstances, "Slavery was not an aberration—it was an extreme. . . . To some this may be elemen-

tary—but it is important to take it all in, the disconnections and the connections." For to do so would be to better understand the closed economy within
which traffic and trade in identities take place; within which, when the carnival turns bitter, the road march becomes the constraining reality of a chain
gang and gender shuffle—and why, incidentally, the rod of correction can lay
about with a caned sweetness. In short, the pattern of disconnections and
reconnections makes very clear indeed the inexorable logic of the Same which
binds veiled slavery to slavery-in-fact. ⟨. . .⟩

In Michelle Cliff's arrangement of things woman does not, indeed cannot,
exist outside so dynamic a conception of history. *Abeng* does not deliver her
packaged and contained in an ahistorical "essentialism." What we have is,
instead, *Subject-in-History* participation. And it is one which, incidentally, can
be very much conquistadorial. After all, in 1958 Jamaica had two rulers: "a
white queen and a white governor." The former was a "rather plain little white
woman decked in medals and other regalia—wearing, of course, a crown. Our-
lady-of-the-colonies. The whitest woman in the world" (*Abeng*: p. 5).
Historical engagement can also be other than conquistadorial. It is in this second context, with its ab-original female types and island-in-between resistance, that Michelle Cliff recreates in Maroon Nanny (at long last!) the
complement to and anticipation of Toussaint and of Nat Turner; of Macandal
and Christophe. For before all of them, she, Maroon Nanny, was. *Abeng's* con-
ceptualization of the essential historical gesture is thus determined by the
active Subject-in-History which Maroon Nanny was and becomes. She
remains indivisibly present in the intricate weave of *Abeng's* genealogies and
disconnections within which she is always represented as person-in-reality and
re-presented as spirit of the deep crevices of the Blue Mountains: of "Cockpits.
Places to hide. Difficult to reach. Not barren but deep and magnificent inden-
tations populated by bush and growth and wild orchids—collectors of
water—natural goblets" (p. 21). In effect, she was: "there is no doubt at all that
she actually existed." But then, because Cliff's conflation of the phenomenal
and the numinous is meticulous, (having been) Maroon Nanny remains as historically singular as she is bio-cultural continuity and symbolic expression
⟨. . . .⟩ Michelle Cliff's mountain stronghold thus continues the hold out for a
line of ab-original and female descent through Jamaica's Maroon Nanny, she
"who could catch bullets in her buttocks." "A small and old Black woman
whose only decoration was a necklace fashioned from the teeth of white men"
(p. 21), Maroon Nanny serves to counterpoint that other "rather plain white
woman decked in medals. . . . The whitest woman in the world."

Abeng then, through Nanny and her sister Sekesu, makes a point of tracing
its genealogy of New World consciousness to a foundational memory-event.
The narrative of Clare Savage's developing Caribbean consciousness thus

introduces us, in a narration as ectypal as it is archetypal, to quite elaborate and woman-centered processes of myth-making and *mythos*-recovering: "It was believed that all island children were descended from one or the other. All island people were first cousins" (p. 18).

—Lemuel A. Johnson, "A-beng: (Re)Calling the Body In(To) Question," *Out of the Kumbla: Caribbean Women and Literature*, ed. Carole Boyce Davies and Elaine Savory Fido (Trenton, N.J.: Africa World Press, 1990), 122–24

M. STEPHANIE RICKS

In *Bodies of Water*, Michelle Cliff draws from both historical and modern sources to zoom in on the individual as outsider in the United States. Her stories are spare, their rhythm staccato. The details sometimes overlap in stories and offer multilayered passages that are slowly peeled away as the narrative progresses.

"A Woman Who Plays Trumpet Is Deported," is dedicated to Valaida Snow, a concentration-camp survivor who played the trumpet. It begins with abrupt, terse prose, its rhythm analogous to a solo trumpet riff. "A woman. A black woman. A black woman musician. A black woman musician who plays trumpet. A bitch who blows. A lady trumpet-player. A woman with chops."

In language that is piercing, clear, and fluid, the story follows the progress of this woman musician from America to Europe. Happy for the solitude and the opportunity to play, the woman is eventually picked up on a Copenhagen street in 1942 and lined up with other women and children with her trumpet clasped to her side.

The story of the book's title, "Bodies of Water" opens with Jess, an older woman fishing on a frozen lake. She is singing to attract the fish and to keep herself awake. Recently widowed by her lover and companion, Jess ultimately reflects on a childhood incident that continues to haunt her.

Michelle Cliff's writing whooshes like the breeze through autumn leaves, making the air crackle and the leaves quiver. Her stories are sometimes rich in details, other times painfully bare but always full of humanity, feeling, and truth. Cliff successfully weaves the divergent themes of oppression and empowerment, with all of the many shadings in between, into an enriching literary endeavor.

—M. Stephanie Ricks, "Tales of the 'Other,' " *Belles Lettres* 6, no. 2 (Winter 1991): 15

ANN R. MORRIS AND MARGARET M. DUNN

Historically, England has been the 'motherland' to the peoples of the West Indies and, even in a post-colonial era, England is occasionally referred to in West Indian writing as the 'motherland' or 'mother country'. Such a reference is usually ironic, however. As the fiction and poetry of West Indian writers makes clear, it is Dominica or Jamaica or Barbados or Antigua that is truly the homeland, the motherland.

For the Caribbean woman, the notion of a motherland is especially complex, encompassing in its connotations her island home and its unique culture as well as the body of tropes, talismans and female bonding that is a woman's heritage through her own and other mothers. The land and one's mothers, then, are co-joined. If a woman is able to claim a connection to both, she is well prepared for the journey toward self-identity and fulfillment. But if she has been denied a developmental bond with her own mother, then the 'mothers' land' itself may provide a surrogate. ⟨. . .⟩

Clare Savage wanders in a disconnected state for many years. Clare is clearly the protagonist of Michelle Cliff's 1987 novel *No Telephone to Heaven*, yet a large early section of the book focuses equally on Clare's mother Kitty who is Jamaica-born and never wants to live anywhere else. While still in Jamaica, Kitty marries Boy Savage and has two daughters. But then Kitty's mother, Miss Mattie, dies, and Boy seizes the opportunity to move his family to New York. For Kitty, the new life is a living death. She misses the climate, the foods, the music and patois, the customs and traditions of Jamaica. With no warning and no explanation, Kitty moves back to the islands, taking Clare's dark-skinned sister with her but leaving Clare and her father, both of whom can presumably make lives for themselves because they can 'pass for white'.

For Clare, however, Kitty's abrupt rejection is traumatic. She is left unmothered, while still a child, 'not feeling much of anything, except a vague dread that she belongs nowhere' (p. 91). Between Clare and her father a gulf exists that only widens with time, Boy Savage having embraced his adopted country when he arrived in Brooklyn and completing his rejection of all things Jamaican by eventually marrying a white New Yorker of Italian descent. After Kitty dies, Clare's sister comes to visit in New York. But there is no bond between the two young women, and Clare is unable to find out from her sister why their mother took one of them and left the other, Clare, without so much as a word of farewell or explanation. Feeling rootless and alone, Clare begins an odyssey that takes her from New York to London and eventually across Europe, with intermittent returns to Jamaica. As Cliff writes about her protagonist, 'There are many bits and pieces to her, for she is composed of fragments. In this journey, she hopes, is her restoration' (p. 87). ⟨. . .⟩

The Jamaica to which Clare returns is ravaged by poverty, crime and civil insurrection. Yet in the midst of all this, Clare begins to find her roots. ⟨. . .⟩

⟨. . .⟩ In returning to her mother's land, Clare finds her mother. Equally important, she finds herself. At one point an old island woman thinks that Clare *is* Kitty, and this seems to Clare an appropriate sign that the years and miles separating mother and daughter are diminished. In response to a question as to why she returned, Clare says, 'I returned to this island to mend . . . to bury . . . my mother . . . I returned to this island because there was nowhere else . . . I could live no longer in borrowed countries, on borrowed time' (pp. 192–93: the ellipses are in the original). Having found her mother and herself, Clare goes on to make a personal and political commitment to Jamaica and its people. For the first time since leaving Kingston many years ago, Clare has found the place where she belongs.

—Ann R. Morris and Margaret M. Dunn, "'The Bloodstream of Our Inheritance': Female Identity and the Caribbean Mothers'-Land," *Motherlands: Black Women's Writing from Africa, the Caribbean and South Asia*, ed. Susheila Nasta (London: The Women's Press Limited, 1991), 219, 232–34

FRANÇOISE LIONNET

Michelle Cliff chooses the *abeng* as an emblem for her book because, like the conch, the book is an instrument of communication whose performative function seems to be valorized. The story she tells is meant to inform and educate Jamaicans and non-Jamaicans alike, and she goes to great lengths to demystify the past in order to imagine, invent, and rewrite a different collective and personal history for the protagonist. The narrative weaves the personal and the political together, allowing the protagonist Clare Savage, who is but a thinly disguised alter ego of the author, to negotiate the conflicting elements of her cultural and familial background. She thus succeeds in reclaiming the multifaceted identity her family and society had "taught [her] to despise," namely, her mixed racial heritage, her femininity, and her homosexuality.

The narrative sets up an uneasy and duplicitous relationship with its audience. It begins with the standard disclaimer, "This work is a work of fiction, and any resemblance to persons alive or dead is entirely coincidental," despite its clearly autobiographical themes, which echo and repeat similar themes treated from a first-person perspective in Cliff's poetry and essays. But *Abeng* discloses far more about the author than does the poetry, while engaging the reader in a dialogue that confronts the fictions of self-representation. ⟨. . .⟩

The use of Creole accentuates some of these structural ambiguities. Numerous instances of patois fragment the linguistic unity of the book, and limit the range of textual understanding for the non-Jamaican reader. Cliff, however, includes a glossary of Creole terms as a posttext, without giving any prior indication of that fact; this is tantamount to a gesture of inclusion/ exclusion that forces the reader to situate him- or herself with regard to his or her particular understanding of Jamaican Creole. Thus American readers who approach this book for the first time may well remain unaware of the glossary, and feel "excluded" unless they flip through to the last page of the book while reading. This move from Standard English to Creole speech is meant to underscore class and race differences among protagonists, but it also makes manifest the double consciousness of the postcolonial, bilingual, and bicultural writer who lives and writes across the margins of different traditions and cultural universes. For Cliff, to attempt to define her own place is also to undermine all homogeneous and monolithic perspectives—especially those constructed by the official colonial historiography—and to situate her text within the prismatic field of contemporary feminist discourse. ⟨. . .⟩

When Michelle Cliff strives to reinvent the past, she is guided by its traces as they exist and show up in the everyday world. More often than not, these traces are present in language in the form of words whose etymology is "foreign" and often unknown to the majority of the people using them. In such cases, the vernacular is "parasitic," its existence depending upon the relative unrecognizability of its origins. That is why Cliff takes on the role of cultural translator, stating: "The people . . . did not know that their name for papaya—*pawpaw*—was the name of one of the languages of Dahomey. Or that the *cotta*, the circle of cloth women wound tightly to make a cushion to balance baskets on their heads, was an African device, an African word" (p. 20). Interestingly, words such as *pawpaw* and *cotta* function as noise in *both* Standard English and Jamaican Creole. Although commonly used in everyday speech, and assimilated into the language, they retain a radical difference that can point to their submerged origins on the palimpsest of history. Now, in Anglocentric "literary language," *pawpaw* and *cotta* could of course be recuperated as "folkloric" cultural detail, but for Cliff they become polyvalent signifiers, lifelines to a different past, the means by which a different art form, closer to an oral tradition of storytelling and self-representation, can begin to take shape.

    —Françoise Lionnet, "Of Mangoes and Maroons: Language, History, and the Multicultural Subject of Michelle Cliff's *Abeng*," *De/Colonizing the Subject: The Politics of Gender in Women's Autobiography*, ed. Sidonie Smith and Julia Watson (Minneapolis: University of Minnesota Press, 1992), 323–24, 333–34.

MARIA HELENA LIMA

Clare, like Jamaica Kincaid's Annie John, exists in dialogue with *Jane Eyre*. Like Jane Eyre, Clare is motherless; she is solitary and left to wander, having "no relations to speak of except [like Jane Eyre] an uncle across the water" (116). Cliff, however, goes a step further than Kincaid and incorporates Bertha Mason into Clare's intertextual identity: "Captive. Ragout. Mixture. Confused. Jamaican. Caliban. Carib. Cannibal. Cimarron. All Bertha. All Clare" (116). ⟨. . .⟩

Clare's separation from her mother signals the rupture from the "African" and the collective in her, since Boy, Clare's father, counsels his daughter on invisibility and secrets and has "no visible problems with declaring himself white": "Self-effacement. Blending in. The uses of camouflage" (100). Kitty leaves her daughter and her husband in the U.S. because she feels she *has* to return to her island, her "point of reference—the place which explained the world to her" (66). Clare's loss of both mother and island clearly structure the novel, which is ultimately about her futile attempt at return and wholeness. There are many bits and pieces to Clare, Cliff writes: she is composed of fragments. Clare's journey back to Jamaica, she hopes, will be her restoration (87). ⟨. . .⟩

⟨. . .⟩ The images Cliff creates to trace Clare's movement back to her homeland, however, are quite disturbing:

> The albino gorilla moving through the underbrush. Hiding from the poachers who would claim her and crush her in a packing crate against the darker ones . . . Make ashtrays of her hands, and a trophy of her head. She cowers in the bush fearing capture. . . . Not feeling much of anything, except a vague dread that she belongs nowhere. . . . She does not gather branches to braid into a nest. She moves. Emigrated, lone travel . . . Time passes. The longing for tribe surfaces—unmistakable. She is the woman who had reclaimed her grandmother's land. (91)

Feelings of displacement characterize not only the exile but the post-colonial condition whose homelessness Cliff figures with images of absence of colour (the albino gorilla) instead of conferring upon her character a mestiza identity (and colour). "Gorilla" and "longing for tribe" convey the primitivism often associated with "African" and evoked in her own name. Clare's return to Jamaica also follows an almost biological urge: the island is female and the "albino" child is finally reunited with the lost mother. From a post-structuralist cultural feminist perspective, Cliff reifies "African," "female experience," and "woman." It is this essentialism which makes her project, the possibility of revolutionary social transformation, and its figuration ultimately incompatible.

As a crossroads character, Clare belongs at least in two worlds. Her first name, Cliff tells us, "stands for privilege, civilization, erasure, forgetting. She is not meant to curse, or rave, or be a critic of imperialism. She is meant to speak softly and keep her place" ("Clare Savage" 265). Her surname evokes the wildness that has been bleached from her skin. Cliff emphasizes how she uses the word *savage* to mock the master's meaning, "turning instead to a sense of non-Western values which are empowering and essential to survival and wholeness" ("Clare Savage" 265). As a colonized child, Clare understands that it is her bleached skin which is the source of her privilege and her power. A knowledge of her history, the past of her people, however, has been bleached from Clare's mind (the history Cliff attempts to recover with *Abeng*).

Whereas Walter Benjamin and Georg Lukács refer to the link between allegory and the annihilation of history, in Cliff, the allegorical serves to inscribe an alternative history as she makes clear how this female power originates in Nanny, the African warrior and Maroon leader who has been left out of most textbooks. At her most powerful, Cliff writes, the grandmother is the source of knowledge, magic, ancestors, stories, healing practices, and food. She assists at rites of passage, protects, and teaches (267).

—Maria Helena Lima, "Revolutionary Developments: Michelle Cliff's *No Telephone to Heaven* and Merle Collins's *Angel*," *Ariel* 24, no. 1 (January 1993): 38–41

BELINDA EDMONDSON

⟨The⟩ status of Michelle Cliff, a contemporary "Jamaica white" (a Jamaican of mostly white ancestry) West Indian woman writer who explicitly seeks to revalue black identity in her novels, is debated by West Indian feminists and intellectuals, many of whom feel that even as Cliff is described as a black feminist novelist in America (where she lives and writes) her novels are not truly part of an Afrocentric Caribbean discourse because her project as a feminist emanates from an American feminist sensibility and perhaps more importantly that her discovery of a black identity is a foreign fashion that she has appropriated. Yet I think it significant that it is white *women* in the West Indies who are questioning the terms of their ambivalent status and not the men ⟨. . . .⟩ However, while certainly several feminist critics have used Fanon's model of colonialism to describe the relationship between male (colonizer) culture and female (colonized) status, and feminist scientist Sandra Harding has even suggested that the world views for white women and Africans converge, these do not begin to address the contradictions of white creole women, who are simultaneously both and neither. If we extend the binary logic of these genderized formulations, white creole women embody not simply both "First" and "Third" World sensibilities but also "male" (white, Euro-American) colonizing culture and "female" (black, post-colonial) colonized nature, a conflation of geopolitical and gender categories that is highly suspect.

Thus, the problem of how to situate the white creole writer is further complicated when gender becomes an issue, as we have seen. The contemporary West Indian novel reflects a somewhat different sensibility than its predecessor: a significant percentage of today's West Indian writers are women, and they have recast the familiar project of articulating a national identity to reflect their specific experiences as women. Michelle Cliff's novels are critical to working out the problems of race and gender in this regard because they reflect her search for an Afrocentric identity through her matrilineal ancestry while attempting to come to terms with her father's lineage of planters and slave-owners; thus, the search for a black history/identity is intimately bound up with a latent feminism as well as with a revolutionary social consciousness. ⟨. . .⟩

⟨. . .⟩ Cliff is setting up a dichotomy in the white father/black mother parallel, so that Clare's search for a black identity becomes aligned with a woman-centered, incipiently feminist consciousness. This is borne out by Cliff's rewriting of the Jamaican myth of Nanny, a maroon fighter in the 1800s who was reputed to catch the bullets of redcoats between her buttocks; in *Abeng* she is transformed into Mma Alli, a lesbian obeah woman who teaches the slaves how to escape.

By recreating Nanny as a "woman-centered" figure Cliff is attempting to insert a wedge in the historical narrative of Jamaica which will revalue not simply a black experience but will also provide an empowering history for West Indian women. Similarly, she casts Kitty—and indeed all black women in this novel—as having a direct and unmediated linkage to a positive black history and consciousness. This contradicts the implicit logic of the narrative structure: it hopes to construct an historical identity from fragments and dislocations of identity, yet it leaves Clare as the sole embodiment of historical fragmentation without acknowledging that the imposition of colonial ideology and racial attitudes must have affected *their* relationship to black identity. Kitty, for instance, has, despite her desire to teach African history to poor black children, married a racist white man, yet her sense of black identity is never questioned in the interests of preserving the narrative's clear racial ideology (indeed, Kitty's explanation that she was pregnant and had no choice is meant to be interpreted as further evidence of the black woman's plight in Jamaica but rather smacks of an authorial "quick fix" to deal with such glaring ambiguity). Despite Clare's pivotal role, the power relations in this novel are structured in binary terms of a source of power (white men: Judge Savage and Boy Savage) and reactions to that power (black women: Mma Alli, Kitty). The logic of this arrangement dictates that were the oppressed (black women) to accede to power, the existing organization of class/race relations would be dismantled, an arrangement that does not acknowledge the diffusion of power in terms more complex than simply economic or racial.

—Belinda Edmondson, "Race, Privilege and the Politics of (Re)Writing History: An Analysis of the Novels of Michelle Cliff," *Callaloo* 16, no. 1 (Winter 1993): 181–82, 188–89

SOUSA JAMBA

In the past, to make sense of their current condition, black writers dealing with the Americans—such as James Baldwin or Ralph Ellison—made their mark by delving into the present. There is, however, a younger generation. Toni Morrison among them, whose narratives have gone back into the years of slavery. This story ⟨*Free Enterprise*⟩ of two black women who, in 1858, plot an unsuccessful revolution is one of these.

We first learn of Annie, a Jamaican woman who has left her life of privilege on the island to join the failed revolution and has now settled on the banks of the Mississippi next to a leper colony where the patients while their time away by telling each other stories. When it is Annie's turn, she tells the story of a Jamaican prophet who had promised his flock he could fly back to Africa. Except for this, the stories at the colony are boring and the characters—as with the rest of the novel—are no more than mere props through which the author tries to make her points. ⟨. . .⟩

⟨. . .⟩ Many of the issues raised in this novel are indeed very relevant to the general debate going on in America about the condition of its citizens of African descent.

Michelle Cliff is at her best when she evokes the horror of slavery. There are memorable passages in this novel. The issues it raises, however, have to be extracted from the highly involved narrative which, I feel, is unnecessary. Every page of this novel seems to be begging desperately to be taken as serious literature.

—Sousa Jamba, "Why the Slaves' Revolution Failed," *The Times* (21 April 1994): 90

CAROLE BOYCE DAVIES

⟨The⟩ migrations between identities, or the articulations of a variety of identities, are central to our understandings of the ways in which ⟨Afro-Caribbean⟩ writers express notions of home in their works. Michelle Cliff, for example, creates the world of the bourgeoise, the Caribbean white vacillating between the metaphoric yard and the big house. And for her, migration issues are also critical and central to the definition of identity, because she becomes racially somebody else, an "other" within the contexts of migration and US racial politics. ⟨. . .⟩

The implications of identity are centrally located in Michelle Cliff's *Claiming an Identity They Taught Me to Despise*. The expressive titling of the book with the issue of identity reclamation, as well as its suggestion that identity is not a singular thing, confronts questions of subjectivity in a discursively lyrical manner. It is a somewhat autobiographical exploration of identity, with gender, heritage, sexuality and the sense of place defining that identity. Landscape, family, historical events, places, relationships, all become features in her exploration. The movement of the book mirrors the migratory pattern, beginning in the Caribbean and childhood and moving to the United States and adulthood. The sections entitled, "Obsolete Geography" and "Filaments" particularly typify the thematics of identity. In the first, we get an extended catalog of Caribbean fruits, vegetation, details of day-to-day experience like the waxing of the parlor floors, the burying of umbilical cords, the slaughtering of domestic animals. Much of the identification with "home" comes from the rural grandmother who maintains continuity with homeland and whose entire being conveys the multifaceted composition of Caribbean society. We see our narrator, however, caught up in the conflict of being privileged, yet poor, white-skinned but culturally Caribbean. Her mother is a distant, intangible, liminal presence in her life. The contradictions of surface appearance versus multi-textured reality, of camouflage and passing are explored. For this reason she feels affinity with Antoinette of *Wide Sargasso Sea* as she does with Tia. The creoleness that is essentially Caribbean identity is the necessity of accepting all facets of experience, history and personhood in the definition of the self. Here, Cliff integrates these into a consciousness of her own identities. Personal history, family history and a people's history and culture all converge.

Even more explicit in her connections are her polemical essays like "If I Could Write This In Fire, I Would Write This in Fire" 〈in *The Land of Look Behind*, 1985〉 where she is definite about the politics of Caribbean identity. Color and privilege are held up and examined. British colonialism and American colonialism are juxtaposed (pp. 67–68). Novels of Black female experience, like Toni Morrison's *Sula* in the African-American context or Ama Ata Aidoo's *Our Sister Killjoy* in the African context, are recalled and deployed. So too are W. E. B. Du Bois's concept of double consciousness and Bob Marley and the Rastafarian assertions on identity questions. Cliff admits intertextual interrogations at many levels.

    —Carole Boyce Davies, *Black Women, Writing and Identity: Migrations of the Subject* (London: Routledge, 1994), 116, 122–23

OPAL PALMER ADISA

Adisa: I know you admire Toni Morrison, and reading *Free Enterprise*, I was reminded of Morrison's work. How, or in what ways, has Morrison influenced your writing?

Cliff: Enormously. I don't think I could have written this novel if she hadn't written *Beloved*. Her imagining of that period, of slavery and its aftermath, opened up my imagination with regard to the rewriting of history, revising the history we've all been taught. And there are touches in my novel that would have been impossible without Morrison's having taken on the whole idea of bondage and resistance.

Adisa: It seems to me that your book is not a novel in the traditional sense of that genre. I have been examining how African, Caribbean, African American, and Latin American writers have been extending the boundary of this genre.

Your novel is a combination of letters, poetry, prose, and even a sense of drama, dialogue. Can you speak about the novel form in relation to your writing?

Cliff: I think part of it is that I come out of an oral tradition, and I come out of a colonial tradition in which we are taught that the "novel" was defined in such and such a way—a rigid definition. We come from an oral tradition that encompasses the telling of history, dreams, family stories, and then we also have the European idea of what the novel is. I have always written in a non-linear fashion. Another thing I owe to Morrison is her statement in *Beloved* that everything is now. Time is not linear. All things are happening at the same time. The past, the present, and the future coexist.

Adisa: What do you want the reader to learn, to think after reading *Free Enterprise*? I mean, you seem to be on a mission. Some might say you are a political writer. Can you speak to this issue?

Cliff: I started out as an historian; I did my graduate work in history. I've always been struck by the misrepresentation of history and have tried to correct received versions of history, especially the history of resistance. It seems to me that if one does not know that one's people have resisted, then it makes resistance difficult.

 —Opal Palmer Adisa, "Journey into Speech—A Writer Between Two Worlds: An Interview with Michelle Cliff," *African American Review* 28, no. 2 (Summer 1994): 279–80

B I B L I O G R A P H Y

The Winner Names the Age: A Collection of Writing by Lillian Smith (editor). 1978.
Claiming an Identity They Taught Me to Despise. 1980.
Abeng. 1984.
The Land of Look Behind. 1985.
No Telephone to Heaven. 1989.
Bodies of Water. 1990.
Free Enterprise. 1993.

MERLE COLLINS

B. 1950

MERLE COLLINS was born on September 29, 1950, to Grenadian parents, Helena and John Collins. Raised and educated in Grenada, Collins attended the University of the West Indies in Mona, Jamaica, where she received her bachelor's degree in English and Spanish in 1972. Collins taught in St. Lucia before returning to Grenada to teach at MacDonald College from 1975 to 1978. She received her master's degree in Latin American studies from Georgetown University in 1981 and returned to Grenada to serve as the coordinator for research on Latin America and the Caribbean for the Ministry of Foreign Affairs.

In Grenada, Collins supported the People's Revolutionary Government, which had taken political control of the island. For Collins the reign of this government worked both to undermine a history of political, economic, and social dependence in Third World countries—specifically Grenada—and to counter the often lingering colonial influences present on the island. When the United States invaded Grenada on October 25, 1983, Collins left the island, moving to Britain shortly thereafter. Collins attended the School of Economics and Political Science at the University of London, focusing on the history of politics in prerevolutionary Grenada from 1950 to 1979. She received her Ph.D. in government in 1990 from the London School of Economics.

Collins's poems, stories, and novels weave traditions of English and French creole languages in Grenada with themes of political and social struggles on the island as well as in other countries in the African diaspora. Her first published poems appeared in *Callaloo: A Grenada Anthology* (1984). The poems in this collection imagine women storytellers as part of a tradition of artistic expression. *Because the Dawn Breaks!: Poems Dedicated to the Grenadian People* (1985), Collins's first published collection of poetry, celebrates the Grenadian population's participation in their revolution.

In 1987, Collins coedited an anthology of short stories, poetry, and autobiographies by women writers from Europe, India, Africa, and the Caribbean and published her first novel, *Angel*. The novel follows two parallel histories: one, the story of three generations of Grenadian women; the other, the story of the Grenadian people's fight for independence. Collins's most recent collection of poetry, *Rotten Pomerack* (1992), focuses on her personal experiences in

Grenada, England, and Ghana, while her most recent novel, *The Colour of Forgetting* (1995), returns to a number of themes from her poetry, complicating stories and memories in various and competing Caribbean histories.

CRITICAL EXTRACTS

NGŪGĪ WA THIONG'O

It is right and appropriate that this collection of poetry ⟨*Because the Dawn Breaks!: Poems Dedicated to the Grenadian People*⟩ is dedicated to the Grenadian people. For the poems—their tone, language, content and vibrant commitment—belong first and foremost to Grenada: the beauty of her landscape; the challenges of her history; and the grandeur of her people. So in the poems one hears not just the voice of Merle Collins, but that of the people of Grenada talking about their struggles, and in particular about their five years' experience of revolution and revolutionary transformation. The poems embody, and celebrate, the people's visions, dreams and hopes during those momentous years of hovering on the brink of tremblingly new and full eternity. And above all is the celebration of beauty—the beauty of the *new* emerging from the *old*. I remember, says the poet, the form of the past foretelling the shape of things to come.

What is that past? It is one of slavery and colonialism and what goes with them: the exploitation, the oppression, the deformation of spirit. Blackness is denied: Africanism is denied; the very landscape of Grenada becomes a matter of shame. Blackness, Africanness, lower class origins reflected in a mirror become, particularly for the petty bourgeois educated, a threat to the self-esteem of those 'caught in the strange dilemma of non-belonging'. The history celebrated in books and the media is that of the colonial conquerors. Gairyism perpetuated this and more. The meek, the exploited and the oppressed, were supposed to wait for compensation in heaven. Blessed are the meek. Deliverance will come from the big houses on the hill!

But that very past is one of continuous resistance by the meek, Fanon's wretched of the earth, for whom 'struggle is the loudest song'. It was out of that fierce and continuous struggle that came the 1979 Grenada Revolution. Merle Collins' poetry captures in telling images and clear languages the new horizons, the new possibilities opened up by the revolution.

—Ngũgĩ Wa Thiong'o, "Introduction," *Because the Dawn Breaks!: Poems Dedicated to the Grenadian People* by Merle Collins (London: Karia Press, 1985), vii–viii

JANE BROOKS

Merle Collins' first novel, *Angel*, explores the interrelated themes of the movement of the Grenadian people towards authentic self-expression, and the development of a popular nationalist system of political self-determination. It would be misleading, however, to suggest that *Angel* is primarily concerned with political personalities. Although one can trace the rise of Eric Gairy through the character of Leader, and the response of the New Jewel Movement and Maurice Bishop through the fictive Horizon group and the character of Chief, the politicians are but distant shadowy figures, whose voices enter the social arena by means of the radio or second-hand report. The novel focuses on the issues which are shown to be the central concern of the people, and primacy is given to the people's response to them. ⟨. . .⟩

The struggle towards a voice and the possibility of true self-expression is under-pinned by the role of dialect in the novel. As a reflection of both the history and the language situation of the island, the text moves between Standard English, Grenadian English Creole, and French Creole, known locally as Patois. Each of these three dialects carries within itself a political, social and cultural history, which is reflected in its perceived value and the concomitant status of its speakers. French Patois, the language associated with Ma Ettie, Doodsie and the elder generation of women, has strong associations with the post-1789 Caribbean slave insurrections, and is linked with such popular revolutionary leaders as Grenada's Fedon, and Haiti's Toussaint L'Ouverture. Angel's generation has English Creole as its *mother* tongue, which, like Patois, is an intimate language learnt in the home, and a language of resistance. Both Creole and Patois are of low prestige. Standard English may be seen as the prestigious *father* tongue, the language of the master/coloniser, and within it are contained the myths used to legitimise racism, dependence and mimicry, which cause the colonised to become alienated from themselves. It is at school that Angel and her contemporaries are taught and examined in the language of 'the other'. The author of *Angel* shows that a necessary precondition for self-expression is a shift in social attitudes towards language. To speak Creole at school was a mark of failure for Angel, whereas for her pupils, while Creole might not be the language of education, their mother tongue was in no way considered inferior. Standard English is banished from the grassroot zonal council meetings of the Horizon party, where the people celebrate their successes after Leader has been deposed in the community's authentic means of expression, Creole.

⟨. . .⟩ The incidents or stories within each chapter are divided up and given heightened significance by the interleaving of Creole and Patois proverbs. These function as a clear indicator of authentically Grenadian frames of perception, and evoke a chorus-type response to events, thus underlining the importance of community. This is certainly reminiscent of the call-and-response tradition so much associated with orature, and in the Caribbean context, with the survival of an African cultural heritage. In the blurring of the divisions between orature and literature, Merle Collins has succeeded in reworking a European form of cultural expression historically linked with the rise of capitalism—the novel—to articulate Grenadian concerns in a form appropriate to that society.

—Jane Brooks, "Struggling Towards a Voice," *Third World Quarterly* 10, no. 3 (July 1988): 1368–70

ANDREW SALKEY

I welcome the demotic sweep and hard-edged characterization of the thoroughly engaging novel *Angel*, which ought to establish its author's position among the best of West Indian novelists who have excelled at writing in the Creole ⟨. . .⟩ and delivering a consummate, artistic folk experience to the delight and appreciation of readers far outside our home area. I welcome too the essential social and political layering of the story line, which contributes a truthful and resonant verisimilitude to the gradually unfolding historical panorama of the narrative.

A Bildungsroman in our own specific West Indian cultural terms, *Angel* tells the story of the eponymous rebel's progress through her Grenadian childhood, her three years at the University of the West Indies in Jamaica, and her return home before the U.S. invasion of her island, which puts an end to her cherished hope of continuing political change for her society, the central challenge of her life up to that time. However, Angel's postinvasion sentiments at the close of the novel, as the long-past colonial *status quo ante* is restored, are: "The spirits gone, you know. The candle not goin out. Their either gone, or they sympathetic. Nothing to fraid." The reader takes this as a clear signal that Angel expects a resumption of her revolutionary fervor, this time to be reborn of a crucial loss of fear.

—Andrew Salkey, [Review of *Angel*], *World Literature Today* 63, no. 1 (Winter 1989): 151

M. J. FENWICH

To the extent that the Prospero/Caliban analogy applies, we can know why the colonial literary tradition honored, with publication and international recognition, only the writers whose expressions most successfully imitated the styles and subjects set by European intellectuals. In fact, like the European tradition and the academic critics, many Caribbean writers themselves still accept the cultural superiority of their colonizers and have sought their literary fame through imitation. ⟨. . .⟩

There is, however, a parallel contemporary movement among the Caribbean writers which stands in defiance of the colonial orthodoxy and offers not an imitation of the European experience but a legitimate art of the Caribbean people and of their cultural and historical aspirations. Whereas Prospero saw language as a means of taming and dominating Caliban, these contemporary writers of the Caribbean have revived Caliban's rebellion and made the language a tool to be used "to curse the master." They have successfully turned the European literary tradition against itself and transformed the "master's" language into a new literary expression that is to be uniquely Caribbean. With conscious irony, they have chosen as their speaker "Caliban," Shakespeare's image of the uncivilized, inarticulate colonial subject, and transformed him into the symbol of the new Caribbean, articulate and prepared to confront world literature on his and her own terms. ⟨. . .⟩

Merle Collins from Grenada, in her poem "The Butterfly Born" (27–33), presents Caliban as a female child: "Afraid of she shadow/of de basket shadow/of she dress shadow/of de fig-leaf shadow/But walkin' alone/all kin' o' hour/Hidin' an' cryin' an' hatin' " for the things she couldn't afford, for being a "woman-chile" taking care of her four younger siblings, for being afraid, for being ashamed, for her self-rejection, and for the adults who scolded her for not knowing her place and for not being obedient, quiet, and respectful. The poem suddenly changes with the Grenadian revolution of 1979 against imperialism, and the new woman Caliban ("the butterfly born") will defy her old fears, step out from "behin'/de blin'/ . . . Not under no table/But out in de open/Demanding equal/recognition/For equal beauty given."

In another poem "Because the Dawn Breaks" (88–90) Merle Collins says of her defiance and historical outrage: "We do not speak/to defy your tenets/though we do/or upset your plans/even though we do/or to tumble/your towers of babel/we speak/in spite of the fact/that we do. . . ." This poem's language shows that the new Caliban has mastered the master's art form, and the tool has become hers to speak directly to the master on his ground, ". . . because/your plan/is not our plan/. . . because/our dreams/are not of living in pig pens/in any other body's/backyard/not of/catching crumbs from tables/not of crawling forever/. . . because/we are workers/peasants/leaders/you see/and were not born/to be your vassals."

The poetry of Merle Collins is not only to confront the master but also to speak to the tamed Caribbean Calibans who "still choose/to skin teet/an' bow head/yes Massa suh/I asks no question suh" ("The Essence," 63–4), to those who welcomed the U.S. intervention in 1983 to re-establish colonialism in her nation. In her poem, "A Song of Pain" (91–3), she writes, "I sing of pain/even as the anger grows/for you have learnt their evil lesson well." She accuses the submissive Calibans of cultural genocide and of ignoring the devastating results of more than three hundred years of colonialism.

—M. J. Fenwich, "Female Calibans: Contemporary Women Poets of the Caribbean," *The Zora Neale Hurston Forum* 4, no. 1 (Fall 1989): 2–5

BRENDA DoHARRIS

Merle Collins, a Grenadian teacher, and a member of Grenada's National Women's Organization until 1983, has sought with varying degrees of success, to weave these dramatic political elements ⟨of the Grenada revolution of 1979⟩ into the fictional fabric of Grenadian working class family life in her novel, *Angel*. ⟨. . .⟩

Perhaps the most compelling aspect of this novel is Merle Collins' willingness to reach deep down into the gut of the survival instinct often characteristic of the most desperately poor. That instinct manifests itself most clearly in her characters' readiness to work at all costs, even in the most humiliating conditions, at greatest inconvenience to themselves—often for the least remuneration. ⟨. . .⟩

Another strong point of the novel is that it reflects Collins' keen ear for her native Grenadian dialect, a talent which she uses to full narrative advantage in the work. The lilting cadence of the dialogue enters one's consciousness as much through the ear as through the mind. Collins is so accurate, so meticulous in her attention to the most minute details of phonetic reproduction that it is easy to imagine even the tone of voice accompanying the spoken words of the dialogue. At times, Collins' authorial voice merges with that of her characters, adopting the dialect form, and expertly submerging narrator and reader in the swirl of events taking place in the novel. ⟨. . .⟩

The work's weakness derives from Collins' attempts to comment on too many aspects of Grenadian social oppression in too limited a narrative ambit. The novelist tries to address questions of racial inferiority, male domination, women's liberation, political oppression and generational differences. The result is that the narrative pace lumbers as the author, somewhat gratuitously and heavy-handedly, injects an element of propaganda into Angel's utterances, Angel's education making her character a perfect vehicle for such talk. ⟨. . .⟩ It is almost as though Collins does not trust her plot and characterization to convey the nuances of ideas.

These flaws apart, however, *Angel* is undeniably a literary hymn of praise to the ingenuity and survival skills of Grenada's working poor.

—Brenda DoHarris, "*Angel*: A Novel by Merle Collins," *The Zora Neale Hurston Forum* 4, no. 1 (Fall 1989): 25–28

Rhonda Cobham

Collins' ⟨*Angel* presents a⟩ wide historical canvas, with its complex sweep of shifting personal and political allegiances over generations ⟨. . . .⟩ Her portrayal of Doodsie, who lives through the social experiments of both the Gairy and Bishop eras, and whose experiences span the degradation of domestic work for white families in Trinidad, and the difficult elation of watching her daughter graduating from university then "throwing away" her future to take part in the revolution, is masterful. ⟨. . .⟩

Much of the action in *Angel* is played out "on stage," so to speak, in long scenes of dialogue only barely structured by an omniscient narrator. Only the sections dealing with Angel's college years, a time of great isolation and alienation, are narrated to any great extent by an introspective narrator. One is reminded of the shifting narrative voices in that other chronicle of a revolutionary moment missed: the Barbadian writer George Lamming's *In the Castle of My Skin*. But where Lamming's novel of childhood ends with the protagonist growing into the castle of his skin as he moves away from village and mother, Collins' Angel returns to reconnect and spin off once more into psychic angst after the revolution.

Or does she? The image of Angel at the end of this chronicle is not of an isolated, disillusioned, unaccommodated individual ⟨. . . .⟩ Angel is physically and spiritually violated, but the way in which her family, still deeply divided over the political tragedy, is able to rally together through this crisis suggests that certain kinship ties remain intact.

Collins' historical sweep has already allowed us a glimpse of the way those ties were able to weather the Gairy betrayal. The novel offers us not so much hope as a quiet affirmation of the endurance of communal ties beyond, in spite of, but also alongside changing political allegiances. Collins' message has a special relevance for American readers for whom it is often difficult to imagine Reagan's Caribbean backyard as a place of real societies with independent political trajectories and deep human loyalties.

—Rhonda Cobham, "Women of the Islands," *Women's Review of Books* 7 (July 1990): 30

Maria Helena Lima

Whereas in *No Telephone to Heaven* the need for change is figured in the allegorical transformation of the island's terrain as "bush" takes over "garden" in Clare's grandmother's land, in *Angel* it is history itself that constitutes the novel's terrain. Collins's novel depicts the history of Grenada against and through the lives of her characters. The testimony of Collins's fiction is one of transformation in attitudes, ideas, and language. Her work is concerned with change—what enables it, what prevents it, why it is necessary.

Although some may perceive Collins's novel as old-fashioned realism, it is revolutionary in bringing together conventionally male and female spheres— public and private, personal and political—to chronicle the history of her country in the spectrum of creole languages available to her, and thus inscribes a "new" kind of self in her reconceptualization of the *Bildungsroman*.

To the individual novel of formation, Collins adds the collectivity of the *testimonio*, a literature of personal witness and involvement designed, according to John Beverly, to make the cause of these movements known to the outside world, to attract recruits, to reflect on the successes and/or failures of the struggle. Because *testimonio* is not so much concerned with the life of a "problematic hero" as with a problematic collective social situation, the narrator in *testimonio* speaks for, or in the name of, a community or group. In keeping with the predominant focus on the collective life of the community, characterization typically exemplifies modes of interdependence among community members. Concerned with continuity, *Angel* seeks to represent what gives the community its identity, what enables it to remain itself. ⟨. . .⟩

Collins's *Angel* bridges some of the differences between the novel and *testimonio* through its powerful oral quality, for it achieves the effect of an ongoing conversation among characters. Collins creates a Grenadian creole which is ritualistic, proverbial, and metaphoric, embedding songs, poems, and proverbs which give the narrative a people's (not an individual's) perspective on events and communicate the complexity of their traditions. More important, like a *testimonio*, Collins's novel represents an affirmation of individual growth and transformation in connection with a group or class situation marked by struggle. The unifying feature of a testimony novel is its consciousness of a collective objective beyond the individual person ⟨J. R. Pereira, "Towards a Theory of Literature in Revolutionary Cuba," *Caribbean Quarterly* 21.1–2, 1975⟩. Collins becomes the living witness to a historical process, faithfully recreating both characters and society in a state of becoming.

—Maria Helena Lima, "Revolutionary Developments: Michelle Cliff's *No Telephone to Heaven* and Merle Collins's *Angel*," *Ariel* 24, no. 1 (January 1993): 43–45

BETTY WILSON

Wilson: ⟨Why⟩ did you choose to have *Angel* in the novel form?

Collins: I think *Angel* also came at a period when I was looking at, looking back at, that whole period of Grenadan history and kind of looking behind the headlines at the things that were happening. Because *Angel* is definitely a product of 1983 and of the crash of October 1983, where Grenada was concerned, where all Grenada was concerned. And about the whole of that trauma and my moving out and looking back at it all and feeling that, as so often happens, the focus remains on the principal actors. The people who are readers, and we, are looking behind all of that at the people who eke out a living from day to day and who do very unpredictable, very contradictory things because they know that their existence is from day to day, and the pressures that they have to go through and how they decide to deal with that, in ways that might be considered by the leaders reactionary or counter-revolutionary or whatever other words. But people, you know, so I just wanted to look at that, without making an overt political statement, just to look at my data. So *Angel* came out of all of that. So that I think I decided on the novel because it was like a period of research for me also, you know in a sense, it's going through all of that and seeing people going through their day to day lives living in that kind of way. It's like reading that whole story.

Wilson: So do you see it as more a personal thing for you, working through the experience, rather than a relationship between you and your audience? Because, as we said, you're very conscious of the community as your audience in your poetry and in your performance . . .

Collins: Yes, I think that's what I'm doing. In fact you're pointing out things to me as the questions come. I think that in a sense that's what I'm doing, because with the short stories now, too, the short stories deal a lot with various people working through their experiences of loss. I think it's a lot about working through experiences of pain, experiences of loss, and the things people do in working through experiences like that. I think probably that's why I chose that form for that theme, because it was a more private interest, more prolonged reflection, in a sense.

Wilson: Because you are so concerned with the collectivity, like wanting to write a play because you want to give the people the images in a form that perhaps might be more easily accessible to them than on the printed page.

Collins: Yes.

Wilson: You know, I can see the intimate connection between you and your audience, the community, as there was in our heritage—the African, the oral tradition—I can see that the link is very intimate, but perhaps you need these periods of introspection as you say.

Collins: Yes, but the interesting thing for me is what happened to the medium; even while I was working it out, while I started working it out like this, it was like having to work through a lot of trauma in my own mind. After the first draft, what changed *Angel* radically was that someone I gave it to to read said, "Yes, I like this, but I think you still have a lot to do." And I felt that, too, but I kind of wanted to hear some guidance, you know, and absolutely, "I think you still have a lot to do." Sometimes you get a voice that you can hear and sometimes you'll use it and you just seem to be talking, it's like you're talking to yourself. He looked at one section and he said, "What you achieve here, I think is wonderful," and he said, "If you read this section to your Grandmother, you know, if you just read it to your Grandmother, she would understand all of it and she would enjoy it. You don't think it might be a good idea to aim at writing most of it in such a way that if you read it to your Grandmother, she would be with you all the way?" And I thought: "That is what I want." And that changed the second draft radically, so that I went back and always tried to imagine that I was reading it to my Grandmother, and she was following. Sometimes I lost it but that's what I tried to do.

—Betty Wilson, "An Interview with Merle Collins," *Callaloo* 16, no. 1 (Winter 1993): 102–3

BRUCE WOODCOCK

Of the Grenadian poets, Merle Collins has received widespread acclaim with her novel *Angel* and her volume of poems *Because the Dawn Breaks*. She has worked closely with a group of African musicians called 'African Dawn', incorporating traditional oral, dramatic and musical forms into the performance of her work. As with other performance poets, her texts on the page are in one sense scores or scripts to be brought to fullness through delivery and enactment. She often takes local experiences as vehicles for what she wishes to deal with. As she herself recognised in the work of other women in her essay 'Women Writers from the Caribbean', 'it is the particular dimension of the experiences as recounted and explored by the women which gives it its special quality and presents a perspective the exploration of which is important to the region's future' ⟨21⟩. Her poem 'Callaloo' uses the image of a popular Caribbean soup as a metaphor of the 'mix-up' in the world, out of which will come some positive transformatory synthesis:

> An' de promise o' de change
> Is sweet
> An' strong
> Like de soup
> When Grannie
> Cover it down dey
> And let it
> Consomme
> Like dat
> Hot

In 'The Lesson', Merle Collins's great-grandmother becomes emblematic of women living under the economic and psychological weight of colonial oppression: she was more familiar with British history than with that of the Caribbean, and thought the name of resistance leader Toussaint L'Ouverture was a curse. The poem envisages a transformation for women as they rewrite history and the future, but emphasises they will 'cherish / Grannie's memory' to include her in the new her-story ⟨Chris Searle, *Words Unchained: Language and Revolution in Grenada*, 1984, 138–40⟩. ⟨. . .⟩

Merle Collins ⟨. . .⟩ has indicated how recent the employment of 'nation language' as a positive cultural force is: her Gran'aunt's reaction to the language of her novel *Angel* was 'We don't talk as bad as that'; so that paradoxically the positive deployment of 'nation language' is possibly a generational phenomenon. It is also, of course, crucially a question of power and the hegemonic force of 'standard English' and the institutional promoters of it in the media and education, the recent discussion papers on the primary national curriculum being merely one contemporary example. The effect of this enforcement of a 'standard' English is not just the marginalisation of languages but of cultures, and it is here that the colonial legacy for Caribbean cultures links with that for the other cultures in Britain and Ireland—Irish, Scots, Welsh, and even regions such as the North of England. All of them have suffered from forms of imperialism, racial or class. What the Caribbean women poets bring to this terrain is the consideration of gender in relation to these other imperialisms ⟨. . . .⟩

—Bruce Woodcock, " 'Long Memoried Women': Caribbean Women Poets," *Black Women's Writing*, ed. Gina Wisker (London: The Macmillan Press Ltd., 1993), 61–62, 68

TUNKA VARADARAJAN

Reading this new novel ⟨*The Colour of Forgetting*⟩ by the Grenadian poetess Merle Collins is like learning a new language.

You begin unsteadily, tiptoeing over phrases such as this: "Is the boy, Carib. Thunder in his head. He fraid thunder. Bad bad." Gradually, you learn this language, parting its folds and peering into a world of unfamiliar names— Caiphas, Mayum, Ti-Moun, Mamag, Willive, Son-Son—and slave-scented, small-island atavism.

This is the story of the Malheureuse family of Paz island, a family with "mixture in the blood"—some slave, some "jefe"—nourished equally on fable and prophecy, like all those who live in Paz. ⟨. . .⟩

Paz, meagre in size, is modelled nimbly on Collins's own Grenada: with nutmeg trees, a revolution by "the young", and a rescue in the end by the Great Country.

The island's most fertile storyteller is Mamag Malheureuse the matriarch, solicitous grand-aunt of the boy Thunder. With daunting breasts and a head-tie "like the red mace petticoat of the nutmeg", Mamag holds the tale together by living longer than anyone else.

—Tunku Varadarajan, "Prophetic Power in a Fabled Land," *The Times* (22 July 1995): 14

MAYA JAGGI

While Collins's first novel, *Angel* (1987), followed the lives of three genera-tions of Grenadian women, *The Colour of Forgetting* gives men a voice. Thunder's father Ned unearths tales for his son of an upbringing in "Nigger Yard" through the tutelage of his wife, Willive. Written mainly in creolized English, with a smattering of the French patois spoken by an older generation of islanders, the novel charts growing "land confusion", as Thunder's family splits when a covetous uncle uses the letter of the law to disinherit his "bastard" nephews, and the nation subsequently divides against itself when a revolu-tionary party tries to impose land reform by barring "uneconomic" smallhold-ings. Through the island landscape, with its tourist intrusions and jets passing overhead, wanders the lone, anachronistic figure of a woman, Carib. Her warning of "blood gone and blood to come" sounds a chorus, or echo, as her ravings prove prophetic: a land protest culminates in bloodshed in the market square.

Even though the setting is mythical, the contours of historical events sur-rounding the Grenadian revolution of 1979–83 can be traced, leading to the split in Maurice Bishop's New Jewel Movement—an event that provided the pretext for the invasion that became the beach-head of US dominance in the region. 〈. . .〉

While Carib's chorus can be repetitive (perhaps a result of transferring a technique from performance poetry—in which Collins excels—too directly to the page), the novel's strength is its rootedness in a communal wisdom. 〈. . .〉 It also draws on a fund of proverbs, reaching back to African folk-tale. 〈. . .〉

The need to confront a bloodied legacy, when the drive to escape from it is often more compelling, is a theme Collins shares with Toni Morrison who, in *Jazz*, sees remembering as the key to preventing a recurrence of the past "as an abused record with no choice but to repeat itself at the crack". In *The Colour of Forgetting*, memory points the path both to Thunder's maturity and to the political maturity of a society.

—Maya Jaggi, "Winter of Discontent," *Times Literary Supplement* (11 August 1995): 22

B I B L I O G R A P H Y

Because the Dawn Breaks!: Poems Dedicated to the Grenadian People. 1985.

Angel. 1987.

Watchers and Seekers: Creative Writing by Black Women in Britain (editor, with Rhonda Cobham). 1987.

Rain Darling: Stories. 1990.

Rotten Pomerack. 1992.

Inside the Ant's Belly: A Collection of Stories for Young People (editor, with Marva Buchana). 1994.

The Colour of Forgetting. 1995.

EDWIDGE DANTICAT
B. 1969

EDWIDGE DANTICAT was born in Haiti in January 1969. Her father, Andre, a taxi driver, left Haiti for Brooklyn, New York, when Edwidge was a toddler; her mother, Rose, a factory worker, followed when Edwidge was four. Edwidge was raised for several years by an aunt in Port-au-Prince, Haiti. Rejoining her parents in 1981, she attended public schools in the Crown Heights section of Brooklyn. In 1990, she received her bachelor's degree in French literature from Barnard College, and in 1993 she received her M.F.A. from Brown University. Her master's thesis was published in 1993 under the title *My Turn in the Fire: An Abridged Novel*.

Danticat's many memories of her life in Haiti provide the substance for much of her work. Most of her memories of that past are filled with death, because, as she recalls in the author's notes to her first novel, "In Haiti death was always around us." She also remembers a ritual similar to female clitoridectomy in Africa, where young women were "locked," or tested for their virginity by the probing hand of a doctor or, in poorer families, by mothers, aunts, and grandmothers. Seeing herself in a long tradition of female storytellers in Haiti—whom she understands as the preservers of history and memory—Danticat feels compelled to use her voice to speak both to the present and to the past.

Danticat's first novel, *Breath, Eyes, Memory* (1994), is the story of Sophie, a Haitian girl who immigrates to Brooklyn. With a number of traceable autobiographical themes, the novel follows Sophie from an early childhood under Haiti's dictatorial Duvalier regime to her immigration to the United States, where prejudice and ignorance led her American classmates to accuse all Haitians of having AIDS. While Danticat's original languages were French and Creole, *Breath, Eyes, Memory* is the first known novel written entirely in English by a Haitian woman; it was nominated for the National Book Award.

While still receiving acclaim for her first novel, Danticat published *Krik? Krak!* (1995), a collection of short stories. Danticat takes her title from a Haitian storytelling tradition in which grandmothers use the single creole word "krik" to ask if the younger generation is ready to hear a story. The children answer, "Krak!" and the tales begin. The stories in Danticat's collection have been described by critics as "spare" and "dreamy." Although much of the action takes place in contemporary Haiti, Danticat also incorporates historical material such as the 1790s slave leader Boukman and the killing of Haitians by the Dominican Republic in 1937 at Massacre River.

Danticat currently resides in the Flatbush area of Brooklyn, researching Haitian cane cutters in the Dominican Republic for her next novel.

C R I T I C A L   E X T R A C T S

WENDY SHEANIN

Edwidge Danticat's haunting first novel ⟨. . .⟩ is a poetic rendering of a young woman's double life as she struggles to find her balance with one foot on American soil and the other on her homeland's. With passion and sensitivity, "Breath, Eyes, Memory" explores the boundaries of love and duty, the necessity of self-definition. ⟨. . .⟩

Although Danticat's language is rich and her characters fully developed, "Breath, Eyes, Memory" falters. New Age rhetoric is carried too far when a sexual-phobia group combines the Alcoholics Anonymous serenity prayer with ethnic healing rituals. Martine's life reads like a soap opera script as one tragedy compounds upon another until the cumulative effect detracts from plausibility.

But Danticat's fresh voices echo off the page. Sophie reflects, "I come from a place where breath, eyes, and memory are one, a place from which you carry your past like the hair on your head. Where women return to their children as butterflies or as tears in the eyes of the statues that their daughters pray to."

Danticat infuses Haitian words into the text and uses Haitian folklore to add depth to her narrative. Sophie and Martine, for example, seem to be direct descendants of Haiti's mythical "people of Creation". ⟨. . .⟩

The author also breathes life into her descriptions of Haiti, celebrating its beauty without disguising its horrors. "The fragrance of crushed mint leaves and stagnant pee alternated in the breeze." In the open market, she witnesses a Macoute, a soldier of the government's occupying army, beat a coal vendor until he lies curled on the ground in the fetal position spitting up blood because he accidentally stepped on the soldier's foot. The descriptions of Haiti capture its spirit in vivid sensory details.

While at times "Breath, Eyes, Memory" veers into melodrama, Danticat has a gift for language and for storytelling.

—Wendy Sheanin, "Haitian Memories Haunt an Emigré in New York," *The San Francisco Chronicle Book Review* (18 December 1994): 6

ETHAN CASY

The recent intensification of the unending tragedy that is Haitian history poses a challenge to writers: how to respond? It is both a new challenge and one as old as the written word. ⟨. . .⟩

What kind of *literary* response does Haiti merit? The topic has become so politicized that the question sounds odd, even dangerous. At least one recent novel failed badly at walking the fine line between literature and political advocacy, in this writer's judgment. But where does "the literary" end and "the political" begin? How to write about appalling realities without succumbing to futility and impotence or acquiescence? ⟨. . .⟩

Into the breach confidently strides Edwidge Danticat, an immensely promising young writer born in a village in Haiti, now living in New York. *Breath, Eyes, Memory* clearly is a *Bildungsroman*, a necessary first effort in what one hopes will be a long and productive American literary career. It is the very personal story of Sophie, first a girl in a Haitian village, later a young woman living with her mother in Brooklyn. Danticat's poise and grace with language and narrative are (pardon the pun) rather breathtaking in someone just twenty-four at the time of her book's publication; she writes with richly suggestive diffidence and uses paragraphing and elision to excellent effect. She also—to use the cliché—writes about what she knows. She is sure to enjoy commercial good fortune in years to come not only by virtue of her "multicultural" background in the vulgar sense, but because her large talent has been blessed with a subject—Haiti—replete with lastingly important implications that American readers need and should want to ponder. In short, she has her work cut out for her.

To a reader with knowledge and experience of Haiti, she consistently strikes the right chords. "Listening to the song, I realized that it was neither my mother nor my Tante Atie who had given all the mother-and-daughter motifs to all the stories they told and all the songs they sang," she writes. "It was something that was essentially Haitian." The portrayal of Haiti in *Breath, Eyes, Memory* offers occasion to consider the "occasional" quality of all writing: Could such a novel have been so poignant—could it even have been written?—had Haiti not been so newsworthy in recent months and years? Yet in a masterstroke of shrewdness and self-discipline, Danticat makes only the most gently glancing of references to her novel's real-life backdrop. "I want that young priest," says the narrator's grandmother. "The one they call Lavalas. I want him to sing the last song at my funeral."

—Ethan Casy, "Remembering Haiti," *Callaloo* 18, no. 2 (Spring 1995): 524–25

INGRID STURGIS

Haitian–born author Edwidge Danticat has given a human face and a personal touch to the painful stories that have come to form our opinion of the country. The author of *Breath, Eyes, Memory* (reviewed in *Emerge* April 1994), comes from a country with a rich oral tradition, where folk tales and mystic rituals are part of the cultural fabric. She offers an authentic voice of the Haitian–American experience. She is, after all, one of the few Haitians to be published in the United States. ⟨. . .⟩

"Haiti has an extensively rich history. It is both glorious and painful, a divided history," says Danticat. "It's something people struggle with every day. We cling to the past. It is our most glorious asset."

But being a writer in such a country is a dangerous career choice, Danticat says. It is a vocation that often comes with a threat of persecution by those who see a woman's words and dreams as witchery—or politics.

"In our world writers are tortured and killed if they are men; called lying whores, then raped and killed, if they are women. In our world, if you are a writer, you are a politician, and we know what happens to politicians. They end up in a prison dungeon, where their bodies are covered in scalding tar before they're forced to eat their own waste."

⟨. . .⟩ *Krik? Krak!*, chronicles the ups and downs of Haitian life. A compilation of masterful storytelling, it reveals the harsh life under dictatorship, the reign of terror by the strong–arm forces, the Tonton Macoutes. The sometimes metaphorical stories are filled with tales of Haitian rituals and legends that resonate with truth and poetry. Make no mistake, these lyrical stories are powerful and political works of art. Unlike *Breath, Eyes, Memory*, Danticat says, "The stories are more of a collective biography. I know someone it happened to or might have happened to. It's a lot of people's stories."

—Ingrid Sturgis, "Young Author Reclaims Haiti's Stories as Birthright," *Emerge* (April 1995): 58–59.

ELLEN KANNER

In many ways, each of these 10 stories ⟨in *Krik? Krak!*⟩ is part of the same tale. Women lose who and what they love to poverty, to violence, to politics, to ideals. The author's deceptively artless stories are not of heroes but of survivors, of the impulse toward life amid death and the urge to write and to tell in order not to forget.

As in her 1994 novel, *Breath, Eyes, Memory*, Danticat focuses here on Haiti's women. "Most of the women in your life had their heads down," she writes.

Like Haiti itself, they still carry a shred of radiance in a time when spirit has been all but extinguished.

The stories are reduced to their essence, to action and symbol, and they bear the authority of folk tales. The characters are almost interchangeable: either young women struggling to find a spark of greatness or love within the limitations of their lives or older women who are wiser and resigned. ⟨. . .⟩

Danticat does not always trust the eloquence of her tales. It is as though she has found the voice of Haiti's women but, at 26, is not entirely comfortable with her own. In several stories, she pushes for a big ending, bigger than her colloquial style warrants. ⟨. . .⟩

The last story in *Krik? Krak!* is the longest and most complex. *Caroline's Wedding* speaks of the precarious balance between cultural identity and American assimilation. Caroline was born and raised in New York, yet her mother and sister feel that by marrying a non-Haitian, "she was divorcing us, trading in her old allegiances for a new one." As long as there is a sisterhood of Haitian women, the past will not be forgotten. Nor will the dead. At their church, they gather to mourn the young Haitian woman and her baby who drowned in *Children of the Sea.*

Danticat's tales are woven together into a tapestry of remembrance, a blending of voices until they become one voice, the voice of a Haitian woman who is all Haitian women.

—Ellen Kanner, " 'You Hear My Mother Who Speaks Through Me,' " *Miami Herald* (9 April 1995): 31

JIM GLADSTONE

Edwidge Danticat's slim yet densely packed first novel chronicles three generations of Haitian and Haitian-American women. Occasionally the matter-of-fact tone of the swift, simple prose in "Breath, Eyes, Memory" seems inappropriate for its subject matter—which includes rape and sexual abuse as well as third world political strife—but Ms. Danticat's calm clarity of vision takes on the resonance of folk art. In the end, her book achieves an emotional complexity that lifts it out of the realm of the potboiler and into that of poetry. Set in both Haiti and New York, where the narrator is sent to join her immigrant mother, the tale is lovingly dominated by powerful female characters who struggle to make better lives for themselves and their families. However, Ms. Danticat also includes two veritable Prince Charmings who go underappreciated by these same women, further evidence of her inclination, even in highly charged scenes, to be fair rather than doctrinaire. Ms. Danticat ⟨. . .⟩ is extraordinarily ambitious in the number of psychological and intellectual themes she introduces in "Breath, Eyes, Memory." She is also extraordinarily successful.

—Jim Gladstone, "In Short—*Breath, Eyes, Memory,*" *New York Times Book Review* (23 April 1995): 20

ROBERT HOUSTON

Readers of the Haitian-born writer Edwidge Danticat's well-received first novel, "Breath, Eyes, Memory," which appeared last spring, will be familiar with the themes in these short stories: oppression (in many forms), hope, fear, poverty, cultural identity and the complex ties among women. Those weary of stories that deal only with the minutiae of "relationships" will rejoice that they have found work that is about something, and something that matters. ⟨. . .⟩

The best of these stories humanize, particularize, give poignancy to the lives of people we may have come to think of as faceless emblems of misery, poverty and brutality. In one, an aging maid in a wealthy Port-au-Prince household, stuck in a childless marriage to an unfaithful husband, seeks solace in a baby she finds abandoned on the street. In another, a prostitute explains to her small son that she dresses up each night because they are expecting an angel to visit, and he sleeps in his Sunday clothes to be ready too.

As a collection, however, the book is quite uneven, which isn't entirely Ms. Danticat's fault. It is not unusual for a publisher to come out with a volume of a new writer's stories after she or he has achieved a degree of name recognition with a novel. Short-story collections are, after all, notoriously poor sellers. In the case of a very young writer like Ms. Danticat, who is 26, that publisher's practice can prove a mixed blessing. The collection has seen daylight, yes, but since some of the stories were written by Ms. Danticat when she was an undergraduate at Barnard College, the level of sophistication in the writing fluctuates greatly. In several ("A Wall of Fire Rising," for example), one can see a talented but developing writer struggling with a good story idea, but just not having the mastery of craft or language to pull it off.

Such stories might be valuable to future scholars in tracing Ms. Danticat's development as a writer, but are out of place in a collection presumed to represent polished, mature work.

—Robert Houston, "Expecting Angels," *New York Times Book Review* (23 April 1995): 22

JORDANA HART

More than anything else, the storytelling of the young Haitian-American writer Edwidge Danticat has given the world honest and loving portraits of Haitian people, both on the island and in the United States. She has smashed the numbing stereotypes created by a barrage of media accounts of Haitian poverty, misery and death. ⟨. . .⟩

Danticat, 26, a teller of stories in the truest sense, takes us heart-pounding into a breathtaking Haiti, whose culture and people are so often diminished, even disfigured, in the writings of those who do not know and love the island.

Of course, Danticat cannot avoid placing her tales within the brutal world of the *Tonton Macoutes*, Haiti's former thuggish soldiers, and the oppressive political system that until recently pushed tens of thousands of Haitians to flee the island by vessel—often only to meet their death or internment in a Florida camp.

It is the details of everyday life, however, the depth of her characters and Danticat's own love and respect for her culture that make her stories at once disturbing yet beguiling.

—Jordana Hart, "Danticat's Stories Pulse with Haitian Heartbeat," *The Boston Globe* (19 July 1995): 70

REBECCA MEAD

While a complicated relation to the mother tongue is an unspoken subtext in Edwidge Danticat's stories, her explicit subject is more often than not the complicated relations between flesh-and-blood mothers and their daughters, both in Haiti and in the diaspora. In *Krik? Krak!* (the title is a traditional call-and-response that begins a storytelling session), Danticat writes of a daughter visiting a jail in Port-au-Prince, where her mother has been sent under suspicion of witchcraft; she tells the story of a pair of daughters in Brooklyn preparing for the wedding of one of them to a Bahamian man, under the disapproving eye of their traditional mother. Danticat's first book, a novel entitled *Breath, Eyes, Memory*, which was published by Soho Press last year, charts the life of a young girl, Sophie, through her relationships with the women in her family: an aunt; her troubled mother, whom she joins in Brooklyn as she enters her teens; her grandmother, whose beliefs about raising daughters—including a practice called *testing*, in which a mother regularly checks with her own fingers to ensure that her adolescent daughter's hymen is intact—are family secrets painfully passed on through the generations; and her own daughter. Sophie's rebellion is chillingly depicted: To escape the testing, she breaks her own hymen with a kitchen pestle, knowing that she will be thrown out of her mother's home. She must abandon her mother in order to escape her—though being motherless is virtually taboo in Haiti. (The Creole expression *san man-man*—literally, "motherless one"—is used to mean a person capable of any transgression, an outlaw or a vagabond: If he has no mother, there is no one to be shamed by his flouting of rules and customs.)

Though the content of her stories is often disturbing, Danticat's manner is warm and open; she is quick to point out that while, like Sophie, she was long separated from her own mother, the novel's more gruesome elements are not autobiographical. ⟨. . .⟩

⟨. . .⟩ Danticat's stories are about what happens when it is revealed that the invincible mother is a fantasy: that mothers are sometimes absent and are often troubled daughters themselves. That Danticat has found a stepmother tongue in which to tell these tales suggests that realizing mothers are fallible need not be a catastrophe. Even when a mother, or a mother tongue, falls short, there are, after all, alternatives to becoming a *san manman*.

—Rebecca Mead, "Queen Creole," *New York Magazine* (20 November 1995): 50

ERIKA J. WATERS

One of Danticat's strengths is her irony, subtle and penetrating. In "The Missing Peace," the American woman naively believes her American passport will protect her from people for whom human life has lost all significance. While watching the young woman clutch her dead baby in "Children of the Sea," the narrator takes the time to record that her friend has passed his exams at the university. Danticat shows here how desperately humankind clings to the myths and beliefs of civilized society.

Irony is further enhanced by the use of "krik krak" as the title. While that is the standard ending (sometimes opening) for a Caribbean story, the stories are usually anancy stories and folktales with moral lessons. Danticat's nightmarish tales are a far cry from those, but her tales do carry a moral lesson—about the powerful and the powerless, about the failure of good to triumph over evil.

How to write of such evil and not appear to exploit the horrific happenings for their macabre appeal poses a significant question for readers as it surely does for Danticat herself. Related here is the assumption of reality. While reality is generally an irrelevancy in fiction, in these stories, where a large part of the appeal is our insight into an inaccessible world, we somehow expect the view afforded us to be authentic. We don't want our sensibilities outraged by a fictive world.

—Erika J. Waters, [Review of *Krik? Krak!*], *The Caribbean Writer* 9 (1995): 261–62

BIBLIOGRAPHY

My Turn in the Fire: An Abridged Novel. 1993.
Breath, Eyes, Memory. 1994.
Krik? Krak!. 1995.

ZEE EDGELL

B. 1940

ZEE EDGELL was born Zelma Edgell on October 21, 1940, in Belize City, the daughter of an entrepreneur who was also, in Edgell's terms, a feminist. Raised and educated in Belize, Edgell received training as a journalist, and her first job was reporting for the *Daily Gleaner* in Jamaica. In the late 1960s, Edgell taught school and edited *The Reporter*, a small paper in Belize City. Later, as the director first of the Women's Bureau and then of the Department of Women's Affairs in Belize, Edgell traveled extensively.

While traveling in Bangladesh in the 1970s, Edgell wrote her first novel, *Beka Lamb* (1982). A coming-of-age story, the novel places Beka's growth into womanhood in the context of Belize's struggle for independence. Employing creole dialect throughout the novel, Edgell offers a way to negotiate between tradition and change to form a productive and healthy community identity. The novel won the Fawcett Book Prize.

Edgell's second novel, *In Times Like These* (1991), is in some ways a sequel to *Beka Lamb*. The heroine is now a grown woman, who, upon returning to Belize after a time in London, has questions about children and about economic and political practice and principle on her mind. The novel challenges the posturing of many leftist ideologues as well as the opportunism of some professed feminists.

In a recent interview, Edgell explained how the issues of gender and race operate in her books. While concerning herself with women's struggles and oppression, Edgell maintains a "balanced view" of men: "I also have a father, a husband and a son," she asserts. On the question of race, Edgell sees her work as entering a long tradition of bitter protest by black American and Caribbean writers; however, she views her novels as intervening in this tradition and shifting the focus: "Writing from the Caribbean is entering a new dimension," she has said. "Now what needs to be said is what to do and how to do it."

In the mid-1980s, Edgell served as a UNICEF consultant in Mogadishu, Somalia. More recently, she has worked as a lecturer in English language and literature and journalism at the University College of Belize, while serving as a public education consultant in Belize City.

CRITICAL   EXTRACTS

EVELYN O'CALLAGHAN

Beka Lamb, Zee Edgell's recent Belizian novel, deals specifically with the pressures that young black women have to face, and with the 'crazy house' that claims some who cannot take these pressures. ⟨. . .⟩

⟨. . .⟩ In Edgell's novel, Beka's best friend, Toycie, gets pregnant by the son of a respected 'Pania' (Spanish stock) family. The boy refuses to marry her, she's expelled from the Catholic high school where she had been excelling, and with no future left, withdraws into madness and later, hidden away with relatives in the bush, dies in a hurricane. ⟨. . .⟩

⟨The⟩ novel succeeds ⟨in that⟩ it takes an everyday Caribbean social phenomenon, personalizes it and anatomizes the agony of those involved, drawing hope from the fact that Beka (symbolized by the bougainvillea stump that puts out new shoots) will survive and learn from another's mistake. Where Edgell fails is in trying to do much more—for example, her attempts at political allegory by the identification of Beka with Belize ('sometimes I feel bruk down like my own country, sister,' p. 115), and the hazy link between Beka's maturity and her country's nationalistic awakening at the end of the novel. Images that are organic to the description of Beka's development become laboured when stretched to fit the political theme as well: Beka's inner turmoil is constantly imaged as a tidal wave about to break, and her growing distress is described in terms of natural turbulence reaching a crisis in the hurricane in which Toycie dies. The attempt to broaden the application of the image to include political upheaval also, tends to lessen the overall effect.

Similarly, the transparent juxtaposition of Toycie's renunciation by the 'superior' Villanueva family with political rhetoric about the exploitation of Belize by the colonial elite, is too obviously calling attention to the novel's message.

Another minor flaw is the author's concern for the 'foreign' reader, which leads to unintegrated cultural explanations ('cultural cushioning') that bear little relation to the narrative's progression. An example is the passage on the history and racial make-up of Belize sketched in (p. 11) with obvious educative intent and little connection with what has gone before in the chapter. It could also be this concern for the non-Belizian reader that causes Edgell to anglicize her dialogue, trying for a compromise between English and Belize creole that is sometimes stilted and sometimes inaccurate—no Belizian uses the word 'Carib' as Beka's mother does (p. 70): since 1968, the term 'Garifuna' has been the norm.

Edgell's style is straightforward: she uses a conventional flashback structure for Beka's cathartic reconstruction of the past, and a simple narrative language to achieve the effect of understatement suitable to Beka's adolescent consciousness. It is only on closer inspection that we realize there is more than appears on the surface, and this also befits Beka's growing maturity, her awareness that life's 'meanings' have to be groped for before they are grasped with any certitude. Despite its flaws, *Beka Lamb* is a rewarding novel and a welcome contribution to the growing body of West Indian novels by and about women.

—Evelyn O'Callaghan, "Driving Women Mad," *Jamaica Journal* 16, no. 2 (May 1983): 70–71

YAKINI KEMP

⟨For⟩ Beka Lamb, educational achievement is something that strengthens the relationship she shares with her paternal grandmother. When Beka wins the essay contest at her convent school and when she successfully passes First Form, after failing the previous year, Beka's sense of self-worth and accomplishment grows immensely. The relationship between her and her Granny Ivy grows to a new level also.

Granny Ivy is the family matriarch who is Beka's link between the present and "before time." The view of Belizean society that Granny Ivy presents to Beka is one that is colored by her position as a poor, hard-working Black woman who has lived in colonial Belize all her life. She is outspoken, has an independent spirit, and she takes an active role in the political battles of her community because she is a fierce nationalist and wants to see her country free. Granny Ivy wishes for political change, but the reality of colonial politics and the entrenched class divisions which are exacerbated by the various racial mixtures and prejudices in the society, continually informs her that achieving independence will be a serious battle within her country.

Beka goes to the PIP's (People's Independence Party) meetings with Granny Ivy and actively discusses the issues with her. Only after Beka becomes absorbed in her schoolwork and the essay contest do they realize that their political discussions are a vital part of their bond. Fear of losing Beka to schools which teach Belizean youth "to look outside instead of in" prompts Granny Ivy to lash out at Beka when she shows no interest in the political happenings anymore. "Who ever heard about any black girl winning so much as a pencil at that convent school? Do you see any black nuns?" (*Beka*, p. 151). Although Granny Ivy wants change in the society and wants her granddaughter to succeed, she sees that education, especially the Catholic centered education of the convent school, alienates the youth from their roots which leads many of them to become condescending toward their kin or exiles from their land. In order to compensate for her own fear and frustration, Granny Ivy continually calls forth one of the primary contradictions in the Belizean educational system and Catholicism in general, namely, their practice of discrimination against Belizeans of African descent.

—Yakini Kemp, "Woman and Womanchild: Bonding and Selfhood in Three West Indian Novels," *Sage* 2, no. 1 (Spring 1985): 25

BRUCE WOODCOCK

Beka Lamb explores the 14-year-old Belizean girl's life at the point when the colony was struggling for its own national identity. It is a theme familiar from other earlier Caribbean novels, dealt with through male characters in Vic Reid's *New Day* (1949) and Lamming's *In the Castle of My Skin* (1953). Zee Edgell similarly weaves together the living sense of the political struggle of the people and her central character's own struggles, often exposing the contradictions between the two. Late in the novel when Beka is fighting to succeed at school by entering an essay competition on the history of the Sisters of Mercy in Belize, Beka's Gran asserts the need for direct involvement in the efforts of the People's Independence Party to win self-government for the country, rather than trying to win 'that fool-fool contest' ⟨151⟩. It is a nice touch since Beka herself is shown earlier as having adolescent aspirations to be a politician. The effect of her education is increasingly to detach her from her family context. When she wins the essay competition, she goes home with her medal and meets an anti-government demonstration led by her Uncle Curo. Overcome by this direct evidence of a different kind of fight, she asks 'Is this the end of everything then, Uncle Curo?', to which he replies with a booming belly laugh, 'The end, pet? Belize people are only just beginning!' ⟨167⟩.

Zee Edgell's intimate awareness of the ambiguous tensions in her society is matched by the immediacy of her writing. Her clear images can often adopt strong emotional overtones which are located in the specific context of Belizean life: 'A rain breeze was rising, and her heart thumped in her chest like a pestle pounding plantain'; 'for most of her life, the members of her family had surrounded her tightly, like sepals around a bud'; 'In Beka's mind, of late, a tidal-like wave was always there, and she lived in constant tension between the drawing back of the water, and the violence of its crashing against the shore. And when it crashed, the sound in her brain was the squawking of pelicans, and she was always afraid' ⟨7, 27, 43, respectively⟩. Equally sure is the handling of narrative. After the first four chapters, the book works as one long flashback of Beka Lamb's life over the last seven months, an act of memory ostensibly performed as a wake for her dead friend Toycie. Within that framework, numerous other intercuttings of narrative are handled with skill and flexibility.

—Bruce Woodcock, "Post-1975 Caribbean Fiction and the Challenge to English Literature," *Critical Quarterly* 28, no. 4 (Winter 1986): 88–89

RICHARD DEVESON

One of the attractions of Zee Edgell's first novel, *Beka Lamb* (which shared the Fawcett Society Book Prize in 1982), is that its aim is straightforwardly to put on record a time and a place and a group of people: the life of a creole family in Belize City at the end of the Second World War. In Gordillo's Grocery and Dry Goods Store "the smell of kerosene, onions, cheese and briny pigtails made the shop stink". The family's garden is filled with roses, maidenhair ferns, bushy crotons, oleander, stephanotis, bougainvillea, "red hibiscus flowers with their tongues hanging out". For meals there are yams, red snappers stewed in coconut milk, corn tortillas and black beans, chillies, escabeche soup. . . . It is perfectly all right to enjoy the exoticism of all this, while acknowledging that for the author its meaning is very different.

Beka Lamb's story is the characteristic Caribbean one of the bright child who grows up and away from her family. But the other attractive feature of the novel is that Beka's growing-up, less characteristically, happens without causing virulent conflict or alienation. She is a dreamy child; her family is happy; the womenfolk are dominant, but her father is also decent enough. It is Beka's friend Toycie who succumbs to unmarried pregnancy and insanity—a victim of the blighting of female ambition and hope which Edgell unstridently shows was another of the pervasive charms of the Belize of her childhood.

    —Richard Deveson, "The Life of the Political Past," *Times Literary Supplement* (24 October 1986): 1187

ELAINE CAMPBELL

Beka Lamb might be called a heroine of the seventies. Published in 1982, Edgell's novel is a showpiece of Belizean literature. Late in its development beyond oratory and journalism, the literature of Belize has been an unknown constituent in the larger world of West Indian Literature. Alan McLeod has pointed out that the literature of the country has been confined largely to rhetoric and poetry because of Belize's history of public meetings as the conventional means of communication and persuasion. McLeod hopes that Belize, so cut off from the more England-oriented West Indian island nations, might explore "avenues not yet entered by the [other] Anglophone Caribbean countries, developing in the process a new esthetic ("The English Literature of Belize," *World Literature Today*, Summer 1982, 443). Whatever may be the future of Belize's late developing literature, Edgell's novel does not indicate a new esthetic. *Beka Lamb* is a competently written work which in no way reflects the magical realism of its Latin American neighbours. If anything, it is a solid specimen of the traditional novel, employing flashback to recount the sad ending of a likable seventeen-year-old who finds herself pregnant out of wedlock. The villain of the piece is a rather self-satisfied young member of Belize's Hispanic population; the novel's weight is thrown heavily in favour of the Black creoles. Beka's own triumph over her tendency to lie—the declared main action of the novel—does not engage the writer to the same degree as does Toycie's story.

The story of Toycie's fall from virtue is really a frame from which to hang a considerable amount of information about the everyday life of Belize's newly emergent urban middle-class, a population still too close to poverty to have developed a set of bourgeois assumptions. Despite Edgell's understandable desire to explain contemporary Belizean events, despite the highly traditional form of the novel, and despite the material of yet another West Indian novel of childhood, *Beka Lamb* could signal a significant change of pace in the West Indian novel because it by-passes what have become the pieties of the times. Beka's engrossment in her milieu calls to mind the novels of Michael Anthony, novels singularly devoid of a sense of estrangement. Anthony's characters are totally integrated West Indians, so absorbed in life's little moments that they bring to West Indian fiction a quality of sweetness rare in the literature of commitment. While Edgell's conservative style may somehow be a function of Belize's position outside the mainstream of West Indian affairs, she cannot be accused of naivete as she has lived in Jamaica, Britain, Nigeria, Afghanistan, Bangladesh and the U.S.A.

—Elaine Campbell, "The Dichotomized Heroine in West Indian Fiction," *Journal of Commonwealth Literature* 22, no. 1 (1987): 142–43

LORNA DOWN

Set within the framework of a colonial society, a society aspiring to independence, *Beka Lamb* examines the dialectical relationship between that society and the individual. The personal stories of the girls Beka and Toycie are used as ways of examining the colonial society. The relationship between Toycie and Emilio in particular suggests the exploitative colonial one. And Beka's journey to self-assurance compares with her country's move to independence. In addition, the traditional ways are shown in conflict with the values promoted by the Church and educational institutions. The result is dramatic change whose impact, emphasized by the constant references to "befo' time" and "tings bruk down," is seen in the disintegrating society, its former wholeness and stability eroded by the colonial experience. But disintegration is only part of the life cycle. Edgell's heroine learns this truth, and by implication independence is therefore a real possibility for her country.

The more important emphasis, however, is on the highly personal odyssey of Beka from early adolescent dependence and uncertainty to self-definition and integration. The novel begins in the present, revealing Beka's success and achievement. It then moves to the past, recalling the major events of her life in order to explain and give meaning to the present. Edgell appropriately uses a folk ritual—The Wake—to place this journey. The Wake operates on two levels: it is a way of mourning what is gone; it is also an attempt to discover and celebrate what has been gained. So Beka, in having a private Wake for Toycie, is paying her respects to the dead and allowing herself to grieve; but in recalling Toycie's life, she is also gaining insight into her own life and that of her society. The Wake is essentially a medium through which the events of the past are recounted, sifted for their fine truths, and appropriated. In doing so, Beka is engaged in ordering through memory the fragments of the past, finding its patterns and recreating self. ⟨. . .⟩

In *Beka Lamb*, Edgell portrays the importance of adolescent girls' private relationships. And while she admits to the tension that society creates she demonstrates that finally it is the girls' personalities and their means of resolving conflicts that determine their growth. The mother-daughter relationship in its various forms also provides central support for the adolescent. There is a direct relation between its presence and the adolescent's definition of self. In addition, Edgell examines stereotypical female means of coping—emotional and passive. Such ways are shown as negative: heroines who practice them fail to attain wholeness. In contrast, there are strong and independent women who through an active creativity impose their will on their world. Edgell has affirmed emotionality and passivity are not the only feminine ways of coping.

Beka Lamb offers us a more complex picture of the female adolescent. Through Toycie and Beka, Edgell examines the conflicts she faces with her awakening sexuality and society's increasing expectations. Such expectations are often ambiguous. They acknowledge her visible growth and supposed maturity but not her sexuality. Beka and Toycie are thus most vulnerable in that area. Miss Flo makes oblique references to Beka's sexuality and Miss Ivy's confession helps her. But generally, the adult women remain silent about their daughters' sexuality. And while Edgell does not claim that biology controls a girl's perception of self and the choices she makes (that is, that biology is destiny), she does take into account the pressure society exerts on a woman to conform to its image of femininity, especially during adolescence. Like other women, Beka must confront and surmount these pressures to achieve selfhood.

—Lorna Down, "Singing Her Own Song: Women and Selfhood in Zee Edgell's *Beka Lamb*," Ariel 18, no. 4 (October 1987): 39–40, 50

CHARLOTTE H. BRUNER

It is difficult to assess the impact of the women's movement and the sexual revolution on world literature today. Nonetheless, the recent rise in the number of women writing, publishing, and focussing on woman's lives as a literary motif is startling. In African and Caribbean literature, the eighties have brought forth new writings, not only by new writers in first novels, but new themes. A new motif of girlhood is emerging and proving to be significant enough to warrant extended fictional treatment. ⟨. . .⟩

Zee Edgell has set her novel, *Beka Lamb* (1982), in the Caribbean colony, now Belize. The story of a few months in the life of fourteen-year-old Beka, recounted as a flashback, is symbolically Beka's own wake for her friend, Toycie. Beka's failure to pass a grade in school and her later success in winning an essay contest form a parallel frame to the recounting of Toycie's story of unwanted pregnancy and death. So actually two girlhoods are contrasted in the one narrative. ⟨. . .⟩

The recalled episodes do build to a climactic effect as the supposed child protagonist becomes increasingly aware of outside events. The cultural milieu impinges on her consciousness as she matures. The reader, along with the heroine, can look back to the naiveté of childhood exuberance or pain and at the same time understand the concurrent events as they are witnessed but not interpreted by the child viewer. Each episode, then, has a two-fold richness of interpretation, often the poignancy of tragedy foreseen. The particularized details of many of the recounted episodes are very personal, very individual. Very likely the author is recapturing, at least in part, a lived experience. Zee Edgell has said, "I enjoyed using the memories of my childhood. It was fun trying to understand my reactions to the experiences of childhood by placing them alongside the historical, economic, political, and sociological data of the period" ⟨letter to Charlotte H. Bruner, 29 January 1984⟩.

—Charlotte H. Bruner, "First Novels of Girlhood," *CLA Journal* 31, no. 3 (March 1988): 324, 328–30

Lizeth Paravisini and Barbara Webb

The socio-historical context of *Beka Lamb* (Belize, 1980) is similar to that of colonial Trinidad in ⟨Merle Hodge's⟩ *Crick Crack Monkey*. The adolescent heroine comes of age in the politically turbulent years that gave rise to the Belize independence movement. The author, Zee Edgell, contributes a detailed social portrait of this neglected area of the Caribbean. Formerly British Honduras, Belize is noted for its extremely heterogeneous population of Blacks, Hispanics, Mayas, Caribs and Asians. Although English is the official language, Spanish, Maya and Carib are also spoken. This racial and linguistic variety, combined with the country's location on the Yucatan peninsula and Guatemalan territorial claims have produced a national "identity crisis" in Belize that rivals that of most other Caribbean societies.

On the surface, Zee Edgell's treatment of the extreme ethnic diversity of Belize society is amazingly devoid of any urgent sense of conflict. Although the author tends to emphasize national pride and unity despite apparent group prejudices, there is an obvious discrepancy between the national ideal and reality; for Belize is a society always on the verge of "breaking down". Young Beka Lamb compares this situation to her own sense of emotional upheaval when she observes, "Sometimes I feel bruk down just like my own country . . . I start all right but then I can't seem to continue. Something gets in the way and then I drift for the longest while" (115).

Although the Lamb family reflects the underlying social tensions of Belize, here too Edgell emphasizes inner strength and unity—perhaps in an attempt to counter the stereotype of the unstable, matriarchal family structure of the predominantly black societies of the Caribbean.

—Lizabeth Paravisini and Barbara Webb, "On the Threshold of Becoming: Caribbean Women Writers," *Cimarron* 1, no. 3 (Spring 1988): 110–11

ENID BOGLE

The use of madness is prevalent in literature as a medium of spectacle, or as inherent in the development of the plot, often either providing entertainment or symbolizing disillusionment. Although the term is grounded in psychology, the intent of this paper is not to present an indepth psychological interpretation. Neither is madness used here to reflect feigned mental anguish such as Hamlet's nor that of a physically diseased mind. This madness is not to be associated with the label given to people who are referred to as being mad because they "march" to a different drummer; instead, the term is used here to mean a conscious or unconscious mental withdrawal from reality. ⟨. . .⟩

Both Rema ⟨in Roger Mais's *The Hills Were Joyful Together*⟩ and Toycie ⟨in *Beka Lamb*⟩ are optimistic heroines whose lives end tragically after they have been driven to madness. Both girls trusted unequivocally their male lovers who in each case failed to live up to what was expected of them. But is the male/female relationship the real source of the problem? Or is it merely an instrument that serves to orchestrate a greater problem? What are the real factors that drive these women to madness?

Young ladies who have "fallen into disgrace" have been referred to as "Shamey Darlings," a common expression in rural Caribbean and also, in rural Jamaica, a term used to refer to the *Mimosa Pudica*, a sensitive plant whose leaves, composed of many pairs of leaflets, when disturbed, fold upward and droop. Reference is made to a plant with similar characteristics, after Toycie faints at the news of her expulsion. Beka finds a "clump of grass, with the tiniest purple-white flowers. . . . Each dainty, olive-green branch supported a dozen tiny oval leaves. She touched one branch watching the shy leaves close like the wings of a butterfly" (112). If we make an analogy between the withdrawal of the leaves and that of Rema and Toycie, since they, like the sensitive plant upon being disturbed withdraw from the real world, then we might say that the withdrawal serves as a natural protecting instinct. But in less than five minutes, the sensitive plant will assume its former posture. This behavior of the plant lends credence to R. D. Laing's claim in *Politics of Experience* that madness is an invention of people to enable them to live in an unbelievable situation and that the condition is temporary. ⟨. . .⟩ If in the world of nature this withdrawal is simply an immediate reaction to protect, and if once the danger is passed, some semblance of the original form is restored, why is it that Rema and Toycie were not allowed to return to their former state? Perhaps unlike the world of the plant, the external factors that were responsible for the condition are still present. Seemingly the signal that Toycie awaits to return to normalcy does not appear, or if it did, she had gone too far inside herself to understand; thus the possibility of regaining sanity is remote. If this is so, then precisely for this reason, the disturbing forces must be removed for human beings, unlike the *Mimosa Pudica*, may not be capable of this voluntary return. Rigney's assessment that madness is more a "cultural phenomenon rather than an anatomical inevitability" seems valid. ⟨. . .⟩

Unlike the *Mimosa Pudica*, both Rema and Toycie withdrew forever from the real world. For both, their love affair catapulted them into a web of circumstances from which they did not escape. The hopelessness that confronts them as a result of their own actions destroys them. Neither one of them seems to have had the will to survive, and to be sane is having the ability to cope with the vicissitudes of the real world. It is as if madness is inevitable when self-love and self-preservation give way to self-effacing. It is a madness that is inevitable when the desire to satisfy external forces takes precedence over those of the inner self.

—Enid Bogle, "Driven to Madness: Psycho-Social Tensions in Two Caribbean Female Characters," *The Zora Neale Hurston Forum* 4, no. 1 (Fall 1989): 9, 14, 16–17

MIKI FLOCKEMANN

The traditions of the Western *Bildungsroman* ⟨. . .⟩ are subverted in the texts by Edgell, ⟨Tsitsi⟩ Dangarembga and ⟨Farida⟩ Karodia. A dual focus is given by the interaction between the protagonist and her friend, cousin or sister; this acts as a strategy for bridging the uncomfortable and problematic relationship between insider/outsider, self/other in writing by black women in the postcolonial contest, where women have been traditionally positioned as object (or native/other). ⟨. . .F⟩ilm-maker and critic Trinh Minh-ha points out how complicated the concept "identity" is for the black, Indian or Asian woman who comments on other "Third Worlders":

> The moment the insider steps out from the inside she's no longer a mere insider. She necessarily looks in from the outside while also looking out from the inside. Not quite the same, not quite the other, she stands in that undetermined threshold place where she constantly drifts in and out.

In other words, the inside/outside opposition is undercut or blurred, and I hope to show how Edgell, Dangarembga and Karodia effect a similar subversion. ⟨. . .⟩ in their attempts at ⟨. . .⟩ providing women-centred alternatives to traditional Western genres such as the *Bildungsroman*, in a post-colonial context. ⟨. . .⟩

Education is viewed in all three works as an escape from poverty, and as an entry into the racially determined class hierarchy. In *Beka Lamb* the stifling atmosphere of anachronistic Victorian morality surrounding St Cecilia's Academy is introduced in the very first paragraph by the description of its close proximity to "His Majesty's Prison". Yet the power implicit in the Academy is also suggested in the same paragraph where, on learning that Beka has won the essay prize, her family feel that she has overnight "changed from what her mother called a 'flat-rate Belize creole' into a person with a 'high mind' " (p. 1). So highly do her family rate education (Beka is given opportunities denied to them) that she feels compelled to lie about failing her exams. When she finally owns up, the political importance of education is noted: her admission, "Daddy, ah fail", is prefaced by an announcement on the radio her father is listening to:

> The commissioners, under the chairmanship of Mr S.D. Hartley, have recommended in the proposed new constitution that universal adult suffrage be introduced in the colony. All prospective voters will be required to take a literacy test. (p. 23)

Beka's failure at school is of course a reflection on the education system, rather than a judgement on her abilities. One of the reasons she "fails", is because she questions the values taught at school. This is particularly evident in her rejection of Catholicism which is used as a form of imperial control. Her clash with Father Nunez, a native Belizean, points to the conflict of cultures, the tensions between tradition and modernity, prevalent in the society ⟨. . . .⟩

Beka first experiences her own questioning of her "superiors" as an indication that there is something wrong with her, which implies that she has internalized the values of St Cecilia's to some extent at this stage. Nevertheless, her spontaneous rejection of these values causes her to identify herself with the entire Belizean society, which is repeatedly referred to as "breaking down": "Sometimes I feel bruk down just like my own country" (p. 115). ⟨. . .⟩

Beka's growing understanding of the social and political implications of her rejection of educational and religious structures occurs when she witnesses Toycie's disintegration or "breaking down" after she is expelled because she is pregnant. This is not only an indictment of the school's outdated moral code, but, more importantly, reveals the extent to which Toycie, unlike Beka, has identified herself with these values, seeing them as her means to escape poverty, and repaying her aunt for the sacrifices made to keep her at school. It should be remembered that Beka comes from a middle-class, upwardly-mobile creole family, while Toycie lives alone with her impoverished aunt Eila who struggles to pay for Toycie's schooling. Toycie's ambition is to be assimilated into the privileged class and she dreams of living in a quarter where "few real Belize people . . . lived": "One of these days, Beka Lamb, I am going to live right da seafront, hurricane or no hurricane" (p. 15). (Significantly, Toycie is killed during a hurricane.) Beka's ambition, however, is to be a politician— partly influenced by her Granny Ivy's fervent support of the People's Independence Party (PIP) who favour independence from Britain. Granny Ivy prophesies that Toycie's ambitions will miscarry because "Toycie was trying to raise her colour, and would wind up with a baby instead of a diploma" (p. 47), and Beka too is dismayed by Toycie's infatuation with the pania (Spanish-speaking) Emilio Villanueva—the name itself suggestive of the family's bourgeois aspirations—and warns: "panias scarcely ever marry creole like we, Toycie" (p. 47). As Beka watches Toycie's humiliation and despair when she is abandoned by Emilio and denied further access to the Academy, she is confronted with the implications of her own potential failure, as well as the dangers inherent in womanhood.

—Miki Flockemann, " 'Not-Quite Insiders and Not-Quite Outsiders': The 'Process of Womanhood' in *Beka Lamb*, *Nervous Conditions* and *Daughters of the Twilight*," *Journal of Commonwealth Literature* 27, no. 1 (1992): 38–41

RENEE HAUSMANN SHEA

Contemporary women novelists from the Caribbean are writing a new chapter in the literature of adolescence—a study of connections. Although few of these novels and short stories were written expressly for adolescents, their authors acquaint us with bright, often rebellious, intractably clever, and always strong-willed adolescent protagonists struggling to define themselves in a world whose political and cultural reality is also in transition. These protagonists are growing up in different countries, some still under colonial rule, others newly independent, but they share a tradition of defining themselves within a web of relationships. Their adolescent struggle to come of age is what psychologist Carol Gilligan calls "a crisis of connections." ⟨. . .⟩

⟨. . .⟩ ⟨*Beka Lamb*⟩ is a study in family and community relationships, in the interaction between private lives and political action, and in a folk culture rich in tradition and manifest in Edgell's use of the Creole language. By no means a feminist tract, *Beka Lamb* offers a gallery of portraits of strong, independent women along with a number of positive male characters. The center of interest, though, is Beka and why she comes through her crisis while her dear friend Toycie succumbs. ⟨. . .⟩

Beka is the successful counterpart, but her success is hard won. Gilligan points out that young women often see an "opposition between self and other, tied in the end to dependence on others and equated with responsibility to care for them" (1982, 139). Thus they feel that they must choose to be "good" (that is, to choose through self-denial not to hurt others) or to be selfish (that is, to hurt others by choosing to be selfish). Early in her story, when Beka is once again caught lying, a sure sign of disconnection with the self, she tells her father she is sorry. When he asks her if she is sorry "for me or for you," she admits that she does not know. At this point, she is not certain to whom she is most responsible—the self or the other. Beka's relationships to family and friends are certain, yet in her adolescence the terms are shifting.

A central event in the novel is Beka's entering and winning an essay contest. This triumph marks another stage in her development because, although she writes the essay and can ultimately and rightfully be called its author, her writing process is a truly collaborative one: Granny Ivy suggests a local man to interview, Beka's mother provides her with an elegant fountain pen and exercise book in which to write, and Beka drafts her essay sitting on the floor surrounded by her family. Further, when Granny Ivy becomes ambivalent about Beka's winning, anticipating her leaving the family, Beka asserts herself and perseveres. She has found a way to develop her independent self yet sustain connections; she has, in Gilligan's terms, exchanged dependence for interdependence. In one of my student's words, "Beka grows to be more independent, while Toycie remains dependent on the hope of others' approval to give her value."

Beka Lamb, like so many of these novels and short stories by contemporary Caribbean women, extends the concept of connection and relationships to the larger domain of politics.

—Renee Hausmann Shea, "Gilligan's 'Crisis of Connections': Caribbean Women Writers," *English Journal* 81, no. 4 (April 1992): 36, 38–39

B I B L I O G R A P H Y

Beka Lamb. 1982.
In Times Like These. 1991.

BERYL GILROY

B. 1924

BERYL GILROY was born August 30, 1924, in Guyana (then British Guiana). She attended the Government Educational Institute, receiving her teacher's certificate in 1945, and moved to England six years later. There she worked as a factory clerk and maid before she was able to return to academics. After receiving an advanced diploma in child development in 1953, Gilroy attended London University, earning her bachelor of science in psychology in 1956; she went on to receive her master's degree from Sussex University in 1979 and a Ph.D. in 1987 from Century City University. Gilroy has worked as a writer, psychologist with a private practice in counseling, freelance journalist, teacher, and headmistress in Guyana and London.

Gilroy began writing when, as a teacher in London, she realized that her students' readers had few, if any, black or nonwhite characters. To fill this void, she wrote a number of books and stories for young children that reflected not only her students' diverse cultural backgrounds but also their interests, fears, and feelings in a context with which they could identify. Many of these stories were published in the Nippers and Little Nippers series. Gilroy created her books for older children, including *In for a Penny* (1978), to help teenagers examine their self-perceptions in relation to the social pressures they faced daily.

Frangipani House (1986), Gilroy's first novel for adults, won a prize in the Greater London Black Council Literature Competition before it was published. The novel follows Mama King, an aged and sick woman in Guyana. Weak in body, though not in spirit, Mama King is sent to a rest home. Her eventual escape and survival allow Gilroy to protest institutions that isolate those whom society views as weak and nonproductive. *Boy-Sandwich* (1990), Gilroy's second novel, builds on the tradition of migration stories in Caribbean literature, following an island family settled in Britain for three generations. *Sunlight on Sweet-Water* (1994) continues this story, employing historical references as a frame for her story.

Gilroy has published a number of other books, including an autobiography, *Black Teacher* (1976), and a collection of poems, *Echoes and Voice* (1991). She is currently working on a contemporary novel, *In Praise of Love and Children*, and on a historical fiction, *After Columbus: Inkle and Yarico*. She lives in London and is attached to the Institute of Education at the University of London.

CRITICAL EXTRACTS

RICHARD DEVESON

A country doesn't, of course, necessarily become independent by becoming Independent; and in the same way it is hard for the literature of an ex-colony to avoid being ex-colonial. The political past lives on, a factor in the intellectual present. The writer is very likely an exile, in Europe or America—at any rate an advance guard of decolonization, an outsider looking in. And yet the past has receded all the same, and the writer, besides looking in, may also turn out to be looking back. Separation, if it isn't turned to artistic account, can breed both nostalgia and distress. ⟨. . .⟩

Frangipani House is a new novel, also a first novel, also a prize-winner (in the GLC Black Literature Competition). Beryl Gilroy's heroine, Mama King, is a Guyanese grandmother who has been consigned to an old-age home by her children, selfish émigrés in New York. The home is a prison, ruled by a monstrous wardress, and Mama King, after going through cantankerousness and despair, escapes from it to join a troop of beggars. Although her flight is not the final resolution of the story, it does read like an attack of wishful symbolism, and there is something forced, generally, about the way in which Mama King is supposed to stand for matriarchal dauntlessness. In the eyes of most of the younger generation, Mama King is the old country; she *is* the past. The old country is "just pain and hatred of poverty, hardship and useless mud and dung, pain, mosquitoes and old age". This may be selfishness speaking, but with one half of itself the novel doesn't dispute the point. Mama King had two children; like most men in the story, her husband cleared off "when the belly show". If the men are not violent, they're not around. Yet at the same time the novel seems to want Mama King to stand for the existence of a good past, a lost world of mothers and dependent young children, a provisional moment of inevitability after and before uncertainty and suffering. It wants to see virtue in that oppressive past precisely because courage and struggle were necessary if it was to be survived. Beneath the rightful protest there is a curious undertow of emigrant's regret.

—Richard Deveson, "The Life of the Political Past," *Times Literary Supplement* (24 October 1986): 1187

JULIAN RATHBONE

Frangipani House is ⟨. . .⟩ securely rooted in a perception of reality that acknowledges the worst but triumphantly asserts the best in us. Beryl Gilroy's book is the tale of Mama King, put into an old people's home by children and grandchildren who have left the Caribbean to work abroad. The first 50 pages are heart-searing as Mama King struggles to cope with the unthinking cruelty of the staff, the dreadful helplessness of being forced to do nothing after a lifetime of activity, and with the humiliations, mental and physical, that come with tired old age. Frangipani House, typical of 'homes' all over the western world, is on the point of winning, of turning her into a mindless vegetable, when a visit from a grandson resurrects her almost vanquished spirit. With the cunning of the very old she absconds with a troupe of mendicants and sets in train the events which restore her to a life of dignity. One unusual criticism: it is too short. Not just the story of Mama King's battle with Frangipani House is here, but her whole life as well, and that of her children and grandchildren and neighbours, and a further 50 pages is not enough.

—Julian Rathbone, "One and All," *New Statesman* (24 October 1986): 30

ANDREW SALKEY

Frangipani House ⟨is⟩ an elegantly written and heartening novel by one of our distinguished women novelists ⟨. . . .⟩ Beryl Gilroy's Mrs. Mable Alexandrina King (affectionately called Mama King by friend and frightened foe), old, ill, but splendidly her own woman, is put away by her family in Frangipani House, a Dickensian rest home on the outskirts of Georgetown. It's the kind of place that the city folks point to and say, "Over yonder—Frangipani House! People dies-out dere! They pays plenty to die-out inside dere! Death comes to lodgers in Frangipani House!"

But not to the redoubtable, sexagenarian Mama King! She opposes Matron Olga Trask, "the honey brown predator" and administrator of the house, by using every means at her circumscribed disposal: anguished silence, fits of depression, outright rebellious conduct, and teetering insanity. In the end Mama King walks away from Frangipani House, is violently mugged, hospitalized, and finally goes to live as a comforter to the destitute among the very poor in the city.

Beryl Gilroy's aptly, understatedly honed, symbolic inference, together with her driving social conscience, makes of all Guyana an allegorical Frangipani House, and certainly one either to escape from or to be changed radically.

—Andrew Salkey, [Review of *Frangipani House*], *World Literature Today* 61, no. 4 (Autumn 1987): 670

ERIKA J. SMILOWITZ

Mama King lives in Frangipani House, supported by her two daughters who lead prosperous lives in America. As Gilroy describes the nursing home:

> Sleepy headed windows dressed in frilled bonnets of lace, and fine, white cotton, hibiscus shrubs that danced their flower bells to the songs of the wind, and a mammee apple tree that kept the grounds clean by never bearing fruit, marked the house as a place of professional comfort, care and heart's ease. (p. 1)

For the most part, the women in Frangipani House live in the past where, as Gilroy said in a recent interview in London, "bits of memories, like condiments, feed their lives." They make futile attempts to assert themselves, but they are cowed by Matron, who is hypocritical, alcoholic and, as we later learn, utterly miserable. ⟨. . .⟩

Gilroy's language adds greatly to the work. Here analogies, often based on tropical landscape, are original, uniquely appropriate and often startlingly poetic. The novel opens on the description of a road as "brown as burnt sugar and tender as old calico." At one point Mama King is crying: "Her heart was so full of hatred . . . that at the slightest touch she would split open like a ripe calabash dropped on stone." Mama King's complaints are "swept aside like rotten wood in rough wind," and Matron withdraws after a reproach "the way a baby turtle draws in its head."

The minor characters, the nurses in particular, are not as clearly delineated and their roles in the novel are contrived. (For example, one nurse plans to marry one of Mama King's grandsons, a coincidence which seems to serve no fictive purpose.) But this is a minor lapse in a memorable, haunting book. *Frangipani House* grapples with disturbing, real-life issues while remaining enjoyable and optimistic—a considerable feat. Mama King finally triumphs over the evil Matron to live a life she chooses. With the help of her loving family, she herself makes it happen.

—Erika J. Smilowitz, "Tales of the Caribbean," *Women's Review of Books* 5 (November 1987): 14

ROBERTA Q. KNOWLES

It is with the insight of a psychologist, the eloquence of a poet, and the compassion of a kindred spirit that Beryl Gilroy, in her latest novel, chronicles the confinement of Mama King, an elderly, infirm grandmother, in Frangipani House, an old-folks home in Guyana.

Lucid and feisty when she arrives, Mama King soon becomes pained by the unvarying routine and the paralyzing constraints ⟨. . . .⟩

In this grim present with nowhere to retreat, Mama King escapes to a magical past, which soothes her with romantic dreams of her husband Danny, who, we discover from the objective recollections of her old friends, was brutal and indifferent. The delicate color of sweet-scented frangipani petals, "snippets of ribbon strewn across a green baize carpet," reminds her of costumes worn by her daughters, daughters who now have abandoned her to the care of strangers, and she stares out into the distance "allowing spools of recollections to unwind." Also, in this dream state, that recurs during her stay at the home, she relives old traumas: the disappearance of her husband, the drowning of a grandson, and a painful accident, which ended her work as a brick-breaker, her only hedge against starvation.

A visit from her grandson Markey jolts her out of her confused reveries and lures her into present-day fantasies. She now dreams of escape and of Markey's return to rescue her. When this escape materializes and Mama King is freed from the indignities of Frangipani House and the fierce grip of her interior world, the narrative force of the novel trails off considerably. We leave the psychologically complex probing of Mama King's depression and delusions, the intricate weaving of past and present, and the vivid character sketches of the other residents, demented and senile, of Frangipani House to join Mama King as she roams with a band of beggars, is the victim of a "choke-and-rob" attack, and ends up in a hospital, visited by her children and grandchildren, who have returned to intensely debate what should be done with her. ⟨. . .⟩

Billed as a protest novel, *Frangipani House* exceeds the confines of that genre and does more than merely explore gerontological crises. The characters it delineates are three dimensional—ranging from the hypocritical matron of "practised sincerity," whose eager, seeking hands would "confiscate the copper pennies on the eyes of a corpse" to the sensitive grandson, who is overwhelmed to see his once vigorous grandmother reduced to "a haunted ghost with a haunting past." On the whole the men are refreshingly complex and humane, far removed from flat stereotypes.

—Roberta Q. Knowles, [Review of *Frangipani House*], *The Caribbean Writer* 2 (1988): 92–93

LUCY WILSON

Typically, we think of exile as a fundamental dislocation brought about by distance from one's home and roots, intensified by race, religion, ethnic origins, class, as well as gender. Another kind of exile, however, is the separation and alienation that results from the inevitable and inexorable process of aging. It is exemplified by a character like Beryl Gilroy's Mama King, who has lived her entire life in one place. ⟨. . .⟩

⟨. . .⟩ Life in Frangipani House has systematically robbed Mama King of everything that gave her life meaning. In *Vital Involvement in Old Age*, Erik Erikson, Joan Erikson, and Helen Kivnick discuss the difficulty some elderly people experience as a result of mandatory retirement: "for those whose creativity and involvement in work has been of major importance and whose identity is largely derived from that work, there can be a bitter and deprived feeling of being expelled and depreciated" (299). This is certainly true of Mama King, whom a nurse scolds saying she is lucky because "Life is a tread-mill. You been on it for years and years. You daughters push you off. Don't grumble. Don't complain. Count your blessings" (16). But Mama King will not be placated. "More than anything else she wanted to work. Her body needed it as it needed food and clothes. And now, time and life, her daughters and the matron had all conspired to deprive her of her faithful friends, work and hard-ship" (19). The "treadmill" of hard work that Nurse Douglas spoke of so dis-paragingly was the source of the old woman's pride and strength:

> Mama King thought of all the distance she had walked in the life, all
> the loads of wood and bags of charcoal, buckets of water, trays of
> washing and heavy fruit she had carried on her single, strong head,
> which in spite of everything had kept its shape. Feeling her head as if
> to reassure herself that it had not been changed in any way by over-
> use and years of faithful service, she marvelled at its strength. (24)

But work is not the only thing Mama King misses. During a rainstorm, Mama King identifies with "a picture card at the mercy of the rushing water," with "no control over its route or its fate" (31). When an old acquaintance, Ben Le Cage, visits her, he asks, "Why do they do this to her? As long as she lives, she has to be active. Sitting around made her mad" (34). Miss Ginchi, Mama King's friend since childhood, comes to the same conclusion: "Confinement and do-nothing destroy people. She like to hustle. She hustle all her life" (48). When one of Mama King's grandchildren, Markey, flies in from his naval base in the Caribbean, he is appalled by the change in her:

> He remembered her dark-haired and strong, able to get the stopper
> from a bottle with her teeth. She was purposeful and positive. Now
> here she was, a haunted ghost with a haunting past. The family had
> imagined her happy, interminably giving and caring and sharing in
> friendship and community. Never getting older. Immortal. What had
> the years done to her? True, she had been ill. But this was more than
> illness. She was old, but age did not enhance or dignify her. What
> had they done to her? (46–47).

What "they" had done to Mama King was to deprive her of work, control, action, community, hardship, and self-actualization.

—Lucy Wilson, "Aging and Ageism in Paule Marshall's *Praisesong for the Widow* and Beryl Gilroy's *Frangipani House*," *Journal of Caribbean Studies* 7, no. 2–3 (Winter 1989 and Spring 1990): 189, 192–93

A. L. McLEOD

Most West Indian fictions about migration have been concerned with an individual's adjustment to a new social environment and have been written in the autobiographical mode. *Boy-Sandwich,* however, expands the range of this type of writing by considering the experiences, aspirations, and reactions of three generations of an island family long settled in Britain, though it retains the form of an autobiographical narrative embellished with astute social observations and penetrating analyses of interracial and interpersonal behavior.

The narrator is an eighteen-year-old boy of Guyanese heritage burdened with the responsibility of caring for his institutionalized grandparents, who have lived in Britain longer than most of their neighbors and who are Empire loyalists who have worked hard, paid their taxes, been frugal, and raised a family that includes a grandson now ready to go up to Cambridge. As the protagonist Tyrone Grainger comments, "I was the filling and they were the slices of bread." Such figurative language abounds in the novel; in fact, the texture of the style is a delight in a time when language is not always valued and crafted in fiction. The bananas in an old people's home are described as "like fingers covered with large neglected sores," and an elderly inmate is said to be "tucking pain away in his body like a coin in his purse." Fear is "a solid rock inside people's hearts." Dialect, not always handled convincingly, is here used with great skill as an elucidation of character and role; it is neither an entertainment nor a decoration. Language, perhaps more than any other element, differentiates the three generations of the family and the family from others.

There are the usual embarrassing members of the extended family, but their peccadilloes are treated sympathetically if not understandingly; the range of characters is extensive, yet none is superfluous. On returning to the Caribbean, Tyrone realizes that "I don't belong here . . . I am British." Implicit is the idea that British no longer means white-skinned, Anglican, and Eurocentric, but this is offered in a discreet, muted manner as befits a novel that examines the nature of a changing, postcolonial society in a mature and exploratory manner. *Boy-Sandwich* is a fine sequel to Gilroy's *Frangipani House* of 1985.

—A. L. McLeod, [Review of *Boy-Sandwich*], *World Literature Today* 64, no. 2 (Spring 1990): 348

RHONDA COBHAM

Beryl Gilroy's *Boy-Sandwich* and Sybil Seaforth's *Growing Up with Miss Milly* are short novels that recount the growing pains of boys rather than girls. Perhaps it is a consequence of the gender of the authors, however, that, rather than concentrating exclusively on one child's developing ego, the novels focus on the painful, intimate unfolding of the relationships between their protagonists and the adults, especially the women, who help bring them up. Gilroy's boy, for instance, is a teenaged "Black British" youngster who is sandwiched between his two aging grandparents; between his parents and grandparents; between his family and the British community; and between Britain and Jamaica. The novel's painstaking recreation of the process of aging in the lives of the boy's grandparents, and the conflicting emotions he experiences as he shifts out of the role of the indulged grandchild into that of a young adult who must make decisions for two frail elderly people entering their second childhood, is certainly its greatest achievement. ⟨. . .⟩

Both novelists tend to sacrifice pace and narrative control in the interest of following these relationships through all their contradictory twists and turns. At times this loss of control amounts to little more than bad writing—as when, in both novels, the authors pause to bring readers up to date with the plot before plunging back into the web of intricate interpersonal relationships. But at its best this technique can be understood as a challenge to a particular kind of linear imperative in the telling of stories. It reminds us that both children and adults experience life as a many-sided set of constantly shifting, often contradictory possibilities, and that it is a mere convention to insist on representing such experience as a story with a beginning, a middle and an end.

In this connection, Gilroy's decision to use the present tense for her first-person narrator underscores the immediacy of all the sensations with which her Boy-Sandwich must cope ⟨. . . .⟩

Language is also an important issue, and both writers have chosen to attempt faithful reproductions of actual speech patterns. Gilroy, who is originally from Guyana, attempts to reproduce Black British and Jamaican speech patterns, while Seaforth, a Jamaican, experiments with Trinidadian dialects. Given the difficulties Caribbean authors face when they try to represent the forms they themselves use, both writers must be commended for coming up with acceptable representations of these (for them) non-native speech patterns. However, there are moments when, for someone familiar with these Creoles, the dialogue rings false. There is a lack of consistency about using Standard instead of Creole, and occasionally the standard forms seem stilted or verbose. For readers unfamiliar with Caribbean languages such slippage can add to the difficulties of following the narratives.

—Rhonda Cobham, "Women of the Islands," *Women's Review of Books* 7 (July 1990): 29

B I B L I O G R A P H Y

Nippers and Little Nippers readers. 1972–1974.
Green and Gold (four volumes). 1976.
Black Teacher. 1976.
In for a Penny. 1978.
Carnival of Dreams. 1980.
Frangipani House. 1986.
Boy-Sandwich. 1990.
Echoes and Voice. 1991.
Love in Bondage: Stedman & Joanna—Dedicated Love in the Eighteenth Century. 1991.
Sunlight on Sweet-Water. 1994.
Gather the Faces. 1994.
On Living in the Third Age. 1994.
Winnowing Out the Words. 1994.

MERLE HODGE

B. 1944

MERLE HODGE was born in Curepe, Trinidad, in 1944, as one of four daughters of Ray Hodge, an immigration officer, and his wife. Receiving her primary and secondary education in Trinidad, Hodge won the Trinidad and Tobago Girl's Island Scholarship in 1962, which enabled her to travel to England to continue her studies. She received her bachelor's degree in French from the University College of London in 1965 and went on to earn her master's degree. Her thesis focused on the poetry of French Guinanese Negritude writer Leon Damas.

Hodge traveled in Eastern and Western Europe, supporting herself by working as a typist and baby-sitter before returning to Trinidad in the early 1970s. After teaching French at the secondary level for a short time, Hodge was appointed as a lecturer at the University of the West Indies. During this time, she began to pursue her Ph.D. in French Caribbean literature and completed a translation of *Pigments*, a collection of short stories by Leon Damas.

In 1970, Hodge published her first novel, *Crick Crack, Monkey* (1970). It tells the story of Tee, a young girl who moves between two opposed black communities: one reflected by her aunt Beatrice's middle-class values; the other, by her aunt Tantie's lower-class raucousness. Hodge followed this novel with a number of nonfiction essays, including "The Shadow of the Whip: A Comment on Male/Female Relations in the Caribbean," in *Is Massa Dead?: Black Moods in the Caribbean* (1974); and "Social Sciences or Exoticism?: Two Novels from Guadeloupe," in *Revista/Review Interamericana* (1974).

In 1979 Hodge moved to Grenada to work with its new prime minister and leader of the socialist revolution, Maurice Bishop. There she became the director of the development of curriculum, focusing on the implementation of a socialist education program; she also worked with the People's Education and Adult Education programs. In 1981, Hodge published *"Is Freedom We Making": The New Democracy in Grenada*, a nonfiction piece about the new government in her adopted home. Two years later, she was forced to return to Trinidad when Bishop was assassinated and the U.S. invaded the island.

Hodge's most recent novel, *For the Life of Laetitia* (1993), tells the story of 12-year-old Lacey, the first in her family to go to secondary

school. This experience creates a number of conflicts, including difficulties with her father and stepmother and with a cruel teacher.

Most recently, Hodge has worked as a freelance writer and lecturer in Trinidad.

C R I T I C A L   E X T R A C T S

ROY NARINESINGH

Crick Crack, Monkey, which was first published in 1970, belongs to a group of
West Indian novels, such as *The Year in San Fernando* and *Christopher* which deal
with the theme of childhood. The central character, Tee, moves in two
worlds—the world of Tantie and the world of Aunt Beatrice—and those two
worlds are bound together in a coherent and unified way by the response of
the central character, who is also narrator, to the experiences of both worlds.
The child, Tee, moves in a context in which there is strong opposition
between certain social and cultural values, and, as narrator, she recounts the
intensely personal dilemmas of her life in that context. This she does with a
remarkable depth of insight and with a vivid evocation of childhood memories. The reader is made to share in the diversity and richness of Tee's experiences without being able to discern at times where the child's voice with a
child's perception of things slides into the adult voice and vision of the omniscient author. Child vision and adult vision are made to coalesce at several
points in the novel.

The two worlds of childhood which Tee inhabits result from the nature of
her domestic circumstances. Her father, who has emigrated to England, is the
brother of Tantie, and her deceased mother is sister to Aunt Beatrice. Tee oscil-
lates between these two spheres of existence and emerges as a deeply disturbed
being—a plight derived from the essential conflict of life styles between creole middle-class and Tantie's world. The conflict externalized in these two
classes of society generates acute feelings of ambivalence within Tee. Both in
form and content the novel is indeed a response to the inner pressures of a
profoundly felt and complex experience. The vivid exploration of the child's
inner world confers on the novel its essential strength. The child's feelings,
thoughts and actions, as she responds to the social and cultural environment
in which the novel is set, reflect the authenticity of remembered experience.

—Roy Narinesingh, "Introduction," *Crick Crack, Monkey*, by Merle Hodge (London:
Heinemann, 1970), vii

MARJORIE THORPE

For the members of the Afro-West Indian community, the question of cultural identification has proved to be particularly problematic. Culturally uprooted during the slave era, the African was obliged to evolve a new set of conventions which would enable him to survive and function in the West Indian environment. Yet his experiences both as a slave and as a black man living in a society colonized by Europeans have encouraged the Afro-West Indian to deny the worth of the locally-evolved culture and to seek instead to identify himself with a foreign cultural tradition which obstructs rather than aids his attempts at self-realization.

The tension created by the conflict between the Afro-West Indian's personal needs and the values of the adopted metropolitan culture is the subject of Merle Hodge's novel, *Crick Crack Monkey*. The theme is not new; but, unlike the majority of other novels which direct the reader's attention to the cultural dilemma of the Afro-West Indian man, *Crick Crack Monkey* is one of a very small group which seeks to examine the reactions of the Afro-West Indian woman to the problem of cultural identification.

The narrator of *Crick Crack Monkey* is a young West Indian girl, Tee. The narrative covers the years of Tee's childhood. The nature of Tee's experiences suggests that, at one level, Hodge intends her young narrator to function as a representative of the West Indian people, few of whom are indigenous to the region. The novel opens with the death of Tee's mother, an incident which is immediately followed by her father's emigration. These two events deprive Tee of her natural home and make her a type of castaway. The frequency with which the figure of the castaway occurs in West Indian literature during the years in which she makes her home with Tantie, Tee is evidence enough of the general nature of the experience. As members of an immigrant society most West Indians have known, in varying degrees of intensity, the sense of cultural dispossession which Tee experiences when she is obliged to make her home in a completely alien environment. At another level, however, Tee is the representative of the de-culturalized, transplanted, Afro-West Indian community. The action of the novel begins when Tee is still a child, her character unformed. As Hodge traces Tee's psychological development, the reader is made aware of the two cultural systems open to the Afro-West Indian: that of the imported metropolitan culture, imitated by Aunt Beatrice; and that of the indigenous black creole culture, reflected in Tantie's way of life. Hodge, however, does not merely present the two cultural systems. Rather, by demonstrating the difference in the attitudes and values of the two women, and by noting, too, the way in which these different attitudes and values affect the young Tee, Hodge is able to suggest the extent to which emotional involvement in either culture is conducive to the individual's success or happiness.

The external conflict in the novel takes the form of a struggle between Aunt Beatrice and Tantie for the guardianship of Tee. From the outset, then, the two cultural systems are set up in opposition to each other. Yet one notes that Tantie and Aunt Beatrice are both related to Tee in a similar way: Tee's mother was Aunt Beatrice's sister. Her father is Tantie's brother. Thus, by implication, Tee is equally heir to the differing cultural traditions which the women represent. In consequence, as Tee attempts to deny first the one and then the other, the cultural contest which is externalised in the conflict between Aunt Beatrice and Tantie eventually becomes the source of Tee's own psychological dilemma. By having her shuttle backwards and forwards between the homes of her two aunts, Hodge underscores the nature of Tee's inner conflict; but Hodge also goes on to suggest that it is a conflict which can never be resolved as long as the individual attempts to cultivate one system of values to the exclusion of the other. The novel ends with Tee about to migrate to England. It is a form of exile which she welcomes as offering a way out of a perplexing cultural situation. Yet withdrawal can hardly be termed a positive solution; and while the possibility exists that, in a foreign country, away from the pressures of her own society, Tee might in time be able to reconcile the two cultural traditions which she has inherited, there is still the other possibility that, like the school-master Mr. Hinds, her sojourn in the metropolis will merely aggravate her contempt for the local black creole culture, thus removing her permanently to the ranks of the culturally displaced.

—Marjorie Thorpe, "The Problem of Cultural Identification in *Crick Crack Monkey*," *Savacou: A Journal of the Caribbean Artists Movement* 13 (1977): 31–32

YAKINI KEMP

That women are the main purveyors of cultural values and role expectations for their daughters and women-children in general is a given. Yet women in modern societies exist within various classes as all people do. This fact renders a particular problem for Tee, the central character of *Crick Crack Monkey* who spends part of her formative existence with her feisty paternal aunt, Tantie, who is from the Trinidadian urban poor, and part with her maternal aunt, Beatrice, a dilettante and member of the rising middle-class. The clash of values and world view which Tee must reconcile as a result of living with these two different women, is an emotional and psychological torment which she tries to solve by choosing sides. Her choice damages her own developing self-concept and is clearly an eventual link to the type of woman she will be in the future.

Tee and Tantie's relationship is one of nurturance. Tantie serves as mother and provider for Tee and her younger brother Toddan after their mother dies in childbirth. Tantie provides the tangible basics: food, clothing and shelter. But she also provides an education in the basics for human survival among the urban poor of Trinidad: love, rage, "fight-back spirit" and pride. Tantie's sense of order and world view result from her life experiences as a Black woman who is unmarried, head of a household and poor. She survives by her resourcefulness and "gifts" from her various men friends who are "uncles" to Tee and Toddan. ⟨. . .⟩

While living with Tantie, Tee develops a sense of family security. Tantie treats her as a child, using the traditional methods and attitudes of parent-child relationships, which is why Tee records no long or involved conversations between them even as she passes to the upper primary grades.

However, Tantie does begin to prepare Tee for a more mature role by sending her on minor errands and trips to the local Chinese grocer. This helps Tee's developing self-confidence and independence. A trip to the grocer alone at the age of seven or eight is something Tee's middle-class aunt Beatrice would never allow. Of course, Tantie's perception of the responsibilities of a womanchild is different. Tee's successful execution of her small missions, coupled with the pride gained from her passing to First Standard, indicate that she is moving progressively toward the development of a positive self-image while she resides with Tantie.

Tee's feeling of unity which gives her a sense of security and her new-found independence are two of the most significant aspects of her developing selfhood. A third aspect, equally significant, is her achievement in education. Ironically, Tantie's wish for the best possible education necessitates delivering Tee to "The Bitch," Aunt Beatrice.

The relationship between Tee and her Aunt Beatrice is never complete, secure or wholesome. Aunt Beatrice lives and breathes all the biases, rules and affectations of the African-Trinidadian petitbourgeoisie by rote. She heaps these prejudices upon Tee's consciousness. They are reinforced by the snobbery and bias of the teachers of St. Ann's and the cruelty and ostracism perpetrated by Beatrice's selfish daughters. The psychological impact of this social setting upon Tee is dramatic and destructive. She withdraws into herself, having no friends or outlet for solace. ⟨. . .⟩

Although Tee is never secure at St. Ann's or in Beatrice's home, the weightiness of the prejudice and the overwhelming force and advantage of the pettibourgeois lifestyle make Tee opt for the values and worldview it presents.

However, this acceptance robs her of her self-worth, making the attitudes and most values gained in Tantie's household null. ⟨. . .⟩

⟨As⟩ Tee prepares to leave Trinidad, she has no close relationship with either aunt. Her education and her relationship with Beatrice have given her a choice in the perception of the world, but it has also seriously damaged the positive self-image she was developing while she resided with Tantie.

—Yakini Kemp, "Woman and Womanchild: Bonding and Selfhood in Three West Indian Novels," *Sage* 2, no. 1 (Spring 1985): 24–25

ELAINE CAMPBELL

With the advent of Zee Edgell's *Beka Lamb* ⟨. . .⟩ and of *Crick Crack Monkey*, the first novel of Trinidadian activist Merle Hodge, the Caribbeanist expects a new theme and perhaps even a new style in West Indian novels. Hodge and Edgell represent the younger women writers from the English-speaking Caribbean; consequently, one looks for radical departures from the work of earlier women writers: Jean Rhys, Phyllis Allfrey, Ada Quayle, Lucille Iremonger, Sylvia Wynter. While Quayle and Iremonger's preoccupation with White creole degeneration makes *The Mistress* and *Creole* now dated, it would take some talent to surpass the high quality of Rhys's writing or the basically revolutionary content of Allfrey's. (Wynter, of the earlier women writers, remains in a class by herself—her only novel, *The Hills of Hebron*, antedates the literary and social criticism for which she is better known.) *Beka Lamb* and *Crick Crack Monkey*, published thirty years after Allfrey's *The Orchid House*, offer less-than-radical advance over the offerings of the past but they do point to possible new directions. The most significant distinction that Edgell offers is that of a sympathetic depiction of Black middle-class life—something we haven't seen much of in literature from the West Indies with the exception of John Hearne's novels that have often been treated as anomalies for that very reason. Hodge's *Crick Crack Monkey*, well-written as it is, throws the West Indian novel back upon the familiar theme of the exile-at-home. ⟨. . .⟩

⟨. . .⟩ A novel of racial and cultural commitment, *Crick Crack Monkey*'s polarities are similar to ⟨Claude⟩ McKay's in *Banana Bottom*. McKay's clergyman's wife, Priscilla Craig, the White expatriate from England, is replaced by Hodge's light-skinned Aunt Beatrice. Both women display stereotypic nicety of behaviour and a certain lack of sincerity. The peasant or proletarian values are represented by the whole village of Banana Bottom in McKay's novel while Hodge offers Tantie Rosa as the vessel of indigenous worth. Roy Narinesingh points out in his Introduction to *Crick Crack Monkey* that "The central character, Tee, moves in two worlds—the world of Tantie and the world of Aunt

Beatrice . . . The child, Tee, moves in a context in which there is strong opposition between certain social and cultural values, and, as a narrator, she
recounts the intensely personal dilemmas of her life in that context" ⟨vii⟩.
Hodge's valuation of the two antagonistic aunts is crystal clear. Neither ambiguity nor complexity cloud the issue. Good and bad angels stand to Tee's right
and left shoulders. But Hodge updates McKay because she resists the impulse
to settle Tee's dilemma through the *deus ex machina* of a mate. Tee is left in childhood at the end of the novel, too young to address the selection of a mate.
Hodge emancipates herself from the possibility of providing a suitable mate
for the perplexed heroine, thereby leaving her in her dilemma. Tee is the modern youth, product of a dual culture, heiress to a dichotomized psyche. She is
a child of the writer of the sixties. She longs to return to her earthy Tantie, but
she does not. She is left standing on the brink of self-realization. "Everything
was changing, unrecognizable, pushing me out. This was as it should be, since
I had moved up and no longer had any place here. But it was painful, and I
longed all the more to be on my way" ⟨110–11⟩. Recognizing that her growth
has taken her beyond the world that Tantie can provide, Tee is nonetheless
unhappy with that growth. She leaves the reader as she wishes for a plane to
lift her off the ground. Her situation is not easily settled: a solution won't be
supplied by a drayman, a field worker, or a bohemian artist. Nor will there
come a plane to lift her off the ground. The answer will have to be worked out
by Tee herself.
—Elaine Campbell, "The Dichotomized Heroine in West Indian Fiction," *Journal of
Commonwealth Literature* 22, no. 1 (1987): 137, 141–42

LIZABETH PARAVISINI AND BARBARA WEBB

In *Crick Crack Monkey* ⟨. . .⟩ the process of becoming an adult is complicated by
the pressures of assimilation in pre-Independence Trinidad. When young Tee's
mother dies and her father emigrates to England, the women of her family
assume responsibility for her upbringing. And it is in Tee's relationship to her
female guardians that Hodge develops the theme of "double consciousness" so
common in Caribbean literature. Tee is literally "torn between two worlds"
when her Aunt Rosa and Aunt Beatrice compete for her guardianship. ⟨. . .⟩

As in other Caribbean novels of childhood and adolescence, the colonial
school system plays a crucial role in the socialization process. Thus Tantie
must also contend with a school system primarily designed to teach allegiance
to the British Empire, where children learn a general contempt for blackness,
tacit obedience to arbitrary authority, conformity and hypocrisy. At home
Tantie admonishes Tee that she is going to school to "learn *book*" and not to let
her teachers put any nonsense in her head. At first spirited young Tee seems

to maintain a sense of her own self-worth despite her teachers, but it is precisely in *books* that she unconsciously learns her first lesson in duality and self-effacement.

In the wonderful world of books, Tee discovers another reality, which she accepts as superior to her own:

> Books transported you always into the familiar solidity of chimneys and apple trees, the enviable normality of real Girls and Boys who went a-sleighing and built snowmen, ate potatoes, not rice, went about in socks and shoes from morning until night and called things by their proper names . . . Books transported you always into Reality and Rightness, which were to be found Abroad. (61)

In order to become a part of this "Rightness", Tee creates Helen, her double; but as the young narrator observes, Helen was more than her double:

> She was the proper Me. And Me, I was her shadow hovering about in incompleteness. (62)

Thus Tee assimilates the values that Tantie had tried so hard to counteract and sees herself as lacking, inadequate, "incomplete"—not because she is a girl but because she is not the "right" kind of girl. Although Tee is said to have soon outgrown and "discarded" Helen, this experience foreshadows the process of self-estrangement that will take place when she wins a scholarship to attend secondary school and goes to live with her Aunt Beatrice.

—Lizabeth Paravisini and Barbara Webb, "On the Threshold of Becoming: Caribbean Women Writers," *Cimarron* 1, no. 3 (Spring 1988): 108–9

KATHLEEN M. BALUTANSKY

Hodge: ⟨. . .⟩ I'm very often asked if *Crick, Crack, Monkey* is a feminist response to the male novel in general. It is not. I didn't know anything about feminism at the time. I didn't even know that word. That was a hundred years ago! That was the sixties! And I was very innocent: I was a university student. What is very interesting is that so many people, not just in the Caribbean but also in Africa, in both French-speaking Africa and English-speaking Africa, have chosen that device of a child narrator or protagonist. Those novels were produced under the colonial situation.

You know, I think that with the exception of perhaps Michael Anthony's, these aren't really novels about children. *Crick, Crack, Monkey* wasn't necessarily about the child, Tee. I think that this is true about a lot of those novels—as I said, with the exception of Michael Anthony, who generally writes about children and who is genuinely childlike in his perspective and remains amazingly able to climb back into a child's consciousness at his age. There's the fellow from Cameroon, Camera Laye, and there's a heap of writers who have used the child narrator basically as a seeing-eye. Well anyway, in the case of the Caribbean writers—but maybe this extends to the African writers as well—I saw that form as a kind of stock-taking in the face of the non-recognition of our culture and of our environment. I think that to a large extent it was a stock-taking and a validation of our culture. But of course it wasn't a validation of *everything*, because although the child notices and records all, it remains a skeptical view; and there are many things about the social structure which must be recorded but which the writers reject. So I don't necessarily see those novels as being about a child growing up here and maturing. That is probably a theme in a number of them, but I think that the children are almost used.

Balutansky: Yes, the distinction you make is a very good one, since in the novels that we're talking about we also have the stock devices of using the naive eye of the child to present the absurdities of the educational system, of the social structures, etc.

Hodge: I've often thought of those child protagonists as symbols, as representative of the Caribbean culture in its infancy. So the impact of the educational system on the child is really an exploration of the impact of the educational system on the budding culture, because the culture is new and it hasn't been given a name and it didn't get recognized as a culture. Of course, for the novel to be interesting and for it to be meaningful it has to deal with the impact of all these things on *human beings*. So it's the impact on children, but ultimately the idea behind that is that we see the child as a representative of the culture.

   —Kathleen M. Balutansky, "We Are All Activists: An Interview with Merle Hodge," *Callaloo*
   12, no. 4 (Fall 1989): 653–54

SIMON GIKANDI

Merle Hodge, whose novel *Crick Crack Monkey* marks a crucial transition from nationalist discourse to post-colonial writing in the Caribbean, has written on how colonial education, by presenting the lived experiences of the Caribbean people as invalid, negated the very subjectivity of the colonized by taking them away from their "own reality": "We never saw ourselves in a book, so we didn't exist in a kind of way and our culture and our environment, our climate, the plants around us did not seem real, did not seem to be of any importance—we overlooked them entirely. The real world was what was in books" ⟨David Dabydeen, *A Handbook for Teaching Caribbean Literature*, 1988, 78⟩. If existence and significance are defined by the texts we write and read, as Hodge seems to suggest here, then the absence of female texts in the Caribbean canon meant that political independence had not restored speech to the Caribbean female subject. If independence represented the triumph of modernist forms, it had legitimized a situation in which the lives of Caribbean women were still surrounded by a veil of silence perpetuated by a male-dominated discourse. For this reason, the current outpouring of Caribbean women's writing can clearly be seen as the first major challenge to the project of modernity initiated by the colonizer. ⟨. . .⟩

Merle Hodge's *Crick Crack Monkey* was the first major novel by a post-colonial West Indian woman writer to problematize and foreground questions of difference and the quest for a voice in a social context that denied social expression to the colonized self and hence cut it off from the liberating forms of self-expression which define the Caribbean narrative. For Hodge, this emphasis on voice as a precondition for black subjectivity in a colonial situation was necessitated by both ideological and technical reasons. First of all, in the plantation societies of the Caribbean, the voices of the oppressed and dominated slaves and indentured labourers survived against the modes of silence engendered by the master class. For these slaves and labourers, then, the preservation and inscription of a distinctive voice would signify the site of their own cultural difference and identity. Second, the voice was, in radically contrasting ways, an instrument of struggle and a depository of African values in a world in which the slaves' traditions were denigrated and their selfhoods repressed ⟨. . .⟩. In terms of narrative, the recovery of voice becomes one way through which unspoken and repressed experiences can be represented.

In Merle Hodge's novel, then, the voice is a synecdoche of the unwritten culture of the colonized, the culture of Aunt Tantie and Ma, and its privileging in the text signifies an epistemological shift from the hegemony of the written forms; alternatively, the negation of the spoken utterance through education and assimilation is a mark of deep alienation. When Tee opens her retrospective view of her childhood at the beginning of *Crick Crack*, she discovers that the past cannot be narrated without a cognizance of the voices that defined it. The voice is shown to be both central to the subject's conception of her past and as a paradigm that defines the context in which her multiple selves were produced. At the opening of the novel, a moment in which the birth of a new baby is superseded by the death of the mother, the world appears to Tee merely as a relationship of voices: "a voice like high-heels and stocking," "an old voice . . . wailing," "Some quavery voices," "a grumble of

men's voices" (2). Tee's subsequent alienation in the colonial world is prefig-
ured by her inability to identify with these fetishized voices as easily as she
identifies with the voice of Tantie and Ma.

> —Simon Gikandi, "Narration in the Post-Colonial Moment: Merle Hodge's *Crick, Crack
> Monkey*," *Ariel* 20, no. 4 (October 1989): 18, 20–21

RHONDA COBHAM

"Crick-crack monkey" is part of a call and response chanted at the end of folk
tales in the southern Caribbean:

> Storyteller: Crick-crack!
> Listeners: Monkey brek 'e back
> On a rotten pomerac.

The "crick-crack" probably imitates the breaking of a branch as the self-opin-
ionated monkey falls out of the tree and slips on the skin of a pomerac fruit.
But the literal meaning of the phrase is less important than its symbolic function as a marker separating the fantasy world of the story from the "real" world
of the storyteller and her audience. The child protagonist, Tee, shouts this
response to end the Anancy stories her grandmother tells during holidays in
the countryside where, she imagines, the magic of an earlier world not yet
deformed by the demands of growing up survives. But the tag is also used in
the novel by city youths as a means of challenging the stories told by
Manhattan, a member of their circle who claims to be an expert on the
American way of life:

> When the fellows were in a tolerant mood they would let Manhatt'n
> tell of his encounter with the sheriff in Dodge City and how he out-
> drew him . . . But when one day someone maliciously murmured
> "Crick crack!" at the end of one of these accounts in perfect Western
> drawl, Manhatt'n in his rage forgot to screw up his mouth to one side
> before starting to speak. "Crick-crack yu mother! Is true whe ah tell
> yu—yu blasted jealous it ain' you! Crick-crack? Ah go crick-crack yu
> stones gi' yu!" Manhatt'n was seen rather less at the bridge after that.
> (Hodge 7)

Hodge utilizes the deflationary technique associated with the tag implicitly in other contexts to emphasize the hiatus between fantasy and reality in
the options open to Tee. Thus, the fantasy world of respectability and pseudo-
whiteness associated with Tee's prim Aunt Beatrice is undermined when Tee's
younger brother, Toddan, shatters the tea-time idyll with his earthy insistence
that he must make "ca-ca." Tee's raucous, big-hearted Tante, is undermined by

similar devices, in spite of the positive, caring values which distinguish her from Aunt Beatrice. Sexual independence in Tante's life has degenerated into sexual promiscuity; freedom from social taboos has degenerated into alcoholism. This is why the decision of one of her older wards, Mikey, to fight for her honor on the street touches Tante so profoundly. Mikey's intervention on her behalf is his answer to the "crick-crack" challenge of the boys on the bridge to the myth of Tante's respectability. However, his heroic stance does not change the fact that Tante's lifestyle is in many respects as inauthentic as that of Aunt Beatrice and that it offers Tee no viable alternative in her search for a role model. ⟨. . .⟩

⟨. . .⟩ *Crick-Crack* resembles the novels of many male Caribbean writers in that it offers us no way of resolving this contradiction between sterile middle-class fantasy and sordid lower-class reality. But the fact that Hodge sets up the problem by recourse to an oral form suggests that its resolution may be achieved through the folklore associated with Tee's grandmother. This is the spoor followed in ⟨Paule⟩ Marshall's more fully developed narrative ⟨*Praisesong for the Widow*⟩. For the time being, however, it is important to note that Hodge uses the crick-crack tag self-reflexively, to provide the deep structure of the text and to critique the narrative to which it gives shape.

—Rhonda Cobham, "Revisioning Our Kumblas: Transforming Feminist and Nationalist Agendas in Three Caribbean Women's Texts," *Callaloo* 16, no. 1 (Winter 1993): 47–48

VÈVÈ A. CLARK

The *marasa* principle, drawn from traditional Haitian lore, suggests at once a pairing of texts for consideration and a commitment to a creative critical process which illuminates a third or wider field of expression beyond binaries. Following the nature-oriented and mystical philosophies from Asia, Africa, and the Caribbean, this particular theory when applied to comparative literature is based on the notion that $1 + 1 = 3$.

The *marasa* sign clarifies the dynamics of social change, the transformation of cultural oppositions within plantation societies. Movement beyond double-consciousness or the binary nightmare of a psyche divided by memory between Africa and Europe occurred particularly in the development of indigenous religious practices (Vodoun, Santería, Shango, Candomblé), Creole languages and mixed-race identities drawn together rather than apart. Coming to *marasa* consciousness in the late twentieth century means that the structure of analysis is triadic: African/Asian, European, and "New World." This third position looks back at the contradictions of racial definitions of the mixed-blood self as fundamentally black, oppositional stances within colonial

educational systems and new letters and liberation movements by comment-
ing on these phenomena in an environment of continuous change. ⟨. . .⟩

⟨. . .⟩ Hodge's *Crick Crack, Monkey* is oppositional in theme, characterizations, structure, narrative technique, and language. Essentially, Hodge represents opposed class differences, defined as "ordinaryness" and respectability
through the protagonist's aunts, Tantie and Aunt Beatrice. In the opening pages
of the narrative, the protagonist, Tee, and her brother are orphaned. When
their widowed father departs abruptly from Trinidad for England after his
wife's funeral, the children are left in a working-class family with a single head
of household, riotous Tantie, whose vulgar speech in Creole, working-class
wit, and determination dominate the first twelve chapters of the narrative.

Most criticism of the novel focuses on the opposition between the two
worlds of Tantie and Beatrice—the bourgeois city dweller and relative to
whom Tee is sent for continued education beyond the local primary schools.
Using the Caribbean culture's symbolic landscapes—house/yard as sites of
expression suggesting women's domains and respectability, as opposed to the
road/bridge areas of unbridled male behavior—we examined how these para-
digms existed in the narrative, discovering how Hodge expands the landscape
of affiliations described in Roger Abrahams's *Man-of-Worlds in the West Indies*
(1983) by including the bush or the mountain refuges of former maroons as
part of Tee's legacy. This is the place to which Tee returns for the summer
months, to her grandmother Ma, to traditions of storytelling (thus the title of
the novel), and to a fading memory, what Zee Edgell's characters refer to as
"befo' time." Deliberately devoting brief space to memories of Tee's summer
home Pointe d'Espoir, in chapter 4, Hodge suggests that there is no possible
return to communal identity for Tee, even though she resembles her great-
great grandmother, called Euphemia by the countryfolk ⟨. . .⟩ The nickname
has replaced Euphemia's "true-true" name, which Ma has trouble remembering:
"[Ma] couldn't remember her grandmother's true-true name. But Tee was growing into her grandmother again, her spirit was in me. They'd never bent down
her spirit and she would come back and come back and come back: if only she
could live to see Tee grow into her tall proud straight grandmother."
Nonetheless, references to Pointe d'Espoir, and to the world of Tantie's adopted son Mikey, where unemployed men signify on one another at the bridge,
open the narrative to levels of expressive behavior not confined to the glorious and rowdy Creole speech of Tantie or to the repressed anglophile domes-
ticity surrounding Aunt Beatrice. *Marasa* consciousness encourages readers to
appreciate a wider range of expression beyond the obvious binary oppositions
in the narrative.

—VèVè A. Clark, "Talking Shop: A Comparative Feminist Approach to Caribbean
  Literature by Women," *Borderwork: Feminist Engagements with Comparative Literature*, ed. Margaret
  R. Higonnet (Ithaca: Cornell University Press, 1994), 267–68, 275–76

B I B L I O G R A P H Y

Crick Crack, Monkey. 1970.
"Is Freedom We Making": The New Democracy in Grenada. 1981.
For the Life of Laetitia. 1993.

JAMAICA KINCAID

B. 1949

JAMAICA KINCAID was born Elaine Potter Richardson on May 25, 1949, in St. John's, Antigua, the daughter of Annie Richardson Drew and Roderick Potter. Her mother, born in Dominica, was a homemaker and political activist; her father, a former taxi driver, worked at a country club in Antigua; her stepfather, David Drew, was a cabinetmaker and carpenter. Kincaid attended the Antiguan Girls School and Princess Margaret School. In 1966 she immigrated to the United States; in New York she worked as an *au pair*, receptionist, and writer for *Art Director*; she attended Westchester Community College in White Plains and Franconia College in New Hampshire.

In 1983, Kincaid published *At the Bottom of the River*, a collection of short stories about Antiguan life, written in a style that is poetic and rich with imagery yet only elliptically narrative. Cataloging life's everyday occurrences, part of her signature prose in these stories as well as in her three novels, Kincaid offers powerful revisions of the way we look at and understand seemingly insignificant moments.

She again focused on Antigua in 1988, when she published *A Small Place*, a nonfictional examination of Antiguan history. The book speaks back to the hundreds of European-authored travel books about the Caribbean islands that offer Antigua to tourists as a place of unbelievably blue seas and lush tropical geography. Kincaid revises and challenges this view, looking at the island through the eyes of its impoverished black inhabitants. Highlighting the lack of infrastructure and the poor quality of life for most of the island's people, Kincaid faults both colonialism and the neocolonialism that replaced it.

Each of Kincaid's novels troubles and complicates mother-daughter relationships. The first of these, *Annie John* (1985), focuses upon Annie's tenuous and ambivalent relationship with her mother, following the girl's movement from the paradisiacal comforts of childhood to the alienation and disconnection of adolescence. Kincaid won a Guggenheim fellowship in 1989 to work on her second novel, *Lucy* (1990). In it she explores the powerful yet often ambiguous interaction between women, expanding on the mother-daughter relationship explored in *Annie John* to consider other relationships between women, such as those between black and white and between rich and poor. The critically acclaimed novel follows a young woman who leaves Antigua to work as an *au pair* in an American city. Kincaid's latest novel, *The Autobiography of My Mother* (1995), continues her exploration of the mother-daughter relationship; however, in this work a version of the mother who appeared in *Annie John* and *Lucy* tells her own story.

Since 1976, Kincaid has been a staff writer for *The New Yorker*. She currently lives in Vermont with her husband and two children.

C R I T I C A L   E X T R A C T S

JUNE BOBB

In her second novel *Annie John*, Jamaica Kincaid unites the sometimes elusive and fragmented, but always colorful world of *At the Bottom of the River* and creates, on one level, an almost Edenic setting at the heart of which is the relationship between Annie John and her mother. Other characters and incidents are dwarfed by the strange power of this relationship, a power both cohesive and destructive, and in a very real way symbolized by the calm and turbulence of the sea. The song of the Caribbean sea is the backdrop against which Annie John grows to maturity. It is the same sea that transported colonist and slave to the islands, thus creating an obsession with England and things English, and encouraging the separation by color and class, typical of West Indian societies. Finally, in the novel, it is a journey by sea which brings about the literal and metaphorical separation of mother and daughter.

Jamaica Kincaid lures the reader into the mysterious world of the known and the unknown, of reality and myth, a world where white clothes are spread out in the sun to "bleach"; daily breakfast is a formidable meal of "solid" food—porridge, eggs, fruit, bread and butter and cheese—a world of regimentation—lessons in piano and manners, and constant injunctions against behaving like a "slut". Woven into the fabric of this existence is the realm of the supernatural—the spirits who wander through the cemetery at night, the ritual of obeah baths, red candles burning, and the wearing of specially made sachets to ward off evil spirits. ⟨. . .⟩

⟨. . .⟩ The presence of Annie's mother looms over the novel framing it with her power. She is every mother descended from the line of powerful black mothers obsessed with the education of their children, an education which to them is a lifeline guaranteeing a better future.

Annie John's future concerns her mother. Her childhood is merely a preparatory stage during which she is made aware of her accepted role as a women in society. "Playing marbles" is out of the question, but she is taught the way to store linen, to cook and to keep house. In these areas, her mother

is exemplary. Annie John's feelings for her mother are strangely ambivalent. During her early years, she is smothered by a motherly attention bordering on the obsessive, and while she wants to be one with her mother, at the same time, and perhaps subconsciously, she yearns for a separate identity.
—June Bobb, [Review of *Annie John*], *Cimarron* 1, no. 3 (Spring 1988): 169–70

GIOVANNA COVI

If the postmodern claim to represent an attack against the Western tradition is acceptable as a fact, then how does one account for the absence of the voices of the minorities? Therefore we must question the tendency to take for granted the radicality of the postmodern ideology. Being cognizant that postmodernism itself has already been coopted into a canon that excludes and excommunicates, it wouldn't be surprising to discover that there are in fact postmodern minority writers. I will argue that the connotation of political radicalism associated with postmodernism is acceptable in so far as it opens up to include the specificity of those voices which have been historically discriminated against. I contend that Jamaica Kincaid, a black woman writer, is *radically* postmodern precisely because she is *also* postmodern, but not only so. Her voice, in fact, dismantles the symmetry of the metaphysical tradition in that it escapes all attempts to become domesticated under any label.

The main theme of her writings is the inquiry into the feminine role and racial difference. Kincaid criticizes the very existence of sexual and racial difference, rather than the modes of their existence: there's no place left for reform; the change that is invoked is not one of guards, but of structure. ⟨. . .⟩

The tremendous strength of Kincaid's stories lies in their capacity to resist all canons: They move at the beat of drums and the rhythm of jazz, so that we may be tempted to coopt them under the label of Black Aesthetics as formulated by Amiri Baraka. Yet, sometimes the feeling is more like that of a nursery rhyme—we listen to what Elisabetta Rasy has theorized as "feminine language": the nurse's language of sounds and silence which stands before and beyond the rational signifying words of the father. The language of the mother and child is expressed by Jamaica Kincaid in the story "My Mother" in these terms:

> My mother and I wordlessly made an arrangement—I sent out my
> beautiful sighs; she received them. (*At the Bottom of the River*, 56)

All these stories are structured around the figure of the mother: the writer is constantly connecting artistic creativity to maternity in the effort to create a new representation of the feminine which includes the logic of maternal love.

The commitment to this new ethics moves in the direction supported, among others, by Julia Kristeva and Luce Irigaray: bringing the maternal into the discourse of the father represents the new voice outside the dichotomy of sexual difference.

And again there is one more label tempting the critic: under the influence of Gates's formulation of 'signifying' as the main feature of Black Aesthetics, one could conclude that *At the Bottom of the River* is a successful example of this Afro-American rhetorical strategy. Parody, repetition, inversion mark every single movement of Kincaid's narrative.

—Giovanna Covi, "Jamaica Kincaid and the Resistance to Canons," *Out of the Kumbla: Caribbean Women and Literature*, eds. Carole Boyce Davies and Elaine Savory Fido (Trenton: Africa World Press, Inc., 1990), 346–49

M. STEPHANIE RICKS

Jamaica Kincaid's newest novel, *Lucy*, details the first year in the United States for Lucy Josephine Potter, a young woman from an unnamed Caribbean island twelve miles long by eight miles wide. During Lucy's year in New York, she leaves behind the young girl whose mother raised her to be a conscientious and obedient young lady and becomes instead an angry young woman, valiantly striving to define herself. ⟨. . .⟩

Lucy enjoys a distantly friendly relationship with Mariah and Lewis (the couple she works for) and stands as silent witness to the disintegration of their marriage, the ending of which seems preordained to Lucy if not to Mariah. ⟨. . .⟩

Lucy also develops a superficial friendship with Peggy, a working-class Irish woman. But like all of her relationships, including the casual sexual partners she acquires over the course of the year, Lucy remains steadfast in her desire not to allow anyone to encroach on her sense of self and her personal space. Whenever outreaching gestures are made by others, Lucy sternly thwarts them—sometimes cruelly. ⟨. . .⟩

Although connections are easy to draw, *Lucy* is not a sequel to *Annie John*, Kincaid's novel about a young girl growing up in Antigua and her contentious relationship with her mother. Where *Annie John* was lush, richly detailed, and linear in structure, *Lucy* is stark, the writing is spare, and the passages rush forward in time only to stop short and address some earlier episode. But like *Annie John*, *Lucy* addresses the alienation and isolation of its central character. And also like Annie, Lucy emerges as a person more comfortable with disentanglements than forging connections. Lucy is an angry person who proudly grips her anger to her chest. She is an uncompromising and unyielding woman. I

only wish that in this gem of a book, Kincaid had offered some reason for
Lucy's anger—and her pain—to complete the circle around Lucy.
    —M. Stephanie Ricks, "Tale of the 'Other,'" *Belles Lettres* 6, no. 2 (Winter 1991): 16

LAURA NIESEN DE ABRUNA

We have known for some time that Jamaica Kincaid writes with a double
vision. From one point of view, her early fiction and sketches in *The New Yorker*,
her collection of dream visions, *At the Bottom of the River* (1978), and her novel
Annie John (1983) all concern the coming-of-age narrative of a young woman
in Antigua. Much of Kincaid's fiction, especially the intensely lyrical prose
poetry of *At the Bottom of the River* and the autobiographical novel *Annie John*,
focuses on the relationship between mother and daughter and the painful separation that occurs between them. Careful examination of the psychoanalyti-
cal implications of these relationships will surely open up the meanings of
these texts. A psychoanalytic analysis from a feminist perspective, one examining mother-daughter bonding, would point out that the narrators in
Kincaid's fiction resist separation from the mother as a way of denying their
intense fear of death. The fear of separation is further complicated in *Annie John*
because the narrator leaves the island for Britain with the clear intention of
making a break with her environment. Both she and her mother, who is also
named Annie, have left their respective mothers and their own homes to seek
a more comfortable life elsewhere. The process of Annie's leaving her mother
is mirrored in the process of leaving the island. Displacement from an initial
intimacy with her mother's realm is reflected in a growing away from the environment until, at the end of the novel, Annie can only dream of leaving her
own home for England.

   Along with a psychoanalytic-feminist perspective, however, other views
must be taken of Kincaid's fiction. *Annie John*, for example, is not just the story
about a young woman's involvement with her mother and her home. There is
a story behind this story of how and why these conflicts are situated in a West
Indian island recently liberated from British rule. The novel is not the story of
a white, bourgeois mother and daughter but of an African-Caribbean mother
from Dominica and her daughter living in a nine-by-twelve mile island that is
drought- and poverty-stricken and far removed from the privileges of middle-
class life in Europe or the United States.

   That Kincaid thought about these differences when writing her fiction is
clear from a 'Talk of the Town' article for *The New Yorker* which appeared in
1977. Kincaid, who rejected her British name Richardson, recalled that most
of the African-Caribbean people of Antigua worked as carpenters, masons,
servants in private homes, seamstresses, fishermen or dockworkers. She added

that, 'A few grew crops and a very small number worked in offices and banks.' When Kincaid was seven she was herself apprenticed to a seamstress for two afternoons a week. People who worked in offices and banks were white, and the most wealthy ran a country club called the Mill Reef Club. The whites owned the banks and the offices and reserved most of the island's pleasant beaches for themselves. This historical and political context is central to Kincaid's fiction.

—Laura Niesen de Abruna, "Family Connections: Mother and Mother Country in the Fiction of Jean Rhys and Jamaica Kincaid," *Motherlands: Black Women's Writing from Africa, the Caribbean and South Asia*, ed. Susheila Nasta (London: The Women's Press Limited, 1991), 273–75

MOIRA FERGUSON

Jamaica Kincaid's fiction invariably achieves closure in terms of water that cleanses, fertilizes dry ground, and opens up new radical possibilities. Symbolically, water is also a place of indeterminacy where anything can happen: ⟨in *Lucy*⟩ it signifies Lucy's return to amniotic fluid and new beginnings. As the beautiful Caribbean represents her as a black Antiguan and a colonial subject, so now does the ink in her pen; she is the community recorder who connects her life in Antigua with what lies ahead; linking the personal and political dimensions of her life, she displays the effect of colonialism and post-colonialism on an African-Caribbean woman. As the final sentence of the novel suggests, her weeping is a form of erasure: "as I looked at this sentence [about loving someone so much she would die] a great wave of shame came over me and I wept so much that the tears fell on the page and caused all the words to become one great big blur" (164).

On the one hand, talking about water, arriving at it, finding comfort in it returns Lucy to a time of harmony and safety. On the other, Lucy is forced to abide with a watery indeterminacy, "one great big blur" that militates against hard and fast answers. The image of the blur suggests that everything is out of focus; it returns us to a camera metaphor, but one connoting a confusion coupled with determinacy. In Lucy's more mature vision, the oscillation of meanings signifies that nothing is privileged, resolved, or closed off. Through the metaphor of water, Lucy contextualizes the metaphor she used previously when she observed Mariah acting in her normal manner, "which was that the world was round and we all agreed on that": now Lucy knows symbolically that the world is flat and she can fall off if she ventures to the edge. She knows the fraudulence of the overall "consensus" that Mariah is so sure of, and its relation to a blonde, European world, the one that Peggy tries to simulate with her artificial lemon shampoo. In questioning "roundness" and stepping closer to the edge, Lucy realizes she can see both forwards and backwards. Having refused enclosures built by others, she begins to forge a site (sight) of her own. She refuses assimilation and embraces cultural difference and an "alien status," only partly of her own making, in the margins (hooks 23).

In this enactment of cultural revenge, of the dissolution of authority, Lucy claims her right to feel and to drown out cognition for the time being. Revealing the duplicity of the colonizing economy by mapping herself on to earlier texts, she creates a new postcolonial cartography. She is ready to write. Finally, at a symbolic level, Lucy is also Antigua of 1967, a territory freeing itself from the colonizer. In the late nineteen sixties, Antigua was struggling toward partial independence and the United States was becoming a contestational zone of anti-war protesters, just as Lucy struggles successfully toward a form of independence. By the end of the narrative, Lucy has begun to decolonize herself; in that sense, Jamaica Kincaid, a postcolonial subject in her own right, has made an ex-post facto intervention in the description of a colonized subject about to be legally and personally freed. The death-like, gray-black and cold January of the opening transitional period has been transformed through Lucy's awakening and agency into the blood-red, milk-white, Caribbean-blue colors of her writing.

—Moira Ferguson, "*Lucy* and the Mark of the Colonizer," *Modern Fiction Studies* 39, no. 2 (Summer 1993): 255–56

HELEN TIFFIN

In both ⟨Erna⟩ Brodber's *Jane and Louisa Will Soon Come Home*, *Myal*, and in Kincaid's *Annie John* and *Lucy* there is an exploration of this erasure/abuse and the potential for retrieval of the colonised Caribbean body. All four texts trace the processes of female reembodiment and the retrieval of Caribbean voice and body from its entrapment/erasure within European script and from those Anglo-Victorian middle-class values with which an educated Caribbean middle-class were so deeply imbued.

The internalisation of the European text, a process imaged by Kincaid in *A Small Place* through the obedient colonial reader in the European library "taking in again and again the fairy tale of how we met you, your right to do the things you did," is refigured and disrupted in *Annie John* through images of girls in classrooms letting their attention wander from the Anglo-script to sexuality and the body, to female companions and the local boys. Annie and her friends sit on the tombstones of the white planters as they compare and admire their developing breasts. Annie is punished for re-captioning her text-book illustration of Columbus "The Great Man Can No Longer Just Get Up and Go" (78). This is a sentence she has overheard her mother use about *her* father, and it is one Annie redeploys here to suggest her pleasure not just at the reversal of Columbus' fortunes as he is taken back to Europe in chains, but at his strategic disembodiment, his temporary leglessness. Columbus's "discovery" precipitated the atrocities of the slave trade, the kidnapping and transporting of Africans in chains to the Caribbean, and the abuse and erasure of their bodies. In *Annie John* too, Western medical constructions of the body are challenged by competing curative systems, symbolised by the ordering and reordering of medicines in the cabinet during Annie's illness: the first in accord with the more eclectic philosophies of Annie's mother and Ma Jollie; the second by Annie's father (who is more deeply interpellated by the western construction of the body and with medical science's exclusionist philosophy).

—Helen Tiffin, "Cold Hearts and (Foreign) Tongues: Recitations and the Reclamation of the Female Body in the Works of Erna Brodber and Jamaica Kincaid," *Callaloo* 16, no. 3 (Fall 1993): 912

MOIRA FERGUSON

Inextricably linked to the mother-daughter separation, colonialism insistently inflects the text. Coupled with the complicating of female experience, that imperial presence suggests its pervasive, quotidian intersection with gender relations. Only language and memory can conjure up the mother-daughter split. That is to say, although the lost biological mother is a major trope, at a different symbolic level outside womb and home, the lost mother also represents precolonial roots before the advent of a vicious surrogate colonial mother. Seemingly a solitary individual, the narrator emblematizes the colonized and joins herself globally to a school of oppositional thinking. Implicitly, Kincaid suggests that alternate explanations always exist. Thus the mystery and indeterminacy of the text further affirm the absurdity of linearity and fixed meaning. At the same time, Kincaid always insists that magic events do not altogether function with different laws but rather "weave a miraculous occurrence into a rigorously everyday reality." In that sense, *At the Bottom of the River* is counterintuitive, a reverse articulation that deals with disputed epistemologies. Jamaica Kincaid denies complexity of meaning and unfixedness now; whether to believe that scenario of rescripted simplicity is another question. Neither its magical nor its factual elements deny the historicity of the text. Time constitutes a network of convergencies of time past, present, and imminent. From the start, the family to which Jamaica Kincaid constantly refers to is also the macrocolonized Antiguan family, the island population before 1967 and any form of independence. In that sense, all references to a mother allusively resonate with colonial as well as maternal signs.

Put another way, the variant narrators of *At the Bottom* speak internally and externally, exemplifying a personal marginality and an abiding sense of alienation that in the last section slides into epiphany. Nothing conforms to an

everyday conception of time or space; the surreal world mingles interchange-
ably and equally with the world of material reality. Water suggests quotidian
and historical fluidity, the constant transformation of events and experiences
always in process. And precisely that easy fusion of fantasy, memory, and
everyday life creates coherence. Thus a fluid investigative perspective alter-
nates with intimations of postcolonial life and affirms a national cultural heritage. The plural narrator does not accept any demarcation between given fact
and an intuited sense of her world. Claiming the rights of an omniscient storyteller, the speaker transforms (transcends) herself and her inner imaginings.
Neither author, Elaine Potter Richardson, born in Antigua, nor the narrator
who chronicles the events, nor the protagonist living and reliving certain
experiences can live distinctly. The narrator reinstates local and personal history as global.

   These overlapping speakers create a chorus of voices that sound throughout. Because memory is a primary textual cohesion and because the refraction
of that memory is splintered, nothing is fixed, everything is in flux, even the
motion toward the lamp and the pen at the end.
   —Moira Ferguson, *Jamaica Kincaid: Where the Land Meets the Body* (Charlottesville: University
   Press of Virginia, 1994), 33–35

CAROLE BOYCE DAVIES

The exploration of the multiple identities of the growing Caribbean womanchild are intrinsic to the narratives of Kincaid's *At the Bottom of the River* and *Annie
John* and, more recently, her novel *Lucy*. Kincaid seems to present an early
engagement with Caribbean identity, located at a different point on the continuum than ⟨Audre⟩ Lorde, ⟨Michelle⟩ Cliff and ⟨Paule⟩ Marshall. The fact
that she was born and raised in the Caribbean allows a different kind of
engagement with the homeland and Caribbean cultural community which
provides the impetus for the internal critique. Hers is never an uncritical,
unproblematized acceptance of Caribbean identity. In fact, as *A Small Place*
shows, she rejects almost everything that had negatively shaped this home-
place and its people: colonization, corrupt politics, neglect, pettiness. But it is
the rejection of a critical insider/outsider who sees with an eye for detail the
many idiosyncracies, anomalies and perversions wrought on a Caribbean slave
society and their legacy on today's people. It is in this context that she
explores her woman self in "Girl," which resonates outward to diverse experiences of growing up female in many cultural communities. "Wingless" and
"Blackness," also in *At the Bottom of the River*, are not only about racial Blackness
as one expects, but relationships of light and dark and to the inner self stripped
of all the outward trappings of identity. Her relationships to the landscape and

its folklore are explored in "In the Night," "Holidays" and "At the Bottom of the River." The female self is explored in the context of landscape and Caribbean folk culture and as expressed in *Lucy* in the context of migration. Central to all of these is perhaps the best presentation of conflicted mother-daughter relationship in Caribbean literature so far. And the mother is a symbolic figure here because she can also be read as the Caribbean, as well as all Lucy rejects in female subordination.

Female sexual identities are multiply-explored as "Girl" begins the catalogue of rules of conduct for the growing Caribbean girl/womanchild. These merge into surrealistic images of the Caribbean supernatural world, but conclude with her woman-to-woman motif which runs through the text. In *Annie John* a similar landscape is created. Here, the maternal grandmother, Ma Jolie, clearly an ancestral presence, is characterized as a mysterious healer who appears at a time when her granddaughter is experiencing a terrible psychological dislocation which is manifesting itself in physical illness. Much of this dislocation is located in Annie's attempts to define herself against her mother and in the context of Caribbean colonialism. *Annie John*, as an autobiographical narrative, functions as a decoder of much that is unexplainable in the mysterious world of the first book, *At the Bottom of the River*. But in both, the necessity to identify with, yet separate oneself from, the mother is a central issue. "My Mother," in *At the Bottom of the River*, pursues this maternal identification/separation fully. There is a need for bonding as there is a need for separate space. The ability of each to separate and thus grow ensures a different resolution of things.

—Carole Boyce Davies, *Black Women, Writing and Identity: Migrations of the Subject* (London: Routledge, 1994), 123–25

ALISON DONNELL

Probably the most sensitive and hostile of Kincaid's works, *A Small Place* refuses its own soft target of the tourist in favour of a range of more contentious offenders. This is not to suggest that the book shies away from a condemnation of tourism, but rather that it probes more thoroughly and painfully the question of responsibility for postcolonial failures (economic, social, and psychological). As Helen Tiffin has pointed out ⟨in "Decolonization and Audience," 1990, 36⟩ *A Small Place* is a "direct address to Americans, English (or worse, Europeans)," but it is not just a word in the ears of those who go in search of sunshine and exotica; it is also an address to those paralysed by liberal guilt. This passage, for example, explicitly addresses the implied reader/ cultural voyeur: "Have you ever wondered why it is that all we seem to have learned from you is how to corrupt our societies and how to be tyrants? You will have to accept that this is mostly your fault" (35). Surely the narrative voice here presents an exaggerated version, almost a pastiche, of the post-colonial text that plays upon white readers' *Angst*. Moreover, the immediacy and tenacity of the response to this cultural trigger would seem to disclose the acute anxiety, if not critical paralysis, on the part of the cross-cultural reader, who would accept willingly her or his assigned position as oppressor and not dare to read such a statement as ironic or provocative.

By planting such an extreme version of the manifesto guiding certain post-colonial texts, Kincaid is able to disclose the way in which meaning is paral-ysed by cultural censorship. Frozen in a moment of guilt, "outside" critics of postcolonial literatures are too often prevented from asking themselves "what is the value of this text?" because they are so obsessed with the dilemma of whether they have the right to ask that question, or are so assured by its abil-ity to uncover their liberal guilt that they need not question its value further. Equally, this statement is a means to scrutinize the credentials and values of those postcolonial texts that rely on their readers' guilt. By presenting the guiding motivation of these texts in such crude terms, the narrator lays bare a political position that has been both significant and successful in the battle to rewrite the script of colonial encounter in order to provoke a reconsideration of the merits of this strategy.

It is through this unveiling and opening of the seams with which post-colonialism has sought to join writers and readers, ex-colonized and ex-colo-nizers, that *A Small Place* bids for a thorough consideration of how all groups might now ethically and effectively respond to each other. By dislocating the agendas to which many postcolonial readers and writers have subscribed, in addition to the more obvious misapprehensions of the tourist's version of cross-cultural encounter, Kincaid's text draws attention to the ways in which political paralysis might have become the unwitting bedfellow of political untouchability, and thus forces a consideration of how within postcolonial sit-uations (both textual and political) cultural analysis and interaction can be achieved helpfully.

However, if *A Small Place* refuses the easy option in terms of "speaking against" by constantly extending its range of targets, then it is equally uneasy about "speaking for" and offering an insider, legitimate, unambiguous meaning. Indeed, it seems to me that Kincaid is most fierce in her address to the Antiguan people, whom she censures for failing to accept responsibility and to engage critically with their present situation. It is interesting that in one inter-view Kincaid confidently declared, "[t]he thing that I am banded with and the thing that I am denounced for, I claim as my own. I am illegitimate, I am ambiguous" ("Interview" 129); she has been widely chastised for daring to write in such an ambivalent fashion about this "small place," her birthplace, Antigua, while living in the distant and more affluent Maine, USA. The ambiguity of her own cultural location, to which she draws attention in this text, fuels the debate over the value of her text—her perceived betrayal of her "cultural home" itself betraying the expectation of the postcolonial writer's duty to speak for her or his community.

—Alison Donnell, "She Ties Her Tongue: The Problems of Cultural Paralysis in Postcolonial Criticism," *Ariel* 26, no. 1 (January 1995): 109–11

CATHLEEN SCHINE

In the earlier novels, Ms. Kincaid created fierce, godlike mothers observed from an awed daughter's point of view. Now ⟨in *The Autobiography of My Mother*⟩ we encounter the mother ⟨Xuela⟩ on her own terms, and her own terms are those dictated by pure will. ⟨. . .⟩

Xuela's mother was a Carib Indian. Her father was born of a red-haired Scot and a woman "of the African people." Xuela is the motley result of colonialism, defiled even in conception. The racial mixture becomes for Ms. Kincaid a parable of moral impurity. Only Xuela's dead, unattainable Carib mother is ever spoken of with any tenderness. For the others, description is identical to accusation. Nor is there ever a mitigating sense of an outside world in which people get up in the morning, go to work, forget their keys. No one could ever confuse this island with V. S. Naipaul's Caribbean, for in his novels set in Trinidad, Mr. Naipaul relishes his characters, a collection of oddball individuals, sometimes ugly, sometimes lovely, always human, in an unlikely, startling culture. Ms. Kincaid is not interested in individuals, in living or in humanity: only in will. She has constructed a world out of her own power to do so. ⟨. . .⟩

Ms. Kincaid has herself purposefully forsaken the "language of the poet," abandoning compassion as if it never existed, while appropriating poetry's cadences and strategies and power to conquer, to dominate, and at last to destroy. She leaves behind her a trail of icy negation. For whatever she describes, she vanquishes and renders lifeless. In one of the few gentle passages of the novel, Ms. Kincaid allows Xuela's English lover to daydream of his faraway English countryside, and then, out of boredom and scorn, brings him and his idyll to their knees. Xuela's family and lovers, her enemies and friends are her own creations—and she describes them to dismiss them. They exist to reaffirm Xuela's unhappy superiority and isolation as they scrabble through their pathetic lives. Only one thing lives up to Xuela's implacable, magnificent, monomaniacal frigidity: Death. "I long to meet the thing greater than I am," she says on the last page of the book, "the thing to which I can submit."

"The Autobiography of My Mother" is pure and overwhelming, a brilliant fable of willed nihilism. One value of the book is that it shows us what megalomania and paranoia look like when transcribed by a first-rate literary artist.

But chilling as it is, there is also something dull and unconvincing about Xuela's anguish. For as personal as Xuela's account is, with the smell of menstrual blood and the stick of sweat smeared across the pages, the mundane, which is to say the world, is banished from these pages: Xuela is a symbol. She sees herself as a symbol, an abstraction of an entire people's suffering and degradation, and so there is a uniformity to her cold vision and a relentless rhythmic message to her empty life that is disturbing certainly—almost unbearable—without ever feeling real.

—Cathleen Schine, "A World as Cruel as Job's," *New York Times Book Review* (4 February 1996): 5

B I B L I O G R A P H Y

At the Bottom of the River. 1983.
Annie John. 1985.
Annie, Gwen, Lilly, Pam and Tulip. 1986.
A Small Place. 1988.
Lucy. 1990.
The Autobiography of My Mother. 1995.

PAULE MARSHALL
B. 1929

PAULE MARSHALL was born Paule Burke on April 9, 1929, in Brooklyn, New York, the daughter of Samuel and Ada Burke, who had immigrated from Barbados shortly after World War I. Although born and educated in the U.S., Marshall is claimed by both the Caribbean and the African-American literary traditions. Raised in a transplanted Caribbean community, Marshall experienced West Indian culture and was surrounded by its languages. Subsequent travels to Barbados afforded Marshall the intimate connection to its rituals, rhythms, and worldview.

In 1950 Paule Burke married Kenneth Marshall; the couple had one son before divorcing in 1963. Marshall received her bachelor's degree in 1953 from Brooklyn College (now part of the City University of New York) and later worked as a freelance writer, librarian in New York's public libraries, and staff writer for *Our World Magazine*. At the same time, she began writing stories and articles for a variety of periodicals.

Marshall's first novel, *Brown Girl, Brownstones* (1959), set in the West Indian neighborhoods of Brooklyn, tells of a young woman's struggle for identity in the West Indian subculture. A coming-of-age story, it is marked by sensitive character portrayals and by rich language that may be influenced by the oral traditions preserved in the West Indian community of Marshall's childhood. While the novel was a critical success, it was a commercial failure.

In 1960 Marshall was awarded a Guggenheim fellowship to work on her second book, *Soul Clap Hands and Sing* (1961), a collection of tales bound generally by the theme of race. This volume, which won the Rosenthal Award from the National Institute of Arts and Letters, contains four long stories about African descendants in the United States, the Caribbean, and South America and their relations with other immigrant groups. Marshall contrasts traditional African spiritual values with the commercialism and materialism of the New World.

Marshall's next novel, *The Chosen Place, The Timeless People*, appeared in 1969. In this work Marshall examines, with the eye of an anthropologist, the changing society of a third-world Caribbean community as it emerges from under colonial rule. Her third novel, *Praisesong for the Widow* (1983), returns to the theme of the destructive power of

materialism and exhibits Marshall's interest in mythology and historical memory. It won the Before Columbus Foundation Book Award in
1984. *Reena and Other Stories*, which included tales written since 1962,
was also published in 1983.

Marshall's long-awaited fourth novel, *Daughters* (1991), is the complex tale of a New York woman of West Indian heritage struggling to
come to terms with racial tensions in the U.S. and with the family she
left on a small island in the Caribbean. It too was generally well
received by critics.

Marshall has been a lecturer on creative writing at Yale University
since 1970; that same year, she married Noury Menard. She and her
husband now live alternately in New York City and the West Indies.

C R I T I C A L   E X T R A C T S

IHAB HASSAN

"An aged man is but a paltry thing," old Willie Yeats once sang, "A tattered
coat upon a stick unless/Soul clap its hands and sing." Paule Marshall, born of
Barbadian parents in Brooklyn, has chosen Yeats's bitter, impassioned phrase as
the title of her second book, making it the uncommon theme of its four
longish stories. The results are both striking and uneven. ⟨. . .⟩

⟨. . .⟩ Paule Marshall enriches our idea of Memory by gentle, lyrical brooding on the meaning of lives that have been already spent or shaped. Her four
aged protagonists can neither clap nor sing. But they have some kindlings of
rage, and the bitter dignity of knowledge through defeat. In this lies the
unique quality of the book. ⟨. . .⟩

By far the best story is the last. "Brazil," a sharp yet moving account of a
famous comedian about to retire, "O Grande Caliban," as everyone knows him
(his true name and his identity seem lost forever), is Rio's implacable jester. A
tiny man, he seems all his life a "Lilliputian in a kingdom of giants." "The world
had been scaled without him in mind—and his rage and contempt for it and
for those who belonged was always just behind his smile, in the vain, superior
lift of his head, in his every gesture." Caliban's frenzied effort to reclaim his
identity from the posters and cheering crowds, from the stupid, spoiled,
blonde Amazon who is his partner, and even from his young, pregnant wife,
takes him to the center of his personality and the terrifying slums of Rio. Here
all is done with tact and great power.

The example of Caliban shows that an aged man may not be entirely a paltry thing. (Indeed, the sequence of stories in the book reveals a progressive vitality in the characters.) Paule Marshall does not bring new resources of form or startling sensibility to the genre. But she allows her poetic style to be molded in each case by the facts of her fiction; she has escaped the clichés that must doubly tempt every Negro author writing today; and she has given us a vision, precise and compassionate, of solitary lives that yet participate in the rich, shifting backgrounds of cultures near and remote. Her retrospective vision is really a forecast of what we may wake up, too late, to see. There is need for a poetics of gerontology.

—Ihab Hassan, "A Circle of Loneliness," *Saturday Review* (16 September 1961): 30

Edward Brathwaite

Anglophobe West Indian literature—certainly its novels—has been mainly concerned with two main themes: the relationship of the author's *persona* or *personae* to his society, found in general to be limiting and frustrating; and stemming from this, a presentation of that society and an illustration of its lack of identity. West Indian novelists have so far, on the whole, attempted to see their society neither in the larger context of Third World underdevelopment, nor, with the exception of Vic Reid, in relation to communal history. Perhaps this has been artistically unnecessary. West Indian novels have been so richly home centered, that they have provided their own universe, with its own universal application. West Indian novelists, faced with the exciting if Sisyphean task of describing their own society in their own terms, for the first time, have had to provide for themselves a priority list in which, quite naturally, a relating of their own encounter with their environment, society and sensibility, has had to take pride of place. In addition, since most West Indian novelists have become exiles in several centres of the metropolitan West, their concern with a continuing and widening exploration of their societies has been limited by distance, separation and the concerns of a different milieu. They have, most of them, continued to write about the West Indies, but a West Indies stopped in time at the snapshot moment of departure.

The question, however, remains as to whether the West Indies, or anywhere else for that matter, can be fully and properly seen unless within a wider framework of external impingements or internal change. The contemporary West Indies, after all, are not simply excolonial territories; they are underdeveloped islands moving into the orbit of North American cultural and material imperialism, retaining stubborn vestiges of their Eurocolonial past (mainly among the elite), and active memories of Africa and slavery (mainly among the folk). ⟨. . .⟩

This way of looking at West Indian writing has been prompted by a read-ing of Paule Marshall's new novel, *The Chosen Place, The Timeless People*. Had Paule Marshall been a West Indian, she probably would not have written this book. Had she not been an Afro-American of West Indian parentage, she possibly could not have written it either; for in it we find a West Indies facing the met-ropolitan West on the one hand, and clinging to a memorial past on the other. Within this matrix, she formulates her enquiry into identity and change. And it is no mere externalized or exotic investigation. Mrs. Marshall has reached as far into West Indian society as her imagination, observation, and memory will allow. The questions raised and the answers suggested are, one feels, an inte-gral part of her own development while being at the same—and for the first—time, a significant contribution to the literature of the West Indies.

The scope and value of this contribution is no accident. Paule Marshall's background has prepared and qualified her for it. Born of Barbadian parents in Brooklyn, she was brought up in a West Indian/Afro-American environment in New York which she explored in her first novel, *Brown Girl, Brownstones* (1959). Visits to the West Indies, and especially ancestral Barbados, revived and strengthened direct links with the Caribbean, as many of her stories illustrate, including one in *Soul Clap Hands and Sing* (1961). Now in *The Chosen Place, The Timeless People* (1969), we have her first mature statement on the islands—or more precisely, on a tiny, hilly corner of Barbados she calls Bournehills (though there is Port-of-Spain during Carnival and something of the Maroons of Jamaica as well).

—Edward Brathwaite, "West Indian History and Society in the Art of Paule Marshall's Novel," *Journal of Black Studies* 1, no. 2 (December 1970): 225–27

WINIFRED STOELTING

For the first time the oppressed, held in enforced silence so long, are begin-ning to tell their version of the story of man. ⟨. . .⟩ Regarding its importance, Richard Long writes that "those who do not know their history are condemned to repeat it endlessly, and that much of the present ferment in the land and indeed in the world is the punishment inflicted upon the guilty, those guilty of such ignorance, a punishment of which, alas, the ignorant innocent share too great a part" ⟨"Africa and America: Race and Scholarship," *CAAS Occasional Papers*, 1969, 2⟩. For more than anything else, more than any conspiratorial threat, our own "lack of resolve to forge a viable link between the traditions of the past and the needs of the future" compounds our past mistakes ⟨12⟩.

Those past mistakes become tragedy for ensuing generations. Paule Marshall demonstrates this in her novel, *The Chosen Place, The Timeless People*, opening with an acknowledgment of the endless suffering not only to those depressed but to those who must bear the burden of guilt as well. Quoting from the Tiv of West Africa, she records, "Once a great wrong has been done, it never dies. People speak the words of peace, but their hearts do not forgive. Generations perform ceremonies of reconciliation but there is no end."

Mrs. Marshall likens this to the Ancient Mariner reciting some unspeakable human act to the wedding guest. The doomed teller relates the horror over and over; yet the condemned listener cannot comprehend the experience of his tale. The deepening wrong becomes rooted in the unconscious, perhaps no longer resolvable by cognitive means. Thus, neither the teller nor the listener can move from the spot—so deeply does the past impinge on the interminable present.

The Chosen Place, The Timeless People reflects this time past in time present, developing a human, historical, and cultural continuum we cannot deny. The stark land images encompass the lengthening ravages of the past; the living masses begotten of colonial mercantilism bespeak the immobility of depressed peoples; the individualized characters, victims of memory, compulsively tell and sorrowfully listen, but there is no reconciliation. Without compromise, Paule Marshall tells the tale in her own search for "viable links" between the traditions of the past and the needs of the present.

—Winifred Stoelting, "Time Past and Time Present: The Search for Viable Links in *The Chosen Place, The Timeless People* by Paule Marshall," *CLA Journal* 16, no. 1 (September 1972): 60–61

PAULE MARSHALL

I grew up among poets. Now they didn't look like poets—whatever that breed is supposed to look like. Nothing about them suggested that poetry was their calling. They were just a group of ordinary housewives and mothers, my mother included, who dressed in a way (shapeless housedresses, dowdy felt hats and long, dark, solemn coats) that made it impossible for me to imagine they had ever been young.

Nor did they do what poets were supposed to do—spend their days in an attic room writing verses. They never put pen to paper except to write occasionally to their relatives in Barbados. "I take my pen in hand hoping these few lines will find you in health as they leave me fair for the time being," was the way their letter invariably began. Rather, their day was spent "scrubbing floor," as they described the work they did.

Several mornings a week these unknown bards would put an apron and a pair of old house shoes in a shopping bag and take the train or streetcar from our section of Brooklyn out to Flatbush. There, those who didn't have steady jobs would wait on certain designated corners for the white housewives in the neighborhood to come along and bargain with them over pay for a day's work cleaning their houses. This was the ritual even in the winter.

Later, armed with the few dollars they had earned, which in their vocabulary became "a few raw-mouth pennies," they made their way back to our neighborhood, where they would sometimes stop off to have a cup of tea or cocoa together before going home to cook dinner for their husbands and children. ⟨. . .⟩

Those late afternoon conversations on a wide range of topics were a way for them to feel they exercised some measure of control over their lives and the events that shaped them. "Soullygal, talk yuh talk!" they were always exhorting each other. "In this man world you got to take yuh mouth and make a gun!" They were in control, if only verbally and if only for the two hours or so that they remained in our house.

For me, sitting over in the corner, being seen but not heard, which was the rule for children in those days, it wasn't only what the women talked about—the content—but the way they put things—their style. The insight, irony, wit and humor they brought to their stories and discussions and their poet's inventiveness and daring with language—which of course I could only sense but not define back then.

They had taken the standard English taught them in the primary schools of Barbados and transformed it into an idiom, an instrument that more adequately described them—changing around the syntax and imposing their own rhythm and accent so that the sentences were more pleasing to their ears. They added the few African sounds and words that had survived, such as the derisive suck-teeth sound and the word "yam," meaning to eat. And to make it more vivid, more in keeping with their expressive quality, they brought to bear a raft of metaphors, parables, Biblical quotations, sayings and the like ⟨. . . .⟩

When people at readings and writers' conferences ask me who my major influences were, they are sometimes a little disappointed when I don't immediately name the usual literary giants. True, I am indebted to those writers, white and black, whom I read during my formative years and still read for instruction and pleasure. But they were preceded in my life by another set of giants whom I always acknowledge before all others: the group of women around the table long ago. They taught me my first lessons in the narrative art. They trained my ear. They set a standard of excellence. This is why the best of my work must be attributed to them; it stands as testimony to the rich legacy of language and culture they so freely passed on to me in the wordshop of the kitchen.

—Paule Marshall, *Reena and Other Stories* (New York: The Feminist Press, 1983), 4, 7–8, 11–12

Dorothy L. Dennison

First published in 1962 in *Harper's* magazine, "Reena" ⟨like "The Valley Between"⟩ deals with the conflicting attitudes of creative women who struggle with the question of their responsibilities as women, as wives, as mothers. This time, however, the question is entertained by black, middle-class, West Indian/American women and covers the historical and social dimensions which have shaped their particularized responses. It might be argued that Marshall's shift to black characters is a direct reflection of the times, for with the sixties came a cultural resurgence which was soon to change the tone and content of American letters. Black Nationalism, as a political and aesthetic ideology, swept the country and provided for blacks the inspiration for a bold, defiant, and jubilant voice. No longer writing to appeal to dominant white society, the black artist began to focus more specifically upon an audience of color. In seeking to rediscover his unique cultural heritage and to share the positive values he had uncovered, he turned more decisively to the folk heritage. "Black is beautiful" was the popular slogan, and all elements of the black folk heritage began to be interpreted with new insight and pride. In presenting her interpretation of black culture, Marshall was no exception to this trend. But her attention was drawn more sharply to the familiar black immigrant experience described in "Reena." ⟨And⟩ she also began to draw on her knowledge of African cultural survivals as they seemed to function in contemporary black American society. ⟨. . .⟩

At a ⟨. . .⟩ point, Reena is able to use her color to advantage. Speaking at a college debate on McCarthyism, she seems intimidating not because of her radical position alone, but also because of "the sheer impact of her blackness in their white midst." ⟨. . .⟩ Her hair, her clothing, her conspicuous presence—all contribute to Reena's self-acceptance. In embracing her African ancestry, she develops the strength to combat all that the white world refuses her.

That strength is built upon the foundation of the extended family, which may be defined as a "philosophical orientation" toward a group identity ⟨Robert Staples, *Introduction to Black Sociology*, 1976, 124⟩. The priority afforded the community in traditional African societies is widely documented. Marshall seems to acknowledge contemporary kinship patterns as but a variant of that family system. Reena's graduation from college, for instance, represents not just a personal accomplishment, but a triumph for both her mother and father and their parents before them: "It was as if I had made up for the generations his people had picked cotton in Georgia and my mother's family had cut cane in the West Indies" (p. 273). The extended ties are also connected through the relationship between the mothers of the major characters. They had known each other since childhood in Barbados and, further, it was they who initiated—more accurately "forced"—the relationship between Reena and Paulie.

Aunt Vi provides another example. While she is blood related to Reena, she is godmother to the narrator, who also refers to the woman as aunt. Over and over again, Marshall shows us both obvious and subtle connections between individuals who have shared a similar space in time and who have gained from that sharing a special insight about conquering its exigencies to keep their communities intact. Both in fact and symbol, the community thrives beyond temporal measurement to embrace perpetual duration.

While this perpetuity is affirmed in the reunion between Paulie and Reena, it is also celebrated in the wake itself. With the juxtaposition of specific cultural rituals which mark the actual beginnings and endings of life, the author seems to be moving toward an exploration of the cyclical nature of time as perceived by traditional African societies. This is in direct contrast to the linear progression of time as perceived by Western societies. Contrary to the Western notion of death as the termination of life, it becomes for this small West Indian community a celebration of the continuity of life. Again we see a clear example of an African cultural survival.

—Dorothy L. Dennison, "Early Short Fiction by Paule Marshall," *Callaloo* 6, no. 2 (Spring-Summer 1983): 35–36, 40–41

SABINE BRÖCK

The black feminist cultural tradition has been striving to counter ⟨the⟩ actual historical (and metaphorical) denial of space for black women with a persistent, if not always explicitly claimed, determination to transcend this assigned (non)-status; this ambivalence characterizes black women's writing. As Barbara Omolade observes poignantly ⟨in "Hearts of Darkness," 1985, 355⟩: "Black women moved through the white man's world: through his space, his land, his fields, his streets, and his woodpiles," to which one should add, and through the white women's kitchens. This experience is deeply ingrained in the social text of black women's lives, their female lore and oral histories, and their literature as well. The earliest written testimonies have mirrored these images of enclosure of which Harriet Brent's expression "the Loophole of Retreat" is a perfect example. Accordingly, scenes of lack of movement and missing space (in the geographical, cultural, and social sense) pervade the literary canon. But readers will find as well, as I will try to show in my discussion of Paule Marshall's placing of some of her heroines, obsessive, aggressive, and extensive efforts to create a space for women to move and thereby trespass not only the limits of Anglo-American discourse but those of closely circumscribed actual lives as well.

The protagonist in *Brown Girl, Brownstones* stands for a development of consciousness. She learns that as a black woman she does not have a place in white society. In her pubescent vacuum Selina has the freedom to imagine spaces and rooms; throughout the novel we can trace her obsession with open spaces, light, water, nature, "unimprinted spaces" ⟨Annis Pratt, *Archetypal Patterns in Women's Fiction*, 1981, 17⟩. Her immigrant perspective enables her to leave Brooklyn in search of her home country, but not without having thoroughly denounced her own adolescent perception of her surroundings. The novel is vibrant with a tension between enclosed and open, free spaces (which Selina imagines parks and streets to be, and which she is allowed, in the novel's first part, to roam freely, unhampered by negative experiences). Structurally, Marshall sets the novel's theme right at the very beginning in her first-page description of the Brownstone neighborhood as "threat" and "doom." This is followed by Selina's adolescent dreams. Marshall follows her through a period of disillusionment, in which she shows the protagonist exclusively in closed rooms. The climax, Selina's dance performance, is an aggressive, but also somewhat desperate effort to take up space, to fill it with herself, to make room for herself, after which Marshall comes back full circle to her introductory idea: Brooklyn as wasteland.

    —Sabine Bröck, "Transcending the 'Loophole of Retreat': Paule Marshall's Placing of Female Generations," *Callaloo* 10, no. 1 (Winter 1987): 80

ANGELITA REYES

American writers of African descent write from social and cultural perspectives which invariably reflect aspects of the Middle Passage and its complex aftermath of American racism, prejudice, and exploitation of people of color. The Middle Passage has become a paradoxical metaphor of progress and displacement in American literature and correspondingly the metaphor of El Dorado likewise represents an ideology of social enterprise and New World conquest. El Dorado—that search for gold in the New World—was one of the most devastating treasure hunts in history. Decidedly, the quest for El Dorado meant the exploitation of indigenous peoples in the Americas and of people brought to the Americas in bondage. ⟨. . .⟩

Avey Johnson's classical journey ⟨in *Praisesong for the Widow*⟩ occurs on two levels: she is, in essence, the heroine embarking on a quest for spiritual enlightenment and renewed strength to deal with the human world. The journey becomes a validation of Avey's American social consciousness. By the middle age of life, Avey has settled for the illusion of El Dorado; that is to say, she has given in to the complacency of upper-middle class living and values. ⟨. . .⟩

Through a series of carefully directed incidents situated by the author, we see how Avey Johnson returns to the nurturing ground. She must experience symbolic death in order to be rebirthed into a new awareness of self, myth, and history. The old man whom she meets in Grenada, Lebert Joseph, represents (like Great-Aunt Cuney) the African connected consciousness in the Americas. For Lebert Joseph is the African and African-American confluence of the mythic deity Legba. Lebert Joseph corresponds to Papa Legba in Haiti, Papa La Bas in the southern United States, Esu-Elegbara in Nigeria, and Legba in Benin. Brought to the New World during the Middle Passage, Legba is personified by an irascible old man who usually carries a cane and limps. One leg is shorter than the other because part of him is in the spirit world and part of him moves in the world of the living. ⟨. . .⟩ In the context of *Praisesong*, Marshall employs Lebert/Legba to further the ritual structure of the novel: he becomes the messenger, the interpreter, leading the central character further along her journey and finally to the threshold of the spirit world in order to rebirth to the world of the living. It is essentially because of Lebert/Legba, this spiritual messenger, that Avey comes to an understanding of her great aunt's presence in her consciousness. As an interpreter, Lebert/Legba knows that Avey Johnson is one of the people who has lost sight of her spiritual "nation" and needs to be reincorporated.

Throughout the narrative, Marshall continues to juxtapose dreams into a fusion of the past and present. In some instances, the fusion of embedded flashback leaves the reader confused about the time sequence of events especially when Avey is thinking/dreaming of the immediate past of her childhood along with remote past of her ancestors. The symbolic significance of the events in the journey motif are eventually clarified when it is understood that Avey must experience a crossing over and must be led to the Threshold in order to be cleansed and rebirthed.

Led by Lebert Joseph/Legba, Avey Johnson moves closer to the Threshold of historic and mythic time, closer to understanding the implications of Middle Passage and El Dorado history. The excursion to Carriacou symbolizes this psychological return into history—it is the difficult passage for her. The actual turbulence of the excursion invokes not only a symbolic enactment of the middle crossing but the turbulence of American [con]quest and preemption. Avey Johnson must be purged of the unnecessary self and experience the symbolic return to the womb, to the unconquered landscape of the New World and her native land. The women who assist Avey on the boat ride during this turbulence of mind and collective history are like the mother-women of Marshall's own life. They are also the historic culture bearers—the primary interpreters of culture and spirituality. Indeed, the women who help Avey are very much reminiscent of "mothers" in Baptist churches who help passengers who suddenly are possessed by the Holy Ghost from harming themselves. The women on the *Emanual C* (again such obvious symbolic naming implies Marshall's didactic narrative position) assist the elderly widow like spiritual mothers. Like technicians of the unseen, the mother-women know that Avey needs to be protected and needs to be renurtured at this point in her life. They approve of Avey's seasickness. She must be purged of material comforts, make the symbolic return, if necessary even by literally defecating on herself. She is humiliated as an adult in order to regain honor ⟨. . . .⟩

—Angelita Reyes, "Politics and Metaphors of Materialism in Paule Marshall's *Praisesong for the Widow* and Toni Morrison's *Tar Baby*," *Politics and the Muse: Studies in the Politics of Recent American Literature,* ed. Adam J. Sorkin (Bowling Green, OH: Bowling Green State University Popular Press, 1989), 179, 187, 190–91

Abena P. A. Busia

Marshall's concern ⟨in *Praisesong for the Widow*⟩ is to take us through a journey of self-recognition and healing. Her text requires of us that we have a knowledge of ⟨VèVè Clark's term⟩ "diaspora literacy," an ability to read a variety of cultural signs of the lives of Africa's children at home and in the New World. Marshall articulates the scattering of the African peoples as a trauma—a trauma that is constantly repeated anew in the lives of her lost children. The life of the modern world and the conditions under which Afro-Americans have to live, the sacrifices they must make to succeed on the terms of American society, invariably means a severing from their cultural roots, and, as Avey learns to her cost, this is tantamount to a repetition, in her private life, of that original historical separation. This is a sacrifice too high. But to understand the nature of the journey and the magnitude of the sacrifice, it is necessary not simply to mark the passage of Avey's journey but to become fellow travelers with her. It is not only Marshall's heroine, but Marshall's readers as well who need to acquire "diaspora literacy." For to do so is to be able to see again the fragments that make up the whole, not as isolated individual and even redundant fragments, but as part of a creative and sustaining whole.

Thus the first task for the reader is to learn, like the widow whose journey we experience, to recognize the cultural signs of a past left littered along our roads of doubtful progress. The crucial factor about *Praisesong* is that it is a novel about the dispossession of the scattered African peoples from their past and their original homeland and, in the present, from their communities and from each other. The boldness of Marshall's project here is to take us through a private history of material acquisition and cultural dispossession, which becomes a metaphor for the history of the group, the history of the African in the New World. The challenge therefore is not to look at literacy or cultural artifact as abstraction, but as a concrete aspect of our lives, where our meaning—our story—becomes what we can read and what we can no longer, or never could, read about ourselves and our lives. The act of reading becomes an exercise in identifications—to recognize life experiences and historic transformations that point the way toward a celebration, a coming together attainable only through an understanding and acceptance of the demands of the past, which are transformed into a gift for the future.

This project is undertaken by giving us a text full of signs and allusion which each reader responds to differently and thus reflects, each in his or her own way, the experience of the widow. For example, an Afro-American reader who recognizes lines from the songs of Nina Simone, but for whom the Carriacou Tramp has no meaning or resonance, will experience the journey differently from a West African such as myself, for whom the opposite is true; the ceremonies for the dead on Carriacou may resonate with meaning while references to specific blues songs go unremarked. The experience of the widow's journey is relived differently, depending on how many, and which, of the many cultural icons and codes within the text the reader can register.

    —Abena P. A. Busia, "What is Your Nation?: Reconnecting Africa and Her Diaspora through Paule Marshall's *Praisesong for the Widow,*" *Changing Our Own Words: Essays on Criticism, Theory, and Writing by Black Women,* ed. Cheryl A. Wall (New Brunswick, NJ: Rutgers University Press, 1989), 197–98

GAY WILENTZ

In a tribute to her Barbadian grandmother Da-duh, Paule Marshall comments on how her life has been informed by the presence of this ancestor:

> [Da-duh]'s an ancestor figure, symbolic for me of the long line of black women and men—African and New World—who made my being possible, and whose spirit continues to animate my life and work. I wish to acknowledge and celebrate them. *I am, in a word, an unabashed ancestor worshipper.* (*Reena* 95; emphasis added)

She states further in this introduction that in all of her novels, at least one elderly woman functions as an ancestor for the main protagonist in the manner of Da-duh. Da-duh appears as the old hairdresser, Mrs. Thompson, in her first novel, *Brown Girl, Brownstones* (1959), as the healer and protector Leesy and cook Carrington in her second novel, *The Chosen Place, The Timeless People* (1965), and as Avey's Great-aunt Cuney in *Praisesong for the Widow* (1983). In noting this, Marshall places herself within a continuum from her African foremothers to the present through the guiding hand of her female ancestor and those in the Caribbean.

In this article, I focus on Marshall's last novel, *Praisesong for the Widow,* in terms of Marshall's role as storyteller and her debt to the orature of her foremothers, the conflict of values in Black American middle-class life, the understanding of one's heritage by a reverse Middle Passage in the Caribbean, and

the reconciliation of African/American self through the direction of the ancestors. Furthermore, this role of ancestor, which emphasizes the passing on of
stories, legends and cultural traditions to generations of children, remains
within woman's domain. Marshall underscores the need to understand one's
African heritage for an integrated African-American life, especially for relatively successful, assimilated middle-class Blacks; moreover, her novels attest
to the view that this return to an African consciousness is more easily visual-
ized in the Caribbean where, she feels, stronger ties to one's ancestors have
remained.

⟨. . . As⟩ a child of Afro-Caribbean parents, she was brought up with a diaspora consciousness. Through her trips back to the Caribbean to visit her
grandmother Da-duh as well as for her own research, Marshall realized that
this world was a step closer to their African past. She relates her learning
process, developed in her works, to the "Great Circuit" of slave trading which
connected North America and the Caribbean with Africa: "Taken together, the
three books . . . constitute a trilogy describing, in reverse, the slave trade's tri-
angular route back to the motherland, the source" ("Shaping the World of my
Art" 107). In each of her novels, her main female character takes a spiritual
"middle passage back" to rediscover as well as pass on the history and stories
of her people, whether it be Selina's trip to the Caribbean at the end of *Brown
Girl, Brownstones*, Merle's voyage to Africa in *The Chosen Place*, or Avey's jumping
ship and finding herself in the Caribbean in *Praisesong*. Moreover, this search
for one's heritage—in this case, to remember one's tribe—is seen as a woman's
search; telling the tales which must be passed on from generation to generation so as to maintain cultural continuity and wholeness is the function of the
women, both the female characters and Marshall herself.

—Gay Wilentz, "Towards a Spiritual Middle Passage Back: Paule Marshall's Diasporic
Vision in *Praisesong for the Widow*," *Obsidian II: Black Literature in Review* 5, no. 3 (Winter 1990):
1–2

SUSAN FROMBERG SCHAEFFER

Paule Marshall's "Daughters" is that rarity, a good *and* important book. It
attempts to look at black experience in our hemisphere, to praise what
progress has been made and to point to what yet needs to be done. In its willingness to take real stock, to find true answers to complex questions, it is a
brave, intelligent and ambitious work.

Ms. Marshall examines the state of black life through Ursa Mackenzie,
whose heritage—and perhaps nature—is dual. Her father, Primus Mackenzie,
is a prominent official of a mythical Caribbean island, Triunion; he has been
known since his youth as "the PM." Her mother is the American-born Estelle

Harrison, who sends a very young Ursa back to the United States so that her child can learn "to talk the talk and walk the walk." Most of all, Estelle does not want Ursa to grow up to be a Triunion woman, one who waits hand and foot on her man and who has little independence of thought or deed. It is as if Estelle knows that her daughter will have a special role to play in determining the fate of black people in one or both of her countries. She is determined her daughter will make a difference. ⟨. . .⟩

"Daughters" seems to imply that the purpose of many unions should now be mutual struggle; struggle, if necessary, *against* each other but always toward an ideal. Black men, who entered the political and economic arenas earlier than black women, have greater temptations to contend with and are thus more likely to be seduced from their ideals. Through Primus and Estelle Mackenzie, Ms. Marshall shows us how the *women* can—and perhaps should— find themselves becoming men's consciences. Primus *knew* that Estelle was to be his conscience, and in this capacity he welcomed her ⟨. . . .⟩

Many ideas dominate this wonderful novel, but perhaps the most important is that we have been on the wrong road, a "bypass road" that allows us to travel through life without seeing the urgent needs of others. You close "Daughters" feeling as if you have taken a dangerous trip that cannot leave you unchanged. Flawless in its sense of place and character, remarkable in its understanding of human nature, "Daughters" is a triumph in every way.

—Susan Fromberg Schaeffer, "Cutting Herself Free," *New York Times Book Review* (27 October 1991): 3, 29

RHONDA COBHAM

In narratives about so-called marginal groups, madness or socially deviant behavior is a common strategy for representing a character's rejection of the roles assigned by the dominant culture. In works like Charlotte Perkins Gilman's short story, "The Yellow Wallpaper," or Richard Wright's *Native Son*, the price the protagonist pays for such acts of defiance is often the ultimate one of self-destruction. Alternatively, where the protagonist survives the trauma of insanity—as happens in Sylvia Plath's *Bell Jar* or V. S. Naipaul's *Mimic Men*, the worlds to which such protagonists are returned are often places in which their irreversible social isolation seems inevitable. In the novels of Caribbean women, mental breakdowns also occur but they seldom mark the final position of the protagonist at the end of the story. Rather, they are used as emotionally releasing devices which help the female protagonist articulate her sense of social inadequacy and spiritual deprivation. This therapeutic aspect of the psychological crisis is reinforced by its association with the possession and healing rituals of African syncretic religious traditions so wide-spread in the New World.

Within this context the moment of breakdown is not a moment of isolation but a moment of contact: with the ancestral past, with the community, and with the self. For Avey in *Praisesong* the dark night of the soul occurs when she relives the trauma of the Middle Passage on the boat journey between Grenada and Carriacou. Respectable, middle-aged matron that she is, she at first experiences her gross retching out of her stomach's contents as the ultimate indignity. Her incontinence and hallucinations mark a violent rupture with her role of corseted respectability as a wealthy widow. But even as she plumbs the depths of psychic and physical disintegration, she becomes aware of soothing female voices and hands which help her through this traumatic rebirth:

> They held her. Hedging her around with their bodies—one stout and solid, the other lean, almost fleshless but with a wiry strength—they tried cushioning her as much as possible from the repeated shocks of the turbulence . . . Their lips close to her ears they spoke to her, soothing low-pitched words which only sought to comfort and reassure her, but which from their tone seemed to approve of what was happening. "Bon," they murmured as the gouts of churned up, liquefied food erupted repeatedly, staining for a moment the white spume on the waves below. "Bon," they whispered at the loud hawking she was helpless to control and at the slime hanging out of her mouth. "Bon" at the stench. (Marshall 205)

The healing bath and massage to which Avey submits herself in the aftermath of the experience on the boat recalls the laying on of hands within Christian and neo-African religious traditions. Subsequently, Avey participates in the island rituals, purged, cleansed and anointed; a fitting vessel for the spirits of the ancestors. If this scene is compared to the vomiting scene in *The Bell Jar*, the contrast in the effects the two identical situations produce is thrown into relief. In Plath's novel each of the girls who succumb to food poisoning, after a banquet intended to groom them for the social roles they are about to take on, throws up in a separate cubicle. Afterwards each is placed in an identical bed and given an identical present. Plath's strategy dramatizes the girls' atomization and isolation in a world that can even reduce revolt to a commodity. But it leaves her reader with no outlet for the anger, victimization or sense of hopelessness it evokes.

—Rhonda Cobham, "Revisioning Our Kumblas: Transforming Feminist and Nationalist Agendas in Three Caribbean Women's Texts," *Callaloo* 16, no. 1 (Winter 1993): 57–58

CAROLE BOYCE DAVIES

There is a Pan-Africanist focus in the relationships to heritage which Marshall
identifies which makes Brathwaite call her work, for example, "literature of
reconnection" ("The African Presence in Caribbean Literature," 1974). While
accepting (this), I see multiple journeys taking place. I have read *Praisesong* as
activating at least two journeys: one journey into female identity, another into
Black identity. Neither journey ought necessarily to attain supremacy over the
other for, as a Black woman, these multiple journeys embody critical aspects
of her being. One could also offer that an understanding of her sexuality is also
a significant journey in the text. And the issue of migration is critical to any
understanding of how these characters pursue these various identities. In other
words, what it means to be American or Caribbean or woman or wife or somebody's notion of an "older woman" and the traffic between these various identities are pursued narratively here.

This sense of journeying between identities had already taken place for
the younger woman, Selina, in *Brown Girl, Brownstones*. This novel ends with the
protagonist about to embark on her journey back to the Caribbean. *Praisesong
for the Widow* has a mature protagonist whose entire development is centered
around journeying. All of these journeys, from the walks with her Great-Aunt
Cuney to the tourist ship journeys and her journey to Carriacou and her subsequent journey back to the US are central to her being able to place her various identities in context. Avey, beyond the impetuousness of youth, has to be
more fully engaged in the rituals of identification. These identifications are of
gender, nationality, heritage, race, age, sexuality, class.

The traffic between United States and Caribbean identities is a large part
of the focus of Marshall's latest novel, *Daughters*. Here, the marriage of a
United States Black woman to a Caribbean politician stages many of the
dynamics of connection and separation implicit in these identities. The product is a daughter, Ursa, who is born in the Caribbean but is raised to live in
the US. Throughout her life she journeys in different directions across class,
race, sexuality and gender identities as she does physically between the
Caribbean and the US. Trains and taxis and cars of various sorts convey her to
different localities for schooling, work, family situations, friendships, relationships where some of her interactions are staged. Her mother, Estelle's participation, separation and alienation from the Caribbean island which becomes
her home and its people, establish a particularity in difference which is often
lost in monolithic cultural subsuming of identity. At a certain level she maintains an aloof distance from the people. This arises from her class position as
the Prime Minister's wife but also from her own inability to fully become part
of the island. And in other ways as well, her opposition is based on political

grounds which come out of a consciousness honed in US race relations and Black political struggles which force her to reject servility. Because of this, she carries a more acute resistance to US imperialism than her husband. His interest in building a tourist-based facility runs diametrically opposite to the people's needs and, in the end, the information which she provides facilitates his eventual rejection by the people. The mother and daughter's joint recognition and rejection of his politics as they support him is one of the contradictory themes of this novel. The legendary warrior figures of Congo Jane and Will Cudjoe, whom she still must write about, are consistently in the background.

—Carole Boyce Davies, *Black Women, Writing and Identity: Migrations of the Subject* (London: Routledge, 1994), 119–20

B I B L I O G R A P H Y

Brown Girl, Brownstones. 1959.
Soul Clap Hands and Sing. 1961.
The Chosen Place, The Timeless People. 1969.
Merle: A Novella and Other Stories. 1983.
Reena and Other Stories. 1983.
Praisesong for the Widow. 1983.
Daughters. 1991.

JEAN RHYS
1894-1979

JEAN RHYS was born Ella Gwendolyn Rees Williams on August 24, 1894, in Roseau, Dominica, the daughter of a third-generation Dominican Creole and a Welsh doctor. Before moving to London in 1907 to live with her aunt, Rhys was educated at a convent school in Roseau. In London, she studied briefly at the Royal Academy of Dramatic Art. In 1919 she married Jean Lenglet, a Dutch-French poet, and moved to Paris. When her husband was imprisoned for trafficking stolen art objects, Rhys was encouraged by Ford Madox Ford, her literary mentor, to publish her writings as a means of supporting herself and her daughter.

Most of Rhys's fiction was published before 1940. Of these works, *Voyage in the Dark* (1934) and *Good Morning, Midnight* (1939) are best remembered. *Voyage in the Dark* tells of Anna Morgan, a 17-year-old girl who leaves her Caribbean island to live in England. With no ties and no money in her new, unknown world, Anna grows increasingly alienated as she copes with the loss of her father and her first lover. In *Good Morning, Midnight*, Rhys's heroine confronts old age, loneliness, and alcoholism in Paris.

Rhys retired to Devonshire in 1939 with her second husband, Leslie Tilden Smith. Two years after his death in 1945, she married his cousin, Max Hamer—who, like her first husband, spent much of their marriage in jail. By the mid-1950s, many of Rhys's books were out of print and she was thought to be dead. In 1958, however, Rhys was asked for her permission to broadcast a version of *Good Morning, Midnight* on BBC radio.

Introduced once again to the British literary scene, Rhys resumed her writing, publishing *Wide Sargasso Sea* to favorable reviews in 1966. The novel gives voice to one of English literature's most silenced and overlooked characters: Bertha Mason, the mad first wife of Rochester in Charlotte Brontë's *Jane Eyre*. The madwoman's story depicts the ambiguous position of the Creole in the West Indies, who, being neither colonized nor colonizer, is treated as the former by Europeans and seen as the latter by the island's black population. The publication of *Wide Sargasso Sea* sparked new interest in Rhys's earlier works. Whereas her dark novels about defenseless women alienated in a patriarchal world had gone unnoticed during the 1930s, she was now recognized as one of England's most talented writers.

Rhys died on May 14, 1979, before finishing the autobiography she was working on. The incomplete text was published posthumously with the title *Smile Please* in 1979.

CRITICAL EXTRACTS

HELEN TIFFIN

All of Rhys's heroines, whether ostensibly English or actually Creole, share a recognizably colonial sensibility, and since this sensibility is the product of a relationship between at least two peoples and two places, it is generally expressed and explored in liaisons between individuals whose world views differ and who are bound in a destructive relationship involving dominance and dependence. In *Palace of the Peacock* Wilson Harris traces a process of psychic decolonization whereby "the oldest uncertainty and desire in the world, the desire to govern or be governed, rule or be ruled forever" ⟨14⟩ is abrogated in favour of a union between all sexes and all races through the agency of the spirit of place. In her novels Jean Rhys works towards a comparable solution to this colonial dilemma; and if ultimately she lacks Harris' confidence, it is because the white West Indian has the double problem of rejecting former affiliations and power structures and of being accepted into a community from which she seems irretrievably excluded by the hostilities of a history which is, and yet is not, her own.

The white Creole is, as a double outsider, condemned to self-consciousness, homelessness, a sense of inescapable difference and even deformity in the two societies by whose judgements she always condemns herself. "White nigger" to the Europeans and "white cockroach" to the Blacks, she sees herself as a gauche, immature distortion of the Europeans on the one hand, and a pale and terrified "deformed" reflection of her Black compatriots on the other. As the distorted reflection of two images, neither of which is really her but which beckon and taunt her with their normality, the Rhys heroine relies on mirrors and mirror images, and they are central to Rhys's depiction of her dilemma.

Unable to judge their own worth, Rhys's heroines are obsessed with mirrors and the need for outside opinion. All are inevitably outsiders in the European worlds through which they drift, and all rely for financial survival and psychic support on Englishmen who are usually much older than themselves. Indeed their whole sense of identity or conviction of self-worth is entirely dependent, as is their fate, on these men and on external accoutrements. Though the Rhys heroine usually has sufficient sensitivity to despise the arrogant complacency of her English lover, she remains shackled to his every whim. In fact it seems that it is dependence itself to which the women are addicted. When the men tire of the liaison, it is abruptly terminated, and independence is foisted on the reluctant mistress whose unhealthy, child-like need for support has only been exacerbated by the association.

The men of Jean Rhys's novels also share certain characteristics: as Englishmen these lovers are almost by definition cold, cautious, hypocritical, and joyless. They are self-absorbed and self-assured, firmly rooted in a world which mirrors their every characteristic—an urban world of perpetually dark streets, actively hostile look-alike houses, and grim cheerless interiors where reluctantly kindled fires shed no warmth. These men patronize their mistresses, encourage their child-like dependence, but readily abdicate ultimate responsibility for their fate. By contrast to the women they exploit, they have little interest in the impression they make on outsiders, although they are devoted nevertheless to keeping up appearances and to "playing the game." But this insistence is intimately connected with the survival of the values of a closely-knit group rather than with personal survival or identity. These men share a total lack of interest in anything that is not English and not, therefore, immediately comprehensible to them. Their reserved, aloof outlook contrasts with the women's open acknowledgement of emotion, which the men consequently find "fantastic" and "hysterical," and condemn as evidence of lack of maturity and self-control.

—Helen Tiffin, "Mirror and Mask: Colonial Motifs in the Novels of Jean Rhys," *World Literature Written in English* 17, no. 1 (April 1978): 328–29

DIANA TRILLING

By now most readers are acquainted with the Jean Rhys story, at least in its public aspect: The start of her writing career in Paris in the 20's and 30's under the guidance of Ford Madox Ford; the dim response to her early novels, "Quartet" (1928), "After Leaving Mr. Mackenzie" (1930), "Voyage in the Dark" (1934), "Good Morning, Midnight" (1939); her lapse into obscurity, no, into total oblivion, for the next 25 years; then her re-discovery and fame with the publication of her fifth and last novel, "Wide Sargasso Sea," in 1966. Her age is uncertain but she was probably 89 at her death in 1979. ⟨. . .⟩

But more than curiosity about the personal history of so gifted an author, legitimate as that is, is involved in our interest in the life of Jean Rhys. Miss Rhys is an obsessed writer whose novels move scarcely at all beyond their central characters—all of them, despite their altered names, the same woman at different stages of experience—or their theme of female victimization. We now have it in Jean Rhys's own words—"People have always been shadows to me. . . . I have never known other people. I have only ever written about myself"—but it was never difficult to guess that she was herself the subject (or is it the object?) of her fiction. There was the possibility and hope that her memoir might help us understand the mysterious process by which she transformed such an extreme of self-absorption into her lovely art.

But unfortunately this book with the nice title, "Smile Please," is markedly disappointing except as it underscores Jean Rhys's second obsession, with craft. There are a few soft sentences, a few agitated passages but, these apart, Miss Rhys's prose is as astute and unfaltering as ever. In fact, it is only by a miracle that it escapes being depressing in its precision and cautions. ⟨. . .⟩

If, as we are told, Miss Rhys throughout her old age wanted desperately to write an autobiography, surely this doesn't accurately describe the impulse that produced "Smile Please." Rather, Miss Rhys seems to have been impelled by the desire to wring yet one more story out of her life—more than it is an autobiography, "Smile Please" is her nonfiction novel. Once more we are given the hardships of a chorus girl touring the English provinces and once more the already well-covered episode of her first marriage, but nothing of her second and third marriages nor of her still-living daughter, nothing of the relationship with Ford and nothing of the life she must have led between husbands. Even the childhood portion advances us little in insight into her formative years.

But though a faint air of exploitation inevitably surrounds the publication of so deficient a performance, "Smile Please" has at least the negative usefulness of confirming the lack of invention in Miss Rhys's work. Even "Wide Sargasso Sea," which purports to tell the story of the mad first wife of Rochester in "Jane Eyre," simply promotes the heroine of Miss Rhys's earlier novels to new reaches of victimization.

—Diana Trilling, "The Odd Career of Jean Rhys," *New York Times Book Review* (25 May 1980): 1, 17

LINDA BAMBER

Rhys's novels, all of them autobiographical, have one subject: the victimization and self-victimization of a woman drifting along the edges of artsy-bourgeois society. The Rhys heroine has no money, no family to speak of, no particular talents. Out of sexual desperation (for she is always spurned by the man she loves) she picks up men who turn out to be cads or gigolos. These encounters usually take place in Bloomsbury or the Left Bank; the atmosphere is of café life, of cosmopolitan sterility. The heroine lives entirely in the present, and her ambition for the future is to get through the afternoon without crying. When she fails she says to herself, "Now, I'm a gone coon. I've begun crying and I'll never stop." The world shrinks to the size of the heroine's rented room—from which she makes pathetic forays for a brandy and to which she returns, as like as not, to be bullied for her failures by the landlady.

Notably absent from Rhys's account of her heroine is any analysis of her plight in political terms. The Rhys heroine is a natural victim, not a victim of sexual politics or class oppression. As an exile of obscure origins she is more or less classless; and although she certainly feels brutalized by men, she insists that "I'm even more afraid of women." The problem is extremely general: "People are such beasts, such mean beasts," says the heroine of *After Leaving Mr. Mackenzie*. Elsewhere the formula is simply "life is cruel and horrible to unprotected people." The social analysis of Rhys's work stops with the assertion that there are outsiders and insiders, and that the one is entitled to resent the other. But even the resentment is fitful and limp. The Rhys heroine knows that she is largely responsible for her own unhappiness. Whenever something good comes her way—money, a man, the possibility of a good time—she instantly loses it through laziness, obsessiveness, or a kind of petty anger arising from her sense that it isn't enough.

Another notable absence in Rhys's work is the sense of place. We are told that we are in Paris rather than London, or vice versa, but it seems to make little difference. The outside world has withdrawn from the Rhys heroine. As long as there is a room, a street, or a restaurant for her to occupy, she doesn't bother much about the details. That is, of course, Rhys herself, in sympathy with her heroine's depression, makes no effort to find correspondences between the inner and the outer life. Her heroines experience the thinness of life and Rhys means for her readers to do likewise.

—Linda Bamber, "Jean Rhys," *Partisan Review* 49, no. 1 (1982): 93–94

ARNOLD E. DAVIDSON

The argument of the plot ⟨of *After Leaving Mr. Mackenzie*⟩ is not promising, and yet Rhys everywhere gives her story unexpected depth and complexity. We might note, for example, how *After Leaving Mr. Mackenzie* opens with a half-reversal of the usual fate of the usual demimondaine protagonist. Instead of ending with this foreordained victim seduced and abandoned, we commence that way. Or more accurately, we half commence that way. Julia Martin was not exactly seduced in that she readily acceded to Mackenzie's original advances. She is not exactly abandoned in that, six months after he decided to take himself out of her life, he is still paying her three hundred francs a week, which is enough for her to go on living modestly in Paris. But not exactly living either. For the six months following Mackenzie's departure, Julia has immured herself in a room in a cheap hotel seeking mostly "a good sort of place to hide in . . . until the sore and cringing feeling, which was the legacy of Mr. Mackenzie, had departed" (p. 11). Her refuge is also the setting for a sustained but hopeless rage. Often she would "walk up and down the room consumed with hatred of the world and everybody in it. . . . Often she would talk to herself as she walked" (p. 12). As Thomas Staley has observed, references to ghosts run throughout the novel ⟨*Jean Rhys*, 1979, 69⟩. The first ghost is Julia herself haunting her quarters and her own empty existence.

There is a definite point to the protraction of that haunting, which is to say that Rhys has her reasons for beginning the book with the aftermath of a crucial parting and not with the preliminary relationship or even the parting itself. In the first place, the separation is standard, predictable, part of the normal course of affairs. Why note what has often happened before? What has not happened before is Julia's sense of being "done for" after being put down yet another time. The reader might therefore wonder at first what was so special about Mr. Mackenzie (we never learn his first name) that his loss mattered so much. The answer, the novel soon shows, is nothing; Mackenzie is no different from his numerous predecessors; he treats Julia no differently than they all have done. But that "no difference" finally makes a difference, and Julia breaks after being dropped once more in just the same fashion as she has been dropped numerous times before. The retreat from life, the emotional debilitation, the futile rage that Julia sees as "the legacy of Mr. Mackenzie" (p. 11) is also the legacy of all who have preceded him. One unlikely reaction sums up the previous course of a too common life. ⟨. . .⟩

There is one final turn to the ending that Rhys appropriately appends to this subtly plotted work. The symbolic spiral in the painting ⟨Julia looks at⟩ was *"flottant dans l'espace"* (p. 17). It was supported by nothing, rested on nothing. And as Helen Nebeker especially observes, nothing is, indeed, a key issue in the novel ⟨*Jean Rhys: Woman in Passage*, 1981, 34–36⟩. Julia's earliest memories are of being happy because of nothing and then of being frightened by nothing. At one point in Part One she describes one of her failures to give an account of herself: "And I felt as if all my life and all myself were floating away from me like smoke and there was nothing to lay hold of—nothing" (p. 53). By the end of the novel, she better knows the nothing that pervades her life. More specifically, she knows that her role in her family is nothing; that her dreams of her first love were nothing; that her hopes for her next affair have already come to nothing. But if Julia does not quite become, with that awareness, a forerunner of Camus' Sisyphus who can happily roll the rock of her own nothingness up the mountain of the nothingness of existence, neither is she crushed between the weight of those two voids. In that strained survival we see again how completely Rhys envisions the bleak life of her protagonist right down to the small sustaining victory achieved through the way in which

Julia finally confronts the unredeemed darkness of her fate, and we also see how carefully the author structures the novel to sum up the emptiness of both the defeats and the victory.

> —Arnold E. Davidson, "The Art and Economics of Destitution in Jean Rhys's *After Leaving Mr. Mackenzie*," *Studies in the Novel* 16, no. 2 (Summer 1984): 216–17, 225–26

ELIZABETH NUNEZ-HARRELL

Perhaps, as ⟨Elaine⟩ Campbell notes, Shand Allfrey's *The Orchid House* did inspire Rhys ⟨Introduction, ix⟩. Perhaps it was the whole body of Caribbean literature developing in the 1940s that sought to identify, understand, and interpret the West Indian character. But it is possible that it was Rhys's response to the nationalistic mood of the late '50s and '60s, asserting West Indian pride, dignity, and self-determination, that led her to assume her place in West Indian literature and consequently to write the best work of her career. ⟨. . .⟩

> ⟨In a 1968 interview with Hannah Carter, Jean Rhys said,⟩ The mad wife in *Jane Eyre* always interested me. I was convinced that Charlotte Brontë must have had something against the West Indies, and I was angry about it. Otherwise, why did she take a West Indian for the horrible lunatic, for that really dreadful creature? I hadn't really formulated the idea of vindicating the mad woman in a novel but when I was rediscovered I was encouraged to do so. (5)

It would appear then that the very fury that propelled Third World writers to exonerate Shakespeare's Caliban from the charge of lust, sloth, greed, lechery, ignorance, and attempted murder, spurred Rhys to set the record straight on the image of the white Caribbean woman. Indeed, although one could say that Antoinette of *Wide Sargasso Sea* is like many of the women that Rhys writes about, one is struck by her uniqueness. She is oppressed not merely because she is a woman but because she is a certain kind of woman—a white Caribbean woman. And her dilemma is peculiar to that kind of woman.

The first two sentences of the novel make this clear. The young girl Antoinette comments: "They say when trouble comes close ranks, and so the white people did. But we were not in their rank" (17). A white girl, Antoinette nevertheless understands that she is also a creole, a kind of person of whom her English husband, Rochester, will say, "Creole of pure English descent she may be, but they are not English nor European either" (67). Later, comparing her to her black maid Amélie, Rochester reflects: "For a moment she looked very much like Amélie. Perhaps they are related, I thought. It's possible, it's even probable in this damned place" (127). As a child, Antoinette is called "white nigger" by her black playmate Tia, and later, as a grown woman, she is taunted by Amélie with the name "white cockroach."

Thus rejected by the white world, spurned by the black world, Antoinette's challenge is to find her place, her identity, her life's meaning in her native land or to remain adrift in the mythical wide Sargasso Sea, languishing between England and the West Indies. Within the first page of the novel, another white creole makes his choice. Mr. Luttrel, realizing that England would not keep its promise to support the white people in the West Indies after the Emancipation Act was passed, got up "one calm evening . . . shot his dog, swam to sea and was gone for always" (17). It is within this context that Jean Rhys asks her readers to understand the plight of the white creole woman so unkindly treated by Charlotte Brontë in *Jane Eyre*.

—Elizabeth Nunez-Harrell, "The Paradoxes of Belonging: The White West Indian Woman in Fiction," *Modern Fiction Studies* 31, no. 2 (Summer 1985): 286–88

ERIKA SMILOWITZ

It is a common critical assertion that Jean Rhys portrays the female victim in novel after novel, but the archetype must be placed in context. Although her women are victims, they are victimized by both men and society: in fact, the men are the society. ⟨. . .⟩

That Rhys should see the world as divided between male "haves" and female "have-nots" and that the females should be defined by the males is not surprising, given her childhood under colonial rule. Just as her position as a white West Indian woman placed her somewhere between the natives and the English elite and left her isolated on her own island, the institution of colonialism too had its effect. Helen Tiffin draws the parallel, which I will discuss in detail here, between "destructive male/female relationships and between imperial nation and colonial underdog . . ." (329). It is one possible explanation for this recurring pattern of childlike women and paternal men.

Voyage in the Dark, Rhys's first written novel, is about the young Anna Morgan, freshly-arrived in London from the West Indies. During the novel, a *bildungsroman* in its most sordid sense, she begins and ends her relationship with Walter Jeffries and learns to exist alone in the harsh demimonde of London. Having left her safe, protective environment in the West Indies, Anna yearns for a similarly comforting one in her new home. Unfortunately, her stepmother Hester, who lives in England, gradually abandons her. Symbolically, women, for Rhys, are not up to the task of providing anyone with sufficient protection. Without her stepmother, Anna must rely on her own resources—mainly her physical attractiveness. Because her acting jobs on the stage are too infrequent and pay too little, and because she is far too distracted to put her own life in order, Anna searches for a man to protect and support her.

She finds Walter Jeffries, a man her father's age. He wants to take charge of her life, give her singing lessons and help her with her career. Clearly, theirs is a father-daughter relationship: " 'You're a perfect darling,' " he tells her, " 'but you're only a baby. You'll be all right later on. Not that it has to do with age. Some people are born knowing their way about' " (43). Anna is obviously not that sort, but rather a child-woman, the most childlike of all Rhys heroines. Walter's brother, in fact, calls her an "infant" (78). It doesn't take Walter long to tire of Anna, but he continues to support her for a time. She finds another man and then another. At the end of the novel she is having an abortion. Rhys's point is clear: women are not creators or sustainers of life. Anna will continue her pattern of searching for male protection, for she cannot survive on her own in London; she is dependent economically and emotionally ⟨. . . .⟩

One manifestation of her lack of authority and powerlessness is that she experiences life in London in a fog, through a filter of haze; nothing is clear and straightforward. In the first half of the novel, she has a cold. Later she is sleepy, and she gets the flu. When she is neither sick nor asleep, she is drunk. As a result, she doesn't recognize the subtleties; she has to be told, for instance, that her friend is a prostitute. Anna manages to function in such a state because her actions have no import. Because of her upbringing in Dominica under British rule, Anna does not expect to wield any influence or have any power, and in England she is as powerless as she was in her colonial home. She sees herself as a dominated individual. Using Edmund Wilson's image, this is the "psychological wound" of colonization ⟨M. M. Mahood, *The Colonial Encounter*, 1977, 167⟩. ⟨. . .⟩

⟨. . . In⟩ Rhys's canon dependent females are always pitted against power-ful, institutionalized male forces and the parallel to the colonial relationship. But one final point must be noted. In novel after novel, helpless women seek out powerful males for protection—but the men ultimately fail them. Walter Jeffries tires of Anna and eventually abandons her; Heidler and Mackenzie do the same; Sasha searches but finds no one at all—her husband has left her before the novel begins—and Mr. Rochester locks his wife in an attic. Women too are failures at providing protection, even the well-intentioned ones. Hester abandons her stepdaughter, claiming financial constraints: with her male support and protection, Anna's father, dead, she too must struggle to sur-vive. Francine and Christophine do what they can, but as black women they are powerless.

Rhys's final message may be that control by others doesn't work. Women must be adults, autonomous and independent, not perpetual children, seeking adult saviours. Women must resist the trap of false protectionism.

—Erika Smilowitz, "Childlike Women and Paternal Men: Colonialism in Jean Rhys's Fiction," *Ariel* 17, no. 4 (October 1986): 93–95, 102

EVELYN O'CALLAGHAN

Jean Rhys (born Dominica, 1890) sets *Wide Sargasso Sea* (*WSS*) in Jamaica after the Emancipation Act of 1834; like Rhys's own maternal forbears, the white creole Antoinette's family had owned slaves. The breakdown of plantation society and her family's growing poverty isolate Antoinette and her mother, until marriage to an Englishman saves them from economic ruin. But the freed blacks, who had mocked the whites' financial degradation, react with violence to their new wealth and burn the family estate. As a result, the family is split up and Antoinette, after years in the refuge of convent school, is married off to an Englishman, a virtual stranger. The destructive nature of their relationship leads to mutual hatred and to Antoinette's mental collapse. The novel ends with her incarceration in her husband's English mansion, the Thornfield Hall of Brontë's *Jane Eyre*.

This novel deals with the attempt and failure of dialogue and interculturation: between white creoles and expatriate whites; between white, black and 'coloured' West Indians; between males and females, between colony and metropolis—one can take as the structuring principle Antoinette's assertion that "there is always the other side. Always". The mirror image of Antoinette/Tia (p. 38), and the conversation between Antoinette and her husband about the unreality of each other's environment (p. 67), are but two examples of failed attempts to communicate across racial, cultural, social and national barriers. The point is, the effort is made and the *reasons* for failure are skilfully, if subtly, illustrated. ⟨. . .⟩

And Antoinette's empathy with Christophine and admiration of the 'superior' Tia, hints at a desire to identify with them that Rhys herself clarifies in *Smile Please*:

> Once I heard her [mother] say that black babies were prettier than white ones. Was this the reason why I prayed so ardently to be black, and would run to the looking-glass in the morning to see if the miracle had happened? ⟨42⟩

But Antoinette is *rejected* by Tia and viewed with hostility by the blacks because of their recent experience of white exploitation. Look Lai draws attention to the fact that her choice of union with Tia and the black world, at the end of *WSS* is based on an illusory gesture of welcome; just as white creole Anna's communality with the black masqueraders in *Voyage in the Dark* (1934) is achieved only in the realm of dream.

—Evelyn O'Callaghan, "'The Outsider's Voice': White Creole Women Novelists in the Caribbean Literary Tradition," *Journal of West Indian Literature* 1, no. 1 (October 1986): 78–79, 83

LAURA NIESEN DE ABRUNA

The formal qualities of such texts as *Wide Sargasso Sea*, ⟨Rhys's⟩ best work, are poetic compression, orality and metaphor, as well as interior monologues and the importance of dreams and association as representational forms. The primacy of the dream vision ending that novel and the continual use of dreams in *Voyage in the Dark* draw attention to Rhys' modernist use of dreams and to the greater acceptance of dreams as a respected type of reality in the work of women writers. In *Voyage in the Dark* dreams and reveries give the novel its structural principle since the narrator uses these means to return to her past whenever something threatening occurs in her present. The blurring of past and present was a deliberate strategy. In a 1934 letter to Evelyn Scott, Rhys pointed out her desire to make *Voyage in the Dark* a conflation of the present and the past. The novel would show, through the use of dreamlike narrative, that the past and the present exist side by side: 'I tried to do it by making the past (the West Indies) very vivid—the present dreamlike downward career of a girl' ⟨*Letters 1931–1966*, 1984, 24⟩. Rhys' great contribution to full presentation of female life is her exploration of the mother-daughter bond, and specifically the effects of the loss of maternal matrix. The alienation from the mother becomes a metaphor for the white Creole girl's alienation from the mother culture, England. ⟨. . .⟩

In *Voyage in the Dark*, as in Rhys' later novels, there is a woman narrator who is deprived of parental nurturing and suffers from this lack of support. Anna's mother has died before the opening of the novel, and her father dies soon after her arrival in England. Her situation is exacerbated because of her political status as a white Creole and her subsequent alienation as a colonial in England. There she becomes a marginal woman living on the money received in exchange for sex. This is a pattern not only in *Voyage in the Dark* but also in all of her novels, in each of which the female character is rejected first by their mothers and then by a male lover, or series of lovers. It appears in all of these novels that the men in positions of power and wealth are the enemy, but the problems of identity and self-esteem for the women characters stem from their inadequate bonding with their mothers. Unable to form a positive self-identity, they are vulnerable to exploitation by men and other women.

The narrative pattern in *Voyage in the Dark* is therefore one of maternal loss and attempted compensation through memory. In these memories, Anna attempts to recapture the island itself, symbol of the mother. Although the memories seem to be reveries out of Anna's control, they form a pattern. Each time Anna suffers loss or humiliation, she returns to thoughts of the island as an unconscious way of deflecting despair through imaginative attachment to the mother. While the projection of such comfort is an admirable strategy against complete dominance by the colonial power, it is inadequate to save Anna, and we must wait for Antoinette Cosway to find a character capable of turning dream compensation into adequate resistance.

—Laura Niesen de Abruna, "Family Connections: Mother and Mother Country in the Fiction of Jean Rhys and Jamaica Kincaid," *Motherlands: Black Women's Writing from Africa, the Caribbean and South Asia*, ed. Susheila Nasta (London: The Women's Press Limited, 1991), 258, 265–66

ELAINE SAVORY FIDO

When a woman writes her alienation from her mother, she might adopt many different voices, but none will carry that proximity to the mother's culture which marks daughter and mother as two different modulations of the same voice.

I resist the judgment which Judith Kegan Gardner makes in her essay on Jean Rhys, Doris Lessing and Christina Stead ⟨"The Exhilaration of Exile: Rhys, Stead, and Lessing," 1989, 141⟩ in which she says of Rhys,

> . . . the white colonial woman has no secure place of origin. Their
> birth nation is not the home of their culture; England is not the home
> of their birth . . .

In relation to Rhys, this is misleading. Whereas some sense of displacement no doubt does come from the accident of birth, Rhys can sound the Creole voice of her mother, as well as British English.

Rhys' different voice textures cut across each other. Sometimes male and female interact, as in the double narrative of *Wide Sargasso Sea*, and here the English voice contains and isolates the Creole. Sometimes the Creole becomes an African language, often spoken by an alternative mother like Francine in *Voyage in the Dark* or Christophine in *Wide Sargasso Sea*. In this way, Rhys writes her distance from her mother-island-home into the voice of every text. ⟨. . .⟩

⟨. . .⟩ When a daughter loses a mother, she loses lines of communication with other women as well. One solution to distrusting other women is to turn to men, but in the attempt to please them, a false self may be created. ⟨. . .⟩

But the 'false self' is not only the result of patriarchy, but the result of trauma between mother and daughter.

There is a powerful example of this in the accounts which Jean Rhys gives in her autobiography of her mother's preference for black babies as prettier than white ones, and of her own self-rejection as palest of the family and the one called Gwendolyn (white in Welsh). We can see the source of this in the child's reaction to a fair doll she had been sent from England: asked by her mother to give up a similar doll which had dark hair to her sister, Gwendolyn took the pale one into the garden and smashed its face with a rock. This is the clearest declaration of refusal to accept the real self. If the mother does not accept that self, another can be created either in exile or in fiction. It is this self which can confront Kristeva's powerful 'Phallic Mother'.

—Elaine Savory Fido, "Mother/lands: Self and Separation in the Work of Buchi Emecheta, Bessie Head and Jean Rhys," *Motherlands: Black Women's Writing from Africa, the Caribbean and South Asia*, ed. Susheila Nasta (London: The Women's Press Limited, 1991), 334–37

MOIRA FERGUSON

Jean Rhys has recirculated a version of *Jane Eyre* in which she rewrites Charlotte Brontë's story of female identity. She refashions a female literary tradition, destabilizing its paradigmatic consciousness. Rochester is held accountable, and madness is problematized. His decision to lock a woman up for years more than justifies her attack on step-brother Richard Mason when he visits her in the attic and reminds her of her legal status and his original negotiations with Rochester; her "lowering look," attributed by the community to a condition derived from her mad family, is also encoded as a sign at the wedding that she knows what is destined to befall her. Her dreams signify the same way.

The narrative logic of the text upholds the author's planter-descendant politic only if we "believe" the closure of the original text, *Jane Eyre*. In *Wide Sargasso Sea*, instead, Rochester is the Coulibri parrot demanding to know who is there—Qui est là?—fighting him at the end; then he dies with his wings clipped in an act of symbolic justice. Even so, whether African-Caribbeans will celebrate or organize themselves after whites abandon the islands is left as an open question. On that question Jean Rhys also challenges the gender and colonial politics of her own exiled world in Britain.

Before Jean Rhys wrote *Wide Sargasso Sea* in the 1950s, two events occurred that were particularly relevant to her discussion in the novel: First, national, anticolonial independence movements erupted all over the world; second, African-Caribbean people emigrated to Britain in large numbers, a situation that culminated in ugly riots against black people in London and the provinces in 1958. Thus only the suppressed of *Wide Sargasso Sea* hold out the possibility of a macrocosmic victory. Overtly readers witness Antoinette's and Rochester's doubled-edged triumphs: she "wins" because she leaps to Tia and life-in-death but dies anyway. Excluded and unknown, she still terminates his family ties to the islands. He "wins" because, while he is left with her money unencumbered, he is wounded and socially displaced. He lives back home as an insider and outsider, a historical anachronism. If he dies in the fire—an optional reading not excluded in this text—then *Wide Sargasso Sea* is a different story. As it stands the revised text of *Jane Eyre* offers no closure.

At the manifest level, then, the text favors Jean Rhys's class—the former white planter class to which Antoinette belongs. She is meant to be a tragic heroine, and although Rochester is represented as a villain, his family forced him and he was dutiful. Excuses have been concocted since the beginning for his abysmal conduct in locking a woman up *sine die*. At the same time Jean Rhys foregrounds African-Caribbean protagonists and the community as Charlotte Brontë never did. Christophine is a critical hero, although she and other members of the Jamaican and Dominican communities resist being shunted awkwardly out of the text to assert an oppositional agency. From a class, race, and gendered perspective, Jean Rhys cannot allow the implied victors of the text to be articulated as victors. That judgment lies in texts whose vested interest lies elsewhere.

—Moira Ferguson, *Colonialism and Gender Relations from Mary Wollstonecraft to Jamaica Kincaid: East Caribbean Connections* (New York: Columbia University Press, 1993), 114–15

MARIA OLLAUSSEN

An important part of the exploration of the white colonial experience is an understanding of the consequences of the division between black and white. Rhys remembers a fierce longing to be part of the black community, something she expected to happen through a miracle: "Dear God, let me be black" (*Smile Please*, 42), she used to pray. She often describes black women in contrast to white women: "They were stronger than we were, they could walk a long way without getting tired, carry heavy weights with ease . . . Also there wasn't for them as there was for us, what I thought of as the worry of getting married . . . Black girls . . . seemed to be perfectly free" (*Smile* 50–51). Rhys's clearly expressed longing for blackness in her letters, in her autobiography, and in her fiction has caused critics to draw the conclusion that she was concerned with issues of racial justice and that she had taken the side of black people. ⟨. . .⟩

Rhys's rather complicated attitude towards black people should be looked at in the context of her enterprise of writing the Creole madwoman's part of the story. It is the "worrying of getting married" that for her defines womanhood. The specific limitations and complications connected with white womanhood did not apply to black women, and therefore Rhys sees them as "perfectly free." Needless to say, this is not an accurate description of black women's lives but a construction which functions to define the dilemma of the white woman as a biological necessity. For a white woman, blackness as freedom means that the only way for her to be free is by miraculously changing the colour of her skin; biological determinism is thus not limited to sex alone.

This clinging to biological determinism can be understood within the context of Rhys's own lack of a clearly defined identity. Lee Erwin argues that although in *Wide Sargasso Sea* Rhys takes up her West Indian past, she cannot be said to articulate West Indian nationalism. "The novel seems rather to inhabit a limbo *between* nationalism; it exists as a response to the loss, rather than the recovery, of a 'place-to-be-from' " (143). Mary Lou Emery describes Jean Rhys asking: "Am I an expatriate? Expatriate from where?" (13–14). ⟨. . .⟩

In *Wide Sargasso Sea*, the starting point is this placelessness. Although Rhys's novel starts with Antoinette's childhood in Coulibri, its boundaries lie outside the novel in another woman's text. In *Jane Eyre* we have the madwoman Bertha locked up in the attic of Thornfield Hall. We know the ending of the story and thus the restrictions placed on both the narrative and the main character. The significant title "Wide Sargasso Sea" refers to the dangers of the sea voyage. Rochester first crosses the Atlantic alone to a place which threatens to destroy him, then once more, bringing his new wife to England. Both Rochester and Antoinette are transformed through this passage. Rochester gives Antoinette a new name, Bertha, and in England she finally is locked up as mad. Rhys finds her own place in *Jane Eyre*, "a prisoner of another's desire." She sets out to describe that place and, in doing that, she redefines it as her own. In her challenge to *Jane Eyre*, Rhys draws on the collective experience of black people as sought out, uprooted, and transported across the Middle Passage and finally locked up and brutally exploited for economic gain. She uses this experience and the black forms of resistance as modes through which the madwoman in *Jane Eyre* is recreated.

—Maria Ollaussen, "Jean Rhys's Construction of Blackness as Escape from White Femininity in *Wide Sargasso Sea*," Ariel 24, no. 2 (April 1993): 66–68

B I B L I O G R A P H Y

The Left Bank and Other Stories. 1927.
Postures. 1928 (as *Quartet: A Novel,* in 1929).
After Leaving Mr. Mackenzie. 1931.
Voyage in the Dark. 1934.
Good Morning, Midnight. 1939.
Wide Sargasso Sea. 1966.
Tigers Are Better Looking: With a Selection from Left Bank. 1968.
My Day: Three Pieces. 1975.
Sleep It Off, Lady. 1976.
Smile Please: An Unfinished Autobiography. 1979.

OLIVE SENIOR

B. 1941

OLIVE SENIOR was born in 1941 in a village in western Jamaica. Her father ran a small farm, while her mother's family owned land in a different parish. As a child, Senior spent long periods of time with her mother's wealthier relatives. Moving between the two worlds—that of villagers and that of landowners—allowed Senior to experience what she has called the "polarities of colonial society." Both the African traditions of her father's village and the European values of her mother's family are reflected in Senior's stories and poems, underscoring the alienation she often felt as a youth.

Senior attended Montego Bay High School, writing for the *Daily Gleaner* after school and during vacations. She later trained as a journalist under its editor. In 1967, she graduated from Carleton University in Canada with a bachelor's degree in journalism. Since then she has worked as a freelance writer and researcher and has been a publications editor for the Institute of Social and Economic Research at the University of the West Indies.

Several of Senior's poems were first published in *Jamaican Woman: An Anthology of Poems* (1980). Her first published collection of poems, *Talking of Trees* (1985), is divided into two parts, the first dealing with close familial and personal relationships in a rural context, and the second focusing on larger political themes and issues raised by urban life. In 1987, Senior confirmed her importance as a writer by winning the Commonwealth Writer's Prize with *Summer Lightning and Other Stories* (1986), her first collection of short stories. Set in rural Jamaica, the book's 10 tales often feature female protagonists and show how economic and political issues affect individuals and their communities. In 1989, Senior published her second short-story collection, *Arrival of the Snake Woman and Other Stories*, and was awarded the Silver Musgrave Medal for Literature by the Institute of Jamaica. Expanding the scope of her first collection, Senior sets some of her tales in rural Jamaica but also places several in an urban context, offering middle-class perspectives not shown in *Summer Lightning and Other Stories*.

Although Senior may be best known for her poetry and fiction, she has also contributed to critical thought about Jamaican cultural issues through her work as manager and editor of the *Jamaica Journal* from 1982 until 1989 and through her nonfiction book, *A–Z of Jamaican Heritage* (1983).

Since the publication of her second volume of stories, Senior has served as writer-in-residence and visiting lecturer at the University of the West Indies and has been named an international writer-in-residence by the Arts Council of Great Britain (1991). Her most recent work includes a collection of poems, *Gardening in the Tropics* (1994), and a collection of short stories, *Discerner of Hearts* (1995).

C R I T I C A L   E X T R A C T S

EVELYN O'CALLAGHAN

The stories ⟨in *Summer Lightning and Other Stories*⟩ are told from a variety of perspectives—that of the old woman, the adult, the adolescent and most commonly, the child. They are related by an unobtrusive omniscient author or in the more personal first person singular. And the language of narration is either a relaxed, colloquial West Indian Standard English or an equally effortless representation of Jamaican Creole. The total effect is of a particular world illuminated from every angle and, by the time we turn the final page, intimately known.

This illumination can be sudden and brutal, as in the title story. Into the secure, dreaming world of childhood, "the man" comes to visit for a few weeks—"for his 'nerves' they said". Unpleasant, even sinister details about the man accumulate until the reader senses danger, while the young boy, innocently fascinated, is drawn closer and closer to the adult's evil. Tension mounts to crisis proportions—as the summer lightning heralds the threatening thunderstorm—but even in the final scene we are left unsure about the outcome, unsure whether innocence or corruption will prevail. The author's deftness in suggesting atmosphere and shades of feeling rather than exhaustively *describing* them, makes for the story's delicacy in treating a potentially explosive subject. ⟨. . .⟩

There is much the reader can learn from Olive Senior's short fiction—about the rich resources of Jamaican speech varieties, about superstitions and folk beliefs and the details of daily life in rural society. But I think the stories leave us with the two particularly lingering impressions. One is the sense of community that dominates in this rural world, a mutual support system of neighbours, friends and relations, which forms an unobtrusive setting for action in the pieces, most noticeably in "The Boy Who Loved Ice Cream" and "Real Old Time T'ing". The other is the almost magical quality with which reality is imbued by the child's vision, and the often thoughtless manner in which insensitive adults shatter this shimmering world—as, for instance, in "Love Orange" and "Bright Thursdays".

Summer Lightning is a slim well-crafted and beautifully packaged offering of treats to be savoured and enjoyed.

—Evelyn O'Callaghan, [Review of *Summer Lightning and Other Stories*], *Journal of West Indian Literature* 1, no. 1 (October 1986): 92–94

ERIKA J. SMILOWITZ

Summer Lightning marks the impressive debut of poet and *Jamaica Journal* editor Olive Senior. Her entertaining stories offer realistic insights into Jamaican village life, particularly the life of women. Familiar places and believable people emerge from these pages, and their stories are told in lively conversational style, enhanced by the appropriate use of "nation language," as poet Edward Brathwaite has termed the Jamaican patois.

The perspective in this collection is often a child's one, and the world through a child's eye is often grim. Senior follows a strong tradition of the novel of childhood: these stories are reminiscent of Jamaica Kincaid's memories of growing up in Antigua and particularly of Merle Hodge's novel, *Crick Crack Monkey* (Andre Deutsch, 1970), set in Trinidad. Like Tee of Hodge's novel, Senior's young characters are often torn between two worlds—a poor, rural one and a middle-class, urban one—as they struggle to find a comfortable niche in a rapidly-changing, post-colonial society.

"Bright Thursdays" is one example. Although Laura's wealthy father has never acknowledged her existence, her mother is proud of the short liaison which produced Laura. She contrives to have the child taken into the magnificent home of her paternal grandparents. Laura has been made to feel different all her life and in her new home she has become fearful and withdrawn. When her father, described in nearly Messianic terms, arrives from New York with his wife, Laura is at first bewildered. "How does one behave with a father?" she asks herself. "She had no experience of this. There were so few fathers among all the people she knew." She is ultimately devastated by his callous treatment. ⟨. . .⟩

Many of these stories touch authentically on the issues that confront Jamaica today, a changing, upwardly-mobile society. The wealthy aunt in "Summer Lightning," for example, is insulted when Bro. Justice, now transformed into a Rastafarian, refuses to address her as "maam" or "mistress" and in fact refuses to address her at all. More than one character, forced to emigrate to England or America for economic survival, dreams of returning home rich enough to impress former neighbors.

Senior's reality is tempered with ironic humor. In "Ascot," Ascot's abnormally large feet give him away as a banana thief. In "Real Old Time T'ing," Senior pokes fun at attempts by bourgeois Patricia to remake her father's life and at his success in outwitting her. The use in both these stories of Jamaican patois strengthens the humor and builds an intimacy between the storyteller and the reader.

—Erika J. Smilowitz, "Tales of the Caribbean," *Women's Review of Books* 5, no. 2 (November 1987): 13

Evelyn O'Callaghan

Throughout *Summer Lightning*, the niceties of ⟨. . .⟩ hierarchy are adhered to by the decent, strict elite among the community: your race/class determines how and from which entrance you are admitted to a house (1), a Black labourer who turns Rasta is seen as losing the respect which his middle-class employers consider their due (6); self-worth is imaged in terms of possession of a certain life style, that is: "a big house with heavy mahogany furniture and many rooms, fixed mealtimes, a mother and father who were married to each other and lived together in the same house . . . who would send you to school with the proper clothes . . ." ("Bright Thursdays," 36).

Inevitably, social standing is linked with race: "brown skin with straight hair" is superior to "dark skin but almost straight hair," which is superior to black, and so on. One *can* rise socially, through education or money, but this involves adopting the values of the "clear" middle class who fear the encroachment of the Black masses into their territory and who, like Miss Christie, have nothing but contempt for the likes of the "uppity black gal" who "seduced" her son to "raise her colour" (40).

Social mobility, then, involves repudiating all previous connections for a life of limitation and conformity. In this, *all* classes are in agreement and here is the rub of Senior's indictment. That Myrtle, in "Bright Thursdays," should be seduced by "a young man of high estate . . . [who] had come visiting the Wheelers where Myrtle was a young servant" (38), and that the resultant child is neither acknowledged nor supported by him or his family, can be explained in the social context. But that Myrtle should raise her daughter to admire, imitate and aspire to the ways of those "of high estate," at the cost of alienation from her own class and colour, is untenable.

The stories, then, vitiate the values informing the rural peasantry's desire to keep up appearances (16), to associate only with "good" families (18) and their tendency to denigrate their own people and their own race: "everybody know this country going to the dog these days for is pure black people children they pushing to send high school. Anybody ever hear you can educate monkey?" ("Ballad," 109–10). Further, by depicting the confusion, self-doubt and fragmentation which such contradictions wreak on the child's psyche— Lenore, Laura, the narrator of "Confirmation Day"—such attitudes assume evil proportions and lessen the stature of the older women in the community who instil racism and snobbery along with manners and morals.

—Evelyn O'Callaghan, "Feminist Consciousness: European/American Theory, Jamaican Stories," *Journal of Caribbean Studies* 6, no. 2 (Spring 1988): 158–59

ISABEL FONSECA

Summer Lightning, which deservedly won the first Commonwealth Writers' Prize, is ⟨. . .⟩ told mainly from the viewpoint of a child who is having a hard time getting heard above the din of adults. The sense of isolation is further emphasized as someone in each story is alienated by the superstitions, jealousies and cruel intolerance of an illiterate rural community. The menaced characters in Senior's more sombre stories recall Antoinette Cosway, the jittery young Creole heiress of Jean Rhys's *Wide Sargasso Sea*, who, for different reasons and 150 years earlier, was caught and driven to madness in the same inbred, oppressively beautiful Jamaica.

Characters who migrate to Kingston are regarded with suspicion and envy; this response is more pronounced in the case of relatives who have made it all the way to England or America. Upward and outward mobility is obsessively pursued, and sometimes achieved at a startling cost. The "Country of the One Eyed God" ends with an outlawed young thug poised to pull the trigger on his own grandmother because she refuses to hand over the money (stitched to her side) that she has saved up for a gaudy coffin. "I don't want to go into the next world", she explains, "as poor and naked as I come into this one."

Olive Senior uses humour effectively to betray the pathetic snobbery of her characters. Another story involves a lazy boy with big feet (the father's parting words to his son are "No matter how hard yu wuk an how much money yu mek yu will nevva find shoes fo dem doan mek dem in fe yu size"). The boy, inauspiciously named Ascot, dreams only of resting his feet on the floor of a large white Cadillac. He eventually gets to America, and, working as a chauffeur, realizes his dream, more or less. After several silent years, he returns home with his large white American wife, and, ashamed, introduces his father and mother as uncle and aunt. (This is not the only story in which emigration involves repudiation of roots.) Far from being appalled, the parents stand in awe of the American woman with a master's degree. "Dat Hascot", his real aunt purrs, "I did always know he wudda reach far yu know." Not all of the stories succeed, but Senior's achievement is to address ominous issues obliquely, by cataloguing, with wit and affection; the lilting speech and loping gait of the local population.

—Isabel Fonseca, "Dreams of Leaving," *Times Literary Supplement* 435, no. 4 (1–7 April 1988): 364

HILTON ALS

"Somewhere between the repetition of Sunday School lessons and the broken doll which the lady sent me one Christmas I lost what it was to be happy." So begins the narrator in "Love Orange," one of 10 short stories in Olive Senior's remarkable, if uneven, collection ⟨*Summer Lightning and Other Stories*⟩. A brief tale of innocence lost, "Love Orange" succeeds in establishing a tone that draws the reader in as it makes its way toward a painful conclusion: the end of belief is the beginning of maturity. Ms. Senior is a writer who shares with the Antiguan Jamaica Kincaid and the Barbadian Paule Marshall the ability to merge island syntax with British inflection. The result is a language that is deft and lyrical. Ms. Senior's stories, all set in Jamaica, are peopled with characters who believe that their dream life is every bit as significant as their daily one, though this belief makes for seductive prose, not necessarily convincing plot lines. The most winning stories are those in which plot barely makes an appearance, as in the title story. It is when Ms. Senior depicts mood, atmosphere and the inner life of her characters that her work avoids a tendency toward the maudlin or the melodramatic. "Summer Lightning" is an original contribution to the flourishing school of West Indian writers who create rooms we've never seen before, voices we've never heard.

—Hilton Als, [Review of *Summer Lightning and Other Stories*], *New York Times Book Review* (17 April 1988): 42

VELMA POLLARD

Senior's short stories and poetry are the work of a creative talent of great sensitivity which expresses tremendous understanding of the human condition, particularly that of poor people both rural and urban. The attempt to slot her writing into a particular genre immediately gives one an uncomfortable feeling. For the work is knit together by a common landscape and a recurring concern for humanity. Both poetry and prose bring the country paths of Senior's childhood and the urban experiences of her young womanhood into focus. The themes of both concern the experiences of people in these environments who represent different points along a scale of social and financial privilege.

The point of view preferred, particularly in the prose published so far, is the child's eye view, complete with all the wonder and confusion ⟨. . . .⟩ The stories presented here, like the stories in *Summer Lightning*, reflect that preference.

The child's eye view is not childlike. It is a clear vision through which the irrationalities of adults, the inequities in society and from time to time the redeeming features in the environment, are expressed. The exploitation of the child's vision allows Senior space for the imaginative forays her readers find most engaging, and for the dramatic presentation of human foibles seen from the point of view of the little person looking and feeling from under. ⟨. . .⟩

The narrative voice in fact records children's reactions to phenomena, to their own condition, and perhaps more critically, to the adults with whom they interact. "Bright Thursdays" for example describes a small girl's discomfort as she adjusts to the strange and demanding formality in the upper-class home of a newly acquired guardian (an unacknowledged grandmother), after the easy casualness of life with a working-class mother who had in fact been a servant to a member of the family. In "Ballad" the child eulogizes her favorite adult, Miss Rilla, a woman of whose life-style her step-mother heartily disapproves and on whom she expects God to exact punishment. In "Confirmation Day" the young candidate is perplexed by the symbolism of the Anglican communion into which she is being inducted, is no less perplexed by the memory of another more dramatic induction (by water in the village river) into a less sophisticated flock, and finally rejects what both have to offer in the supreme indictment of the Christian religion: "I'd rather be a child of someone else, being a child of god is too frightening. . . ."

Religion and adult attitudes and behavior receive the harshest implied judgment from Senior. These are the areas of greatest confusion for the children in these fascinating stories. In "Bright Thursdays" the Christian God is as threatening and illogical as the requirements of the domestic situation in which the heroine Laura finds herself. Mealtime in the new home is one of the major trials of the child's life. It takes place at "The Table" in the "Dining Room" where three people huddle together at one end of a table which could easily accommodate twelve. Over it hang beribboned and bewhiskered grandparents looking down from oval picture frames. She fears the clouds on the way to school in this environment for they

> reminded her of the pictures she used to get in Sunday School show-
> ing Jesus coming to earth again, floating down on one of these fat
> white clouds . . . these pictures only served to remind her that she
> was a sinner and that God would one day soon appear out of the sky
> flashing fire and brimstone to judge and condemn her. ⟨. . .⟩

Senior's effectiveness lies partly in the precision with which she reproduces the speech of the characters. In her writing she exploits fully the complex Jamaican speech community, making use of the flexibility the different codes allow. There are stereotypes of language and class easily recognizable in these works. Auntie Mary, for example, is funny and distressing partly because she is so real. The imaginative child who tries to dispel her loneliness in "See the Tiki Tiki Scatter" is engaging because we can hear her voice as she dramatizes her grandmother's song:

> Oh burr-EAK the NEWS to MOTH-er
> And TELL her that I LOVE-er
> And TELL her NOT to WAIT for MEEE
> FOR I'M NOT COMING HOOOOOOME.

Her isolation becomes pitiful when the attempt to fraternize with Peggy the maid is thwarted by the finality of Peggy's words, spoken in a code which contrasts with that of the narrative voice and increases the gulf between them: "No. No white people back yaso. Go weh. Back to yu big house." The fit of theme, character and language is impeccable.

—Velma Pollard, "An Introduction to the Poetry and Fiction of Olive Senior," *Callaloo* 11, no. 3 (Summer 1988): 540–41, 544

CHARLES H. ROWELL

〈Senior: . . .〉 While the consciousness in *Summer Lightning* is mainly that of the child, the stories in *Arrival* are also told from the point of view of adults (males and females) as well as children of different races and classes. The experiences described are urban as well as rural; in short, while *Summer Lightning* focused mainly on the peasantry, in *Arrival* I am beginning to explore the lives of the rising black and brown bourgeoisie.

In *Arrival* I am also experimenting—tentatively—with magical realism. I believe it is a form well suited to our societies as it enables us artistically to fuse the mundane with the other world which lurks not too far beyond our everyday existence—the magical, spiritual, whatever you choose to call it. For me, writing, literature, is inextricably fused with magic. Though most of my writing is in a realistic vein, I am conscious at all times of other possibilities lurking just beyond consciousness, of the great ineffable mystery that lies at the core of each life, at the heart of every story.

In recent years I have been much affected by the work of Latin American writers—particularly Jorge Amado, Gabriel Garcia Marquez and Mario Vargas Llosa—and I believe their example is helping me to shape the work that I am writing now.

Rowell: Your poems and stories assume, as does the work of other new Caribbean writers, a voice of certainty or self-assurance. That is, unlike the previous generations of Caribbean writers, you don't concern yourself with public battles against colonialism and white racism. You don't focus on public issues; you concentrate on the interior lives of your characters.

Senior: I am not sure I entirely agree with some of what you are saying here. I don't know that the subject matter of Caribbean literature has changed substantively over the years—there are common threads running through the literature from the forties and fifties which are still there in the work that is being produced today—that is, the search for an identity both personal and national, the exploration of issues of race and class, that is, the subtleties of race and class, the encounter with race . . . and not just battles with "white racism" per se; the attempt to affirm indigenous culture, and so on.

What has changed, I agree, is the form, the way in which some of us are exploring these issues; for instance, the fact that Caribbean women writers have now come to the fore is opening up to us a completely new approach to the topic of the Caribbean mother—one of our great literary preoccupations—and of our relationship with that mother. It is also, I believe, personalizing the socio-political issues.

It is true that I don't focus on public issues, but that doesn't mean that I do not share in the social and political preoccupations. In fact, I would say that a very strong socio-political consciousness informs all my work. I believe that I am dealing with fundamentally the same issue as before—the impact of colonialism, forms of racism, issues of justice, notions of power/powerlessness. But for me, the human being, the individual life, is the primary focus of everything, so all experience tends to be filtered through a particular consciousness. The most creative act for me as a writer is to assume that consciousness and give it expression. I am entering people's lives and recreating their autobiographies. Although my concerns are explicitly existential, I am nevertheless highly conscious of the socio-political environment, the *context* in which we operate.

>   —Charles H. Rowell, "An Interview with Olive Senior," *Callaloo* 11, no. 3 (Summer 1988): 484–85

Nadezda Obradovic

Olive Senior's first collection of short prose, *Summer Lightning*, brought her the Commonwealth Writers Prize in 1987. Her second, *Arrival of the Snake Woman and Other Stories*, offers seven new selections. The setting, as always, is the author's native island of Jamaica, where her protagonists—usually naïve, sensitive, and vulnerable children and women—meet with a real world of evil and ambition and, in the process, find their own way. The heroine of "The Tenantry of Birds," for example, is a young girl always under the domination of someone, first her mother and later her husband; ultimately she finds the courage and will to do as she pleases, freed from parental and marital bonds. The passage from childhood to girlhood is the subject of the tender story "The Two Grandmothers"; the rural ambience of the grandmother's hut, so attractive to the young female protagonist during her early years, becomes so dull to her as she matures that she even leaves her grandmother sick in bed and instead hurries home to watch "Dallas."

The backdrop of all the stories is the mixed society of Jamaica, with its stark divisions among whites, blacks, and others. Senior's presentation of her characters' initial realization that they belong to a despised underclass is fine and sensitive, as when one pampered and conceited young girl is suddenly called a "dirty nigger" for the first time. It is on such shocks of real adult life that Senior—who is also a journalist (*Jamaica Journal*), poet (*Talking of Trees*), and reference-book author (*A–Z of Jamaican Heritage*)—builds her human dramas.

—Nadezda Obradovic, [Review of *Arrival of the Snake Woman and Other Stories*], *World Literature Today* 64, no. 3 (Summer 1990): 514

VELMA POLLARD

The official language of Jamaica is Standard Jamaican English (SJE), a dialect of English as accessible to English speakers the world over as Standard American or Standard Australian English. It is the language of the school and of all the official organisations of the society. The majority of Jamaicans, however, speak Jamaican Creole (JC), a Creole of English lexicon which everyone in the speech community understands. Because of the lexical relationship between the two languages most Creole speakers regard themselves as English speakers. There is, in addition, a code introduced by the Rastafari, a socio-religious group, and adopted by other speakers, particularly the young. ⟨. . .⟩

Because language and social class, in the stereotypical descriptions of these, are closely aligned, creative writers are able to use the codes to identify prototypical characters and attitudes. This is not to suggest a particular self-consciousness in the production of literary writing, for I believe that what we will look at is a reproduction of natural speech. What the artists ⟨including Olive Senior⟩ have done is to select to write about situations requiring the use of the different codes available to speakers. It is precisely because the natural language of the people in the community is reproduced, that we are able to discuss language as it functions within the speech community, using as evidence texts from the writing we are about to examine. ⟨. . .⟩

The narrative voice in Senior's stories depends entirely on the identity of the narrator. In those instances, however, where the language is a version of JC, it is the turn of phrase, the idiom, more than the differences in grammar or lexicon, which signal its use. The non-JC speaker is unlikely to have difficulty understanding the words. Note the opening gambit of perhaps the most popular story of the collection *Summer Lightning*, 'Do Angels Wear Brassières?':

> Beccka down on her knees ending her goodnight prayers and Cherry telling her softly, 'And ask God to bless Auntie Mary.' Beccka vex that anybody could interrupt her private conversation with God so, say loud loud, 'no. Not praying for nobody that tek weh mi best glassy eye marble.' (p. 67) ⟨. . .⟩

Mothertongue, certainly for a writer like Senior, is a number of speech codes: the broad JC of the maid in 'See the Tiki-Tiki Scatter', the English of the middle and upper classes, the hyper-corrected forms sometimes used by the aspirants to competence in English, the barely non-standard forms which make up the relaxed speech of many educated Jamaicans or the mixture of all these as the educated speaker switches from one code to the other, responding to situation or trying for effect. Because she is true to the characters she creates, and because she creates characters across the social boundaries, Senior exposes the reader to a very wide range of possibilities within the continuum between JC and SJE. Any study of this artist's language must take account of this range.

—Velma Pollard, "Mothertongue Voices in the Writing of Olive Senior and Lorna Goodison," *Motherlands: Black Women's Writing from Africa, the Caribbean and South Asia*, ed. Susheila Nasta (London: The Women's Press Limited, 1991), 239–40, 244–45

AMEENA GAFOOR

Many West Indian authors have portrayed various aspects of Indo-Caribbean female experience and ⟨. . .⟩ Olive Senior's short story, "The Arrival of the Snake Woman" ⟨. . .⟩ seems to present a culmination of all the phases of readjustment and accommodation inherent in migration and displacement. It starts at the beginning of the process with the woman as an alien and works its way through the alienation and isolation of the exile, colonial victimization and racial exclusion to the conscious decision to integrate culturally and also to address the issue of her tentative hold on land and home. This ⟨. . .⟩ short story is counter-discursive: it depicts resistance to the colonial power base and questions the centre/margin paradigm of dominant discourse in a manner which characterizes post-colonial writing. Ashcroft, Griffiths, and Tiffin address themselves in *The Empire Writes Back* (Routledge, 1989) to the question of the dismantling of the power hierarchy entrenched in colonial texts, the abrogation of European power and its false premises, the reappropriation of indigenous cultural forms and the recognition that hybridity and syncreticity are the most viable means to recuperation and selfhood in the semiotics of postcolonial writing and, although Senior's short story is not itself a rewriting of a colonial text, it is newer writing which intervenes in and resists dominant discourse about the *other*. It relates how the Indo-Caribbean woman manages in the colonial minefield.

Senior's short story depicts a plural society in what is unmistakably colonial Jamaica, the temporal setting estimated at the first half of the twentieth century. At its heart, the work portrays racial antagonisms, cultural differences, alienation, exclusion, powerlessness, subjection, and conformity, all of which have come to characterize the construction of the colonial world. The text can be read as an interrogation of patriarchal morality, as an imaginative document of the Indian female immigrant experience in a tangled web of human relationships, or as a story of adolescence and growing up in the multicultural prism as the adult male narrator, Ishmael, recaptures his boyhood and adolescent struggles of grappling with the ambiguities and ambivalences, confusions and contradictions of the adult world around him. The most crucial issues in regional literature have been race, class, and identity—not unnaturally so considering the multi-racial, multicultural nature of our social reality—and these issues have impacted significantly in this short story.

—Ameena Gafoor, "The Image of the Indo-Caribbean Woman in Olive Senior's *The Arrival of the Snake Woman*," *Callaloo* 16, no. 1 (Winter 1993): 34–35

RICHARD F. PATTESON

Clearly, the search for an authentic voice for the expression of the "matter" of the West Indies has been in progress for decades, and Senior owes a considerable debt to distinguished predecessors and older contemporaries like ⟨Samuel⟩ Selvon, ⟨V. S.⟩ Reid, and John Hearne. In several of the stories in her first book, *Summer Lightning*, a version of vernacular Jamaican speech—and one not so obviously "invented" as Reid's or Selvon's—is the norm rather than the deviation. Senior's importance as a writer does not rest exclusively upon those stories, but they are among her best, and her bold placement of them alongside ones narrated in standard English is a signal confirmation of her status as a leading post-colonial writer. The dialect stories in a sense validate the others, and the polyphonous voice that emerges moves from one form of discourse to another with facility and commanding assurance. The most immediate effect gained is one of intense verisimilitude, for Senior's prodigious mastery of the varieties of English speech in Jamaica, the "continuum" of Jamaican English, is a brilliant reflection of the linguistic versatility in daily life that is a hallmark of Caribbean creole culture. On a deeper level, the medley of discourses that constitutes her two short story collections represents the countercolonization of a language once associated with hegemonic authority.

Yet even though Senior accomplishes this linguistic feat, she is still the product of a society whose educational, economic, religious, and political institutions are predominantly European in origin and character. And the genre itself—the written fictional story created for its own effect—if not entirely a European or American invention, is at least intimately connected with that cultural matrix. Wilson Harris, along with many others, has roundly criticized the Anglophone Caribbean's most celebrated man of letters, V. S. Naipaul, for his allegiance in his early novels to what Ramchand calls "the mainstream tradition of the English nineteenth-century novel" ⟨Kenneth Ramchand, *The West Indian Novel and Its Background*, 1983, 9⟩. Naipaul and others like him, Harris insists, employ "a 'coherency' based on the English social model to describe a native world" ⟨Wilson Harris, "The Unresolved Constitution," 1968, 45⟩. Harris decries the use of that literary form to render "invalid" the native world and to pander to the wider audience outside the Caribbean by supporting Western notions of superiority. But surely (whatever one may think of Naipaul) Senior's fiction does not aim for or achieve such an effect. Her studies of family relationships, while as conventionally realistic as Naipaul's fiction, are actually subtle attacks on systems of power dynamics analogous to those underlying colonialism itself. And, moreover, her tales owe as much to a tradition of oral storytelling in Africa as to the genre developed by Poe, Chekhov, and deMaupassant. Reflecting on her childhood, Senior has remarked: "My major influence then was the oral tradition. . . . Later came formal exposure to 'English' literature in high school" ⟨Charles Rowell, "An Interview with Olive Senior," 1988, 480⟩. The single word "later" speaks volumes about the subordination of the written and the "formal" to the oral and the vernacular in the genesis of Senior's stories, and their final manifestation as works of literature is still marked by a spoken quality, a sense of a personality telling the story, that emerges from and vitalizes the written text.

—Richard F. Patteson, "The Fiction of Olive Senior: Traditional Society and the Wider World," *Ariel* 24, no. 1 (January 1993): 15–16

B I B L I O G R A P H Y

The Message Is Change: A Perspective on the 1972 General Elections. 1972.
Once Upon a Time in Jamaica. 1977.
A–Z of Jamaican Heritage. 1983.
Talking of Trees. 1985.
Summer Lightning and Other Stories. 1986.

Arrival of the Snake Woman and Other Stories. 1989.
Working Miracles: Women of the English-Speaking Caribbean. 1991.
Gardening in the Tropics. 1994.
Discerner of Hearts. 1995.